THE OWL AND THE PUSSYCAT

The Duke of Valderano

MINERVA PRESS

ATLANTA LONDON SYDNEY

THE OWL AND THE PUSSYCAT
Copyright © The Duke of Valderano 1998

ISBN 0 75410 627 6

First Published 1998 by
MINERVA PRESS
195 Knightsbridge
London SW7 1RE

Printed in Great Britain for Minerva Press

for my good friend Francis Malan with all best wishes

Ronnie

Ronald de Valderano

THE OWL AND THE PUSSYCAT

Aug 2002

London.

Dedication and Acknowledgements

This little book of some of the memories of our lives together, I dedicate to my beloved wife, Honor.

I also wish to express my deep gratitude to all our friends in so many countries and from so many walks of life, not all of whom can be mentioned in this book. We shared in our affection for them all, and can never thank them enough for having contributed so much to a wonderfully happy and eventful life.

Also to Mandy, May and Justine who typed the first draft of this book, and to Bob Lee who introduced me to Peter Riva, and without whose encouragement I might never have published this book.

Finally, and specially, to Colin Beer, who has so generously edited this book and helped me so greatly in writing it; to Amanda Norfield-Jones, who sub-edited and re-typed it, setting it up for publication; and to Rebecca Elsey, for further corrections.

Malta, Rome, London and
St Etienne de Baigorry (Pays Basque) 1995–1996

The Owl and the Pussycat went to sea
In a beautiful pea-green boat,
They took some honey, and plenty of money,
Wrapped up in a five-pound note.
The Owl looked up to the stars above,
And sang to a small guitar,
'Oh, lovely Pussy! O, Pussy, my love,
What a beautiful Pussy you are,
You are,
You are!
What a beautiful Pussy you are!'
Pussy said to the Owl, 'You elegant fowl!
How charmingly sweet you sing!
O, let us be married! Too long we have tarried:
But what shall we do for a ring?'
They sailed away for a year and a day
To the land where the Bong-tree grows
And there in a wood a Piggy-wig stood
With a ring in the end of his nose,
His nose,
His nose,
With a ring at the end of his nose.
'Dear Pig, are you willing to sell for one shilling
Your ring?' said the Piggy, 'I will.'
So they took it away, and were married next day
By the Turkey who lives on the hill.

They dined on mince, and slices of quince,
Which they ate with a runcible spoon;
And hand in hand, on the edge of the sand,
They danced to the light of the moon,
The moon,
The moon,
They danced by the light of the moon.

Edward Lear

Contents

Chapter One

Forbears

My father was not present at my birth in 1918 as he was abroad in the Middle East fighting somebody or other. He was a regular soldier who had joined his cavalry regiment in 1908.

The Germans were always rather put out by the amateurishness of the British Army officers, and they would not have been surprised when my father's colonel said when he first joined the regiment, 'You will be expected to hunt three days a week during the season, and in the polo season you will be expected to play at least three days a week, but apart from that I don't want to see you hanging around the barracks.'

Four and a half years later, when my father was stationed at Aliwal Barracks at Tidworth and was schooling his charger Red Prince II, the horse slipped in front of a jump, hit the top of it hard, turned in the air falling on top of my father, and then rolled. The effect was instantly to transform my father into a pancake! He was picked up, mostly with a shovel, and taken to the kitchen table in his colonel's house, which happened to be nearby. There they operated on what was left of him. His pelvis was broken in seven places, with multiple fractures of both legs, both arms, virtually all his ribs and his skull, as well as a fracture of his spine.

Against all the odds he lived, held together with silver wire and silver plates, and in 1915 reported to his regiment for duty. As he could not ride a horse (although the cavalry were largely dismounted at the time) he was told that the Hussars did not want him. So he went off to join the Royal Flying Corps. I had many photographs of him in cavalry britches, boots and sabre, standing proudly by early fighters of the time. Alas, he was not a great success as a fighter pilot, as at over five thousand feet, the blood from the fractures in his head would rush into his eyes and blind him. There were photographs of him standing beside his aircraft wrecked in the top of a tree, in the roof of a house, in a haystack, in a river. Eventually the commanding officer sent for him and said, 'You are worse than the Red Baron. You are destroying the Royal Flying Corps. I cannot have you here any longer.'

Undeterred, my father went off to join the Machine Gun Corps. Everybody hated the machine gunners because immediately they were located, every enemy mortar and available piece of artillery was concentrated on their destruction. Perhaps in the Middle East, where he was to transfer with them, there were not so many mortars and guns, or perhaps he was just lucky, but he returned at the end of the war – still held together with silver wire, but otherwise unscathed.

On being introduced to me for the first time he is said to have remarked, 'Oh dear!', but whether this was addressed as a term of endearment to my mother or an expression of surprise and horror, I was never told.

The war over, my father was unable to go on fighting and was obliged to leave the service, as more or less one hundred per cent disabled. His brother and two brothers-in-law had been killed in the war, but my grandfather had been too old to serve, having been born in 1859. However, he too had been a Hussar, and had charged with his regiment at Omdurman in 1898. In the words of the citation, 'The Major, having had his horse shot under him, dismounted [presumably a sort of forced landing], and then, drawing his sabre and pistol, he attacked the enemy with a terrible ferocity, killing very many of them.' For this he was awarded the Khedive's Star, or something of the sort, and it was said that he had killed some thirty of the enemy until the rest ran away. He was a man of vast violence, and I suppose that he was very angry because they had shot his horse.

Most people were frightened of my grandfather, who was very dark and saturnine, and had the temper of a fiend (surpassed only by that of his wife, a woman of quite extraordinary beauty, but who when enraged would have terrified Satan himself). It appears that when my grandfather was a young man in Sicily, where we had considerable estates, some person was unwise enough to insult my grandmother in some way. My grandfather promptly challenged this wretch to a duel – and cut off his head. He then did a very odd thing. He picked the head up and took it away with him. He then had it boiled down and trepanned, and had the top half of the skull mounted in massive silver as an ink-well.

He used this for the rest of his life, and I remember it well. When engaged in furious argument with my grandmother, he used to tap it with his pen. My father was somewhat embarrassed by it and when my grandfather died, it disappeared – much to my regret.

The old man did not even die peacefully. He hated doctors and would never allow one in the house. However, when he was dying, the family were gathered around, and when finally he seemed to be dead they agreed that it was essential to call a doctor, if only to certify death. The local doctor was summoned, and started to examine the 'corpse' with his stethoscope. After a minute or so, grandfather opened one eye, then the other; he then leapt out of bed, seized the doctor by the scruff of the neck and the seat of his pants, rushed him down the corridor, down the stairs and through the hall, and literally kicked him out on to the gravel drive. He then went back upstairs and fell down across the doorway of his bedroom. This time he was really dead.

It is extraordinary to think that I knew him really only as an old man, but it was not so very long before the First World War, possibly in the 1880s, that the Italian authorities sent a troop of soldiers up to our castle in Italy to collect taxes. My grandfather had them seized, thrown into the dungeons, and a month later sent them back with a message that if they ever attempted to do the same thing again, he would have them all hanged from the battlements. It is really not so very long ago, yet it was quite a different world.

In fact he spent much time in this grim and sinister castle, and only sold it after the First World War, in about 1924. It is a huge pile with walls several metres thick, which the family built between 1493 and 1494. Prince Massimo stayed there with my grandfather before the First World War, and told me once, 'My dear fellow, I must tell you that it was quite the most uncomfortable place in which I have ever stayed.' I knew the Massimo Castle at Arsoli very well and that was pretty uncomfortable, so my grandfather's place must have been something special. I go to see it sometimes, although I remember only very vaguely when it belonged to us. It is a fortress without any pretensions of being a dwelling house.

During the Second World War it was occupied by the Germans, as it commands a great stretch of the country. The Americans bombed it, the British shelled it and the Poles mortared it, but all they were able to do was to knock down one of the towers, damage another and knock off all the battlements. It is almost impossible to breach stone walls that are in places more than six metres thick. We know that there was a loo; it projected from the top of the castle. My grandmother refused absolutely to live there, and when we took a party of friends there some years ago, they all agreed that not for a million pounds would they spend a night in the place alone; when I suggested to my wife that it would be fun if we could buy it back, she said flatly that if I did, I would have to live in it by myself.

The family is of remote origin from the islands off the south-east coast of Denmark. Tacitus refers to the tribe as the Varini, a Latinised version of Varingar (meaning 'the people of the sea', in the same way that the Vikingar – or Vikings – were the people of the fjords). The tribe spread along the Baltic and as far north as the Varanger Fjord in the north of Norway and Russia, which still bears their name. Some then went to Novgorod, and from there east to the area where Moscow is today; then down the Russian rivers to attack Constantinople in about AD 960 under the Emperor Basil II. They carried on their banners the symbols of the wolf and the winged dragon. Eventually, under their leader, Starkader, they formed the first of the Varangian Guards of the Emperor. Not all accepted this service. Some went east and were never heard of again, except that in the 1920s an archaeologist digging in Baluchistan dug up an iron Norse helmet with the symbol of the winged dragon on it. Another group returned and established itself at Kiev and also in Moscow.

The group from which we are descended accepted service with the Emperor, but not for long. When they heard that the Normans had established themselves in Sicily and southern Italy, they took service under the de Hauteville Kings of Sicily, who with the Normans, had conquered the Abad emirate of Sicily. They were there for barely two generations before they moved to Normandy, to Varanger

Villa – now called Varangeville – where they established themselves. Shortly after AD 1100, they made an expedition to England and seized an island in the Humber and adjoining lands; however, they were at least forty years too late, and all the goodies had gone. A branch of the family stayed on in England, moving about and acquiring Brierlly and two or three other manors, marrying into local Norman families. In the fourteenth century, they returned to Varangeville and also Rouen, where there are fairly complete records of them. They were Sieurs de Varangeville and sometimes Counts of Varangeville, but in about 1485, Robert, Sieur et Comte de Varangeville, fleeing from his creditors and the King's men, returned to Italy and set up as a *Condottiero*.

The family records do not show what the connection was, but certainly there was some family friendship or blood tie with the Gaetani Family. Robert, on arrival at Rome, went to see Prince Nicolo Gaetani at Sermonetta. There he persuaded Nicolo to lend him the ruined fortress in Ninfa on the edge of the Pontine Marshes. In fact, it was on an island. The main castle had been burnt out at least one hundred years previously but the curtain walls still stood, as well as the four towers. There was a village in the centre of the island, with a stream of good water running through it. There Robert recruited his *condotta* of marsh men, little men who were to some extent immune to the malaria that plagued the marshes, and were also expert shots with a short bow, using poisoned arrows. He chose this place as it could not be besieged – the malaria would have killed off the investing troops – and because it was reasonably secure.

All went well and he formed his *condotta* and trained them, but then had the misfortune to have a furious quarrel with Cesare Borgia, the Pope's son and a man with whom it was better not to disagree about anything. Robert returned to Ninfa and reported to Prince Gaetani at Sermonetta, who advised him to leave as soon as possible with his *condotta* and to do so that day rather than the following day. Robert left and went north with his men until he reached Piedmont.

This did not stop Cesare, who came to Ninfa. Finding that Robert had gone, he set siege to Sermonetta, taking it after two years – at which time he killed Prince Nicolo and threw all his family into the Castel St Angelo in Rome.

Meanwhile, King Charles VIII of France had been preparing to invade Italy and to attack the Pope, with whom he had quarrelled. Robert approached the King and offered his services, and that of his *condotta*. The King was delighted: here was a ready-made force of expert archers who knew the country. He asked what Robert would like in return. Robert said that he wished for a Dukedom and the usual pickings of a *condotta*. The King was even more pleased, as this would cost him nothing. Summoning a chamberlain, he instructed that M. Le Comte de Varangeville should have letters patent made out to him as Duke of Valdarno. The French clerk drawing these letters had never heard of the place, and through a clerical error (perhaps he was a Flamand) made them out in the name of the Duke of Valderano. We have been stuck with the wrong name for the past five hundred years.

Charles VIII conquered Italy as far south as Naples, so Robert was able to get the remainder of the Gaetani family released. He built the fortress at Valdarno, which was never taken. He was a successful *Condottiero*, the commander of a private army and what we would call today a horrible mercenary but in those days was a most honourable profession. Charles VIII did not live long, and Robert moved first to Normandy and then for a short time to England. He married Maria della Scala – the last of the great della Scala family, who had been Captains of the

People and Dukes of Verona nearly two hundred years previously but were then living in much reduced circumstances in Livorno. Robert was a colourful character, apparently a huge man who stood near seven feet tall and was of legendary strength.

His grandson, also Robert, the third Duke, married a Princess Bathory in Hungary. Here, following in his grandfather's footsteps as a *Condottiero*, he served with Count Hunyady against the Turks.

Spanish, Italian and French marriages, as well as English, followed throughout the centuries, and the family acquired considerable estates abroad and also in England and Ireland.

My paternal great-grandfather had the foresight to invest considerable sums in the early railways and finance railway building in Belgium, Italy, Brazil, Britain and elsewhere. This paid off very well indeed. He was not so lucky in a joint venture with the Baron d'Erlanger in an early attempt to build a channel tunnel, and his enormous racing stud in England cost him a huge fortune. His best horse, having come second in the Derby, went to stud and promptly fell down dead.

He spent some considerable time in Brazil and put down a large force of bandits that was terrorising the north-western frontier area with Bolivia in the region of the Rio Madeira and Rio de Marmora.

They were interfering with the building of a railway in which he had invested, killing the workers and stealing everything.

Although an elderly man then, he travelled to this remote and very inhospitable area. He soon discovered that the bandits usually spent the nights carousing in the forest, singing, playing guitars and drinking quantities of cane spirit.

He trained and armed a force, equipping them with the latest American repeating rifles, and, attacking at night, annihilated the bandits. He too had been a colonel of cavalry, and had no intention of letting a gang of criminals disrupt the work and kill his men.

Chapter Two

Early Days

Childhood

I suppose that I had a rather unusual childhood. My mother and father carried on a sort of guerrilla war between them, while they moved rapidly from house to house. They seem to have had a particular liking for haunted houses. The first was Brandon Hall where there were apparently several ghosts, although I do not remember any of them. As a baby, I was for long periods with my great-aunt at Morley Manor. I remember being in my pram there and in a play pen. Nanny Reid looked after me in a wing of this large house. There was a very nice lady in a lavender-coloured dress who used to come and sit on my bed at night and talk to me. I was told that she was, in fact, a ghost, but that meant nothing to me. She was for me more real than my family, as I used to see her very often and I saw the family seldom. Occasionally I was taken down for tea and told not to make a mess and to speak only when spoken to. After half an hour or so I would be removed back to my own quarters and shut away from the rest of the house down long corridors and stairs.

There was a huge garden of some forty acres with ponds, terraces, pergolas, a vast rose garden and hothouses for hundreds of orchids. I used to sleepwalk and on one or two occasions I was found by the keepers in the wood a mile or more from the house. As an only child, I have sometimes been asked whether I was lonely. I cannot remember knowing any other boys or girls and there were no children's parties but I was certainly not lonely, nor did I miss the company of other children. From time to time the servants used to flee in the night and there were stories of various ghosts. I suspect that in many cases the ghost was my great-aunt, who used to wander about in the night in a white nightdress. The house was almost entirely panelled in oak and very dark, with mullion windows. Without doubt there were some unexplained things there – such as Jane Pott, a middle-aged serving woman in late eighteenth century dress. She was frequently seen in the dining room, carrying dishes. There was something rather nasty in the serving room outside the dining room. I suspect it was an elemental of sorts. I bumped into it one night while sleepwalking. It was tall (over six feet, although children exaggerate height), it was like a huge sack, covered with rough, long hair, and it stank. Many years later I was to smell the same odour again in the mortuary at Dover. I recognised it instantly: the smell of corruption.

Mill Place, not far from Bristol, was a house where my parents lived for two years. I remember it well. I associate it with the strong smell of stocks in the garden, a huge copper beech on the lawn, Old Bill (the gardener who made me my first bow and arrow) and the mill itself, a dark and rather sinister place. I was four at the time. The disconcerting thing about the house was that fires used to break out on the stairs fairly frequently. Also, when the river flooded my mother had to go through the garden to the mill (which was some four hundred yards away), across the river and up the other bank for three-quarters of a mile to open the sluice gates, and then come back again. At night, in the winter, she did not enjoy this.

My parents moved again – to Rookley Manor, near Stockbridge, which had originally been a hunting lodge built for King John. Here again we had a retinue of ghosts. There was George III and George IV, who used to be seen in the avenue of lime trees, and a headless horse at the bottom of the drive. It was a lovely old house, and here I was introduced to Darkie, a pony. My father was determined that I should become a superb horseman. My sixpence a week pocket money was given to me in pennies, and I had to go over the jumps with a penny between each knee. If I dropped one I did not get it back. I was also instructed in tent pegging with a lance, which I rather enjoyed. Targets were set up over the jumps; they were supposed to represent enemies. Armed with a cavalry sabre, I was taught to use the point left and right and also the blade to cut them down. In the end I became quite a good horseman.

Nanny Reid had been replaced by Miss Dunn. My father disliked her and so did I. My mother had gone in for breeding Sealyham terriers which bit everybody. The cellar used to flood. My father waged an endless war with the electric light machine and with Mr Page from the local garage, who was supposed to make the machine work. Finally, Miss Dunn met the headless horse and had to be removed by men in white coats. She was not seen again. It was from Rookley that my mother finally fled to London. My father sold the house and went after her. He had a Crossley car at that time; of course it had to be started with a handle, and frequently backfired and burst into flames. That too was abandoned when we left Rookley.

My Mother

As we are the product of our genes as well as our education, experience and environment, I should write briefly about my mother's family. On her father's side she was the descendant of a cadet branch of the Grenvilles of Wotton (Sir Richard Grenville of the Revenge). Her grandfather lived at Haynes Park, outside Bedford, which is now, I believe, a girls' school. Her father was a man of Herculean strength who spent most of his life fishing and shooting in Ireland. There is a story about him that when fishing by a river one day he was attacked by a bull. It seems that rather than jump into the river, he advanced upon the bull, seized it by the horns and broke its neck.

Her mother was Irish, and the family lived at Barton Mills, near New Ross. Her mother's father was a Colonel Bridges, who married Anne Gifford of Ballysop. He was a quarrelsome man, and a duellist who could be seen going out in the dawn with his case of saw-handled pistols to shoot his neighbours. Anne Gifford was killed in a hunting accident when she was still in her early twenties and her husband was wed again almost immediately, marrying Anne's sister. This was against the canons of the church and scandalised the local people, who disliked the colonel anyway.

Eventually he was forced to leave Ireland. He took his young family to Canada, and then to America. My great-aunt and her younger sister, who were the two children of Anne, were actually chased over the prairie by American Indians. Unkind people said that when the stagecoach looked like a pin cushion with their arrows, the aunt put her head out of the window and said, 'Go away, you savages! Do you know who you are chasing?' – whereupon the Indians fled in terror. She was a very formidable person, who grew up to be one of the great beauties of her day. She maintained a splendid establishment at Morley Manor, with an indoor staff of some thirty people, as well as ten gardeners, lodge-keepers, the chauffeur who eventually replaced the coachmen, and two or three keepers – some fifty people in all.

It was there that I spent much of my childhood and youth. My mother, like her aunt, spoke a number of languages: English, German, French, Italian and some Portuguese and Spanish. She could read Latin, studied at the Sorbonne and was an accomplished artist: some of her pictures hang in Italian galleries. She had a brilliant, dilettante mind, and once learnt Iranian – reading, writing and speaking it – in less than two months. Alas, she and my father were an ill-matched couple: she with an artistic temperament and interested in antiquities, gardening and politics. Her friends included Freya Stark and various desert explorers, painters and writers. My father's main interests were in country pursuits and although my mother was a fearless rider to hounds, it was a marriage doomed from the first.

My father had acquired a cheetah – perhaps as a counterblast to the Sealyhams, hoping that the cheetah would eat them – but in fact they got on very well together. The cheetah became my particular pet and used to sleep on my bed with me. My father, the cheetah and I followed my mother to London and for a short time we had a house in Ashley Place by the Catholic Cathedral. But there were constant and frightful rows. My father hated who he called her 'dreadful friends', and eventually she left for Italy. They were divorced when I was nine. In fact, I was very much relieved – it put an end to the rows – and by that time I had been packed off to prep school. My mother married again, Colonel Cino Bacchiani, (later a general) and Count of Savarna. He was a colonel of the Alpini, but of Hungarian origin. She bought a villa at Anticoli and lived there for the rest of her life, except for the war years. I loved her very much, but I fear that she did not have a very happy life.

School Days

When I was nine I was sent to a preparatory school at Westgate-on-Sea in Kent. It was run by one of those muscular, Christian clerics, and I disliked it very much. We had to attend chapel twice a day; this fostered in me a dislike of church services which has remained all my life. Once a week we were all given some aperient, whether we needed it or not, and every morning we had to plunge into an ice-cold bath. The school also inculcated in me an intense dislike of missionaries and I was beaten by the muscular headmaster 'for being the only boy in the school who refuses to give his pocket money to the Reverend Odinga for his wonderful missionary work in Africa'. But I certainly was not prepared to give my pocket money to the Reverend Odinga, who used to come every term to collect.

I was supposed to follow my father and grandfather to Eton, but three weeks before I was due to go there my father had a blood row with my prospective housemaster and he decided to send me instead to Stowe, a new public school which had been open for a mere seven years. Set in hundreds of acres of the most beautiful parkland, it was paradise after Westgate-on-Sea. Alas, I did very little work there. In my first year I fenced and shot for Stowe, and played in the school's junior cricket team.

In those days athletic ability was an excuse for academic failure, and I was allowed to get away with doing little or no work. I was also busy poaching in the autumn and winter. There were plenty of pheasants around and as I have always been able to do with little sleep, I used to get out of my dormitory at night, returning at about three in the morning. I kept a variety of guns – a .22 rifle with a silencer being my favourite. I kept it sometimes in a hole in the ha-ha wall some four hundred yards from the school, on the edge of the wood. A roosting pheasant in the moonlight made an easy target. Soon I was shooting too many to carry on my bicycle, so I arranged with a 'fence' in Buckingham to whom I sold them to get me an old car for £15. With this I was able to extend my activities, and soon complaints came flooding into the school from local landowners. A great gun-hunt was organised and some weapons were found, but not mine. The following season there were more complaints and another gun-hunt was organised. Again, a few were found, but not mine. There was suspicion that I was the culprit but no proof, and my housemaster spent many days trying to catch me. A third gun-hunt was organised but again nothing of mine was found.

One night when everybody was in bed and lights were out I was summoned by the house prefect to go to the headmaster's study. This looked bad. J.F. Roxborough was a most remarkable man, and undoubtedly one of the great headmasters of all time. I was called in to be greeted most courteously. 'Sit down, Ronnie,' he said. I thought that I had better do so while I still could. 'Have a cigarette,' he invited, and continued, 'don't bother to say that you never smoke, because I know that you do. Now, I have asked you here this evening because the school is in trouble. The local people are complaining that their pheasants are being poached, and you know and I know who is doing it! Poor Major Howarth, your housemaster, spends endless hours trying to catch you; he never will, but the wounds he had in 1916 are hurting him terribly and I am in deep trouble with the local estate owners. Now, knowing what the situation is and if you think that a gentleman should continue doing what you are doing, go ahead, but if you think, as I do, that a gentleman would not do this, then you will stop. Have another glass of port.' Of course, that was the end of my poaching activities.

I enjoyed Stowe, and later my son was to go there and he enjoyed it also. However, it was not long after I had to stop poaching that my father decided that I should go to France to learn the language. I already spoke English and Italian and some Spanish. In due course I found myself at the Collège de Normandie near Clères. This was a case of being thrown in at the deep end, as none of the boys spoke English and I had to learn French in a hurry. Le Collège de Normandie had been going for some seventy-five years and was supposed to be run on the lines of an English public school. M. Dédé was the headmaster and on showing us round when we arrived he referred to the changing rooms proudly as 'Just like an English public 'ouse'. In fact, the school bore little resemblance to any English public school. We got up at 6.00 a.m. and breakfast was at 6.30 a.m., consisting of bread, cider and camembert cheese which jumped up on to the table of its own accord and could be smelt fifty yards away. Lessons started at 7.15 a.m. and continued until midday, when we had luncheon. On Sundays we had roast horse and on Fridays we had ray (a revolting fish). After luncheon there was 'Le Foot'. A strange game: we either had purple football boots or yellow ones. It was played by any number a side. At a certain moment a master threw in a football. This was the signal to rush at the nearest boy wearing football boots of a different colour to one's own and kick him. The ball was largely ignored. There was also 'Athlétisme', which was less painful. We also played a totally lethal game of bicycle-polo, which was great fun. There was also swimming, fencing and tennis in the summer. We had more bread and cider at 4.00 p.m. and then worked until 7.30 p.m. when there was supper, after which we worked in our rooms until 10.00 p.m. It was a long day and they made us work very hard. There were no punishments as such but in their place there were rewards, and those who did well were given weekend passes to go to Paris. So we all worked very hard. I learnt French quickly and in due course I passed my French

Baccalaureate. I also took over editing the school magazine, an infinitely dull publication.

With two friends, Baron La Caze and Demaret, this magazine was transformed into a political broadsheet advocating the imprisonment of all politicians and the return of the French monarchy. Demand soon exceeded supply and we went to Rouen to hire a hand-printing press; *Le Léopard* was born. It was an instant success and we started selling it in Rouen; for the first and really only time in my life, I was making money. Alas, disaster was not far away: some idiot boy at the school sent a copy to his father, a Socialist Deputy who appeared in the Parliament and, flinging a copy of the *Léopard* on the floor together with his top hat, danced on both, shouting 'Where is this nest of vipers?' At the school we knew nothing of this until one day a convoy of five black Citroen cars arrived, occupied by policemen armed to the teeth, who arrested... the headmaster! Poor M. Dédé, who knew nothing of the *Léopard*, was hauled off to jail. It took him two days to convince the authorities – who then returned and arrested us, confiscating the press. As a foreigner I was expelled from France. I was escorted to the St Briac, the cross-channel boat, and seen off the premises. I thought that my father would be furious, but I returned to a hero's welcome, as my father, himself a mixture of continental blood, was strangely xenophobic.

With Matriculation and the French Baccalaureate, and with fluent French, Italian and some Spanish, I was able to get into Cambridge. I went to Magdalene College, where I enjoyed myself immensely.

University: Peace and then War

At Cambridge I read for the History Honours Tripos, and also some law. With Rob Walker, later of motor racing fame, I bought a 1914 Silver Ghost 40/50 Rolls in Paris for twenty pounds. It had a huge whale-back and an immensely long bonnet. It had brakes on two wheels only and an enormous handbrake outside. It took about a mile to stop it at any speed and in it we thundered down to London to nightclubs, returning at dawn and climbing back into college. I went shooting on the Wash and had quite a good syndicate pheasant school. Those were wonderful days at Cambridge, but all things come to an end and my father eventually sent me off to Baden-Baden to learn German. There I met a pretty and charming girl and quite soon I spoke the language fairly well. I also attended one of the Nuremberg rallies of the Nazi Party. It was extremely spectacular, with cones of searchlights pointing into the night sky and ringing the arena. Battalions of Brown-Shirts marched in singing the Horst Wessel Lied. Eventually Hitler appeared on the podium at the end and gave a long speech relayed at mega-decibel levels through the arena. At the end everyone was shouting '*Sieg Heil*' and giving the Nazi salute, and to my astonishment I found myself doing the same. It taught me a lesson that I have never forgotten about the immense power of hypnosis and the terrible danger of mass hysteria.

Through my girlfriend I had met Dr Schacht, whose brother was the Nazi finance minister, and he arranged for me to meet Hitler at Bechtesgarten. Many of the Nazi leaders believed that English aristocracy had political power, and believing me to be somebody who would inherit a title (although not an English one), he arranged the meeting. It took place at teatime in the mountain retreat where Hitler used to spend some time. He was wearing a brown jacket and appeared a very ordinary little man. Also present were Schacht, Goering, Goebbels and Himmler.

Hitler unquestionably had the ability to charm, but I was not worth his effort. He asked me if I was enjoying my stay in Germany and I replied truthfully that I was. He asked me if the British people wished for friendship with Germany and I said that the British people wanted friendly relations with all countries. There were a few other banalities and that was that. He did not impress me as a person at all, but then he certainly did not think that I was worth impressing. However, it is not everybody who can say that he had tea with Hitler.

I knew Mussolini well. He used to come up for luncheon to my mother's villa near Rome and I met him there on several occasions. He was surprisingly well read, and could be both interesting and amusing. He left his pomposity together with his entourage in the village outside the villa gates. Later I was to meet Franco, Salazar, De Gaulle, Eisenhower and Churchill, although I was never introduced to the latter. I was also for a short time a stand-in ADC to Montgomery, and I had luncheon with Pope John Paul II when he was a simple priest studying in Rome. So I had the good fortune to meet many of the historical figures of my time.

The civil war in Spain was already into its second year when I went to see what was going on and there met Franco for the first time. I believed then and believe now that he was a great man who did an enormous amount for his country, a brilliant man but totally lacking in charisma. He had a cold character and I believe that he never had any close friends. It was a remarkably cruel war, but then civil wars invariably are. The horrors of what I saw then have remained with me all my life, but some of the lessons I learnt were to stand me in good stead later.

It was then decided that I should go into the City and become a stockbroker. I hated every moment of this and was utterly useless. My father became more and more irritated with me, and finally insisted that I should join the Territorial Army. As my uncles both maternal and paternal had been killed in the First World War (having served in the Rifle Brigade and the King's Royal Rifle Corps respectively), I became a rifleman without any great enthusiasm. I discovered that six months leave could be obtained to learn a foreign language, and it was when I went to learn French (which I already spoke fluently) that I visited Spain. In 1939 I went to America while 'learning Italian', which I also already spoke fluently. In fact I was in America when I was summoned to rejoin my regiment: war was thought to be imminent. I transferred to the Hampshire Regiment – later the Royal Hampshire Regiment, and now sadly disbanded.

Chapter Three

Wartime

1939: The Beginning of the Second World War

The regiment moved into Fort Fareham, a damp and very dreary Napoleonic fort. A few days before war was declared I was sent off with a platoon of soldiers to guard the telegraph cable which came up from the seabed at Horsey Island in the middle of Portsmouth harbour. This was much better than Fort Fareham as I was away from the regiment, and away from the adjutant, whom I disliked immensely. We also had Navy rations, which were much better than those for the army. I posted my soldiers around the island and gave them a pep talk on how important it was to prevent German saboteurs from landing and destroying the cable. War was declared on 3rd September, 1939, and that same evening there was a fairly thick sea fog. Through the darkness and the fog one of my gallant soldiers heard the creak of oars, and the dim outline of a small rowing boat. 'Halt,' he shouted. 'Who goes there?' Silence. 'Halt! Who goes there?' Again, no reply. For the third time the sentry shouted, 'Halt! Who goes there... Halt! Or I fire.' Then he fired – and shot a fisherman through the arm. The bullet went out through the bottom of the boat, which began to fill with water. The fishermen on board were hurt, wet and angry, but it was their fault, and they almost certainly had the distinction of becoming the first casualties of the Second World War.

My colonel was not pleased with me, and the vile adjutant even less so. Still, I had obeyed regulations and the sentry had acted correctly. However, worse was to follow. Three weeks later there was a tremendous storm: lightning, thunder, rain and a howling wind. One of my soldiers was patrolling with a fixed bayonet and was struck by lightning. Fortunately, he was not killed, but he was burnt and badly shocked. I got on the telephone to Battalion Headquarters and reported the matter, asking that the medical officer should come out to the island as soon as possible. I then went down to the jetty to wait for them, as I was told that the colonel and the adjutant were also coming. It was a really bad night, with a big sea running. Finally, a small boat set out from the shore and was rowed with some difficulty towards the island.

The jetty was made of wood and projected out about thirty yards from the island. There were some wooden steps leading down to the water at the end. The steps were slippery, and the lashing rain and wind made it difficult to bring the little rowing boat alongside. The colonel shouted up to me to throw down a rope. At the end of the jetty there was a lifebelt with a long rope attached to it, coiled under the lifebelt. It was obvious that it would be useless just to throw down the loose end of the rope, as it would have been blown away in the wind. So I threw the lifebelt down into the boat. I was not to know that it had probably been there since the beginning of time. Whatever was in it must once have floated but had, over the years, turned to concrete. The lifebelt sailed down into the rowing boat and went clean through the bottom. The boat immediately started to sink, and scrambling to get out, the three occupants overturned it.

A few minutes later three bedraggled figures, soaking wet and covered from head to foot in mud and slime, clambered up the steps – whereupon I was instantly relieved of my command at Horsey Island and returned to the dreary fort. I was then sent off on a course to learn about the innards of military transport, which finished with a practical examination. Alas, I did something to the engine on which I was working which necessitated the whole vehicle being sent off to some major ordnance depot to be repaired. The next time I was sent off I returned with a 'D' (distinguished). The battalion was then moved to an enormous deserted mansion not far from Frome in Somerset. Here we went on immensely long route marches; these hurt my feet, which have always been tender, to the extent that my boots filled with blood. I had learnt some rather unorthodox tactics in the Spanish Civil War, including the use of Molotov cocktails and the potential of push and pull booby traps. As I was clearly not making a very good regimental officer, and possibly rather a dangerous one, I became Battalion Intelligence Officer. This was great fun, and I began to enjoy myself.

It was here too that I met again the girl who was to become my wife, and whom I had met many years ago as a child and at her first coming-out dance. The officers' mess gave a party on the lawn of Battalion HQ for local people who had been kind and shown hospitality to the troops, and there she was. Before long, however, we were warned to prepare to go to France; but fortunately the evacuation from Dunkirk came just as we were due to embark. The battalion was moved hastily into a position covering the east coast, but I found myself, to my delight, left behind on the rear party to clear up, and in the general confusion following the withdrawal from Dunkirk and loss of nearly all the army's weapons, we on the rear party were forgotten for three months. I had discovered a cache of several hundred two-gallon tins of petrol hidden in the park. Some of it had been there for a very long time and the tins had rusted through, but there was still enough left to fill my car whenever I wanted, to take Honor and myself to Bath to dance at the Assembly Rooms, go on picnics together and to enjoy that glorious summer of 1940. When eventually they remembered about us and we had to rejoin the battalion near Hatfield Forest, Honor and I were unofficially engaged.

At Hatfield I had the job of camouflaging pillboxes. This gave scope for a good deal of imagination. I transformed pillboxes into public lavatories with 'Men' on a board disguising the loophole for the machine gun on one side and 'Ladies' on the other. Unfortunately, they were not infrequently used for the purpose for which they proclaimed. Others I transformed into rubbish dumps, and others still I hid quite effectively with posters and graffiti.

This was a happy time for me. As Battalion Intelligence Officer I was largely left to my own devices and was able to get away from run-of-the-mill regimental duties. It was a time only clouded for me by my separation from Honor, as we were already discussing our marriage plans.

There was a certain unreality about the war at this time. Although most of the British Army had been rescued from the beaches of Dunkirk, there was very little equipment. Everything was either totally lacking or in very short supply.

We went out on exercises with the brigade, and eventually with the division, but there was an amateurishness about it all. I even found plenty of time to get some shooting round about with local landowners and farmers.

However, this pleasant interlude was not to last very long.

At about this time some imbecile at the War Office decided that we would become 'mechanised infantry'. The idea appealed to me as it suggested that we would not have to go on long marches. As virtually all the British Army transport had been left behind in France, we were put into Midland Red buses, which of course, could be seen miles away; but we went on exercises with them and finally into camp in Hatfield Forest. I got some rather good shooting here, and kept the mess supplied with deer, rabbits, partridges and some pheasants. Soon the rains came, and our Midland Red buses, together with the carriers from the carrier platoon, were immobile in a sea of mud. It was about this time on one of the exercises – a divisional one, I think – that I was asleep in a ditch one night when I was woken by the signals officer with a coded message. Decoded it said simply: 'Cromwell'. This was the word informing us that an invasion was imminent, and on receipt of it we had to move forward into prepared positions on the east coast. I went over to my colonel and shook him. 'Cromwell has come through, sir,' I said. The colonel rolled over and mumbled, 'Bugger off.' I shook him again and said, 'Sir, wake up.' The code word Cromwell has come through.' He sat up straight and said, 'You bloody fool. Don't you know that Cromwell has been dead for nearly three hundred years?'

With the aid of farmers' tractors we were eventually mobile again and moved off nearer London in the area of Harpenden. It was from here that we became 'airborne troops'. That is to say that we force-marched to the nearest airfield where we were eventually embarked on a variety of aircraft, from Tiger Moths to Transports. This air armada was dispersed by a major thunderstorm; some of the battalion arrived in Scotland and some in Cornwall. It was not considered to be a success, so we were sent to defend the white cliffs of Dover. The brigade column was very long and also very visible. Aircraft trails in the sky indicated that the enemy had taken note of our movements. We debussed outside Dover and marched in. The battalion was detailed to occupy the Citadel Barracks, the Grand Shaft Barracks in front of us with another battalion, and brigade headquarters in Dover Castle on the other side of the harbour.

As we marched up the hill to the Citadel, the German dive-bombers came in, and we had our first casualties of the war. I had found the deepest and safest dungeon for my intelligence section, and Dover was noisy.

With great precision the German fighters used to come in low over the cliffs shortly after dawn, cannon-gunning us. They then went away, and at about 10.00 a.m. the dive-bombers would come in. They usually carried one large bomb. They would come over fairly high, turn and dive, release their bomb and then pull up and climb while the rear gunner loosed off with machine guns or a cannon. This would also be the signal for the defences to go into action. The trawlers in the harbour had a sort of stove pipe rigged up on them attached to the steam from the engine room. The trick was to remove the pin of a 36 Mills hand-grenade while keeping the lever held down. Then slide the hand-grenade down the stove pipe and pull the lanyard, which sent a blast of steam into the base of the stove pipe. The grenade was sent hurtling up the stove pipe, and the lever blew off as it left the end of the pipe; the grenade carried on up several hundred feet and then exploded. Following the rule of gravity, the fragments from these bombs showered down everywhere. Then there were the anti-aircraft guns, the pom-pom guns on the warships, machine guns, Bofors 40 mm Light AA guns and God only knows what else.

When the dive-bombers had gone away, the next visitors would be the heavy bombers making for London. They did not bomb us on the outward journey but on their return they dropped any remaining explosives on us. The afternoon also saw the return of the dive-bombers, and then just before dusk the fighters would come over cannon-gunning the cliffs again.

At night we had the cross-channel guns. The Germans had three batteries at Calais and Cap Gris Nez. They fired eleven-inch shells which took exactly one minute from the flash where fired to their arrival at Dover. They made a great deal of noise and caused considerable destruction. Then we had 9.5-inch guns that did not have the range to reach France but were fired at German convoys and E-boats coming up the Channel close to the French coast. We had our own cross-channel guns, too. These lived in railway tunnels and were trundled out, fired, and trundled back again. In short the noise went on day and night, and it was remarkable that we did not have more casualties than we had; but they were many, and the destruction of Dover was considerable.

At Dover I had the somewhat unenviable job of search-ing dead bodies. We had a few most days, mostly airmen, our own and German who had come down in the Channel. Sometimes they had been in the water for some time and were washed ashore and then left lying on the beaches for many days before being found. These bodies had to be undressed, their identity tags recovered and then searched for documents, photographs and anything else. In very many cases the bodies disintegrated and I was left with a pile of bits – arms, feet, heads, legs and so on. I cannot say that I enjoyed this job, and others shunned my company as no matter now carefully I washed I acquired a most unpleasant smell. My arrival in the mess for meals was generally a signal for an exodus of the other officers.

I also developed a certain ghoulish sense of humour, and I remember sending a particularly ripe corpse in a sack to the Brigade Intelligence Officer who had had the bad manners to attempt to court my fiancée! I also started my collection of unexploded bombs and travelled around the area asking unit commanders, with a disarming smile, if they had any such devices for me.

It is probable that the many people who thought that I was mad as a hatter at this time were right. In fact I knew little about bomb disposal, or of their working. Fortunately, they were not so sophisticated at this time as they were to become later, and I had no accidents. In fact, I achieved a minor triumph in that the first explosive incendiary bombs were dropped on Dover, and I was able to collect several which had failed to explode. With my intelligence section, I took them to bits and found out how they worked. I then set up a series of targets at different distances on the main barracks square: a battle dress stuffed with straw, empty jerry cans, one full one with petrol in it, large slats of wood to measure penetration, and so on. In the centre I put my explosive incendiary and, having banged it with a hammer to set off the bomb (which did not explode immediately but only when it was burning furiously), I withdrew to a safe distance. I had posted sentries to prevent anybody coming on to the barrack square, but just at that moment my colonel, who was in a hurry, said to the sentry on the main gates, 'Don't you bloody well know who I am?' – and ordered his driver to go on. He arrived on the barrack square just as the bomb went off. The effect was spectacular; pieces of flaming magnesium were scattered over a wide area and one went through the petrol tank of the colonel's staff car, which immediately exploded in flames. With the speed of light, my colonel and his driver were out of it and running for their lives. Fortunately, nobody was hurt.

I carefully completed my report, with drawings of how the bomb worked and details of the penetration of burning magnesium fragments at different distances – including the fact that it would penetrate the petrol tank of a staff car at some fifteen metres. The report went up through 'the usual channels' and finally to War Office, and I even received a commendation for it. However, my colonel was by now convinced that he had a dangerous lunatic on his hands and determined to send me elsewhere as soon as possible, before I could kill him or blow up the barracks.

His first idea was to transfer me to another battalion of the same regiment, but nobody seemed to very anxious to have me. Likewise the staff had no vacancies for a subaltern officer who was widely known for his interest in unexploded bombs and eccentricity.

Finally he had the idea of offering my services to Major Thompson, the Port Security Officer (an MI5 job), who was engaged in counter-intelligence. That I spoke several languages stood me in good stead, and at the interview I got on well with Major Thompson, who seemed to me then to be a harmless elderly man, in his early fifties.

He was running a counter-intelligence office at Temple Ewell, some miles outside Dover, towards Canterbury. It was based in Pear Tree Cottage, a rather pretty little cottage in the village, while Major Thompson, who was a local landowner, had a beautiful manor house not far away.

War Office approval was requested and was ultimately granted, and so I found myself transferred to the Port Security Section. In fact, I must admit that I made a very bad regimental officer but I was to enjoy myself with Major Thompson, very much more that I ever did with the regiment.

Before taking up my new duties, Honor and I were married; but I will write of that later.

Honor

I first met Honor when we were children together at Sidmouth. I had built a rather fine sand fort on the beach and was admiring my handiwork when I saw a little girl of about five rushing towards me with long black hair, to almost halfway down her back, streaming behind her. She jumped into my fort and began reorganising it, at the same time speaking to me in an unknown language. This had a powerful effect on me. We met again on several occasions with our respective nannies, but then I did not see her again until I went to her coming-out dance at the house of some cousins of hers which was not far from my father's house in the New Forest. We spent most of the evening quarrelling, as she was much taken up with a young Dragoon officer with chain mail on the shoulders of his uniform and a large pink face. I said that he looked like something out of a museum, and she said that my French was bad. In fact I spoke fluent French, but it certainly was not as good as hers: Honor spoke French as a child and was always taken for a French woman when in France. I could never be taken for French, as I had a fairly strong Italian accent. When the party broke up, my car would not start, and I had to come back into the house when all the other guests had left in order to telephone for help. Then Honor and I had quite a long and increasingly amicable conversation (in the absence of the medieval officer).

Honor was the daughter of a group captain in the Air Force, later to become an air marshal. He was one of only three men to have been awarded the Air Force Cross and two bars as well as a DFC, a CB, an OBE and other decorations. On her father's side she was descended from Edward the Black Prince and had mainly English and French blood. On her mother's side she was descended from the Plantagenet Kings and Roger Mortimer of Wigmore and had a considerable amount of Spanish blood.

As her father and mother were very frequently away on foreign postings, Honor was brought up almost entirely by her grandmother, who was an invalid and bedridden. She had a succession of French nurses and governesses, with whom she spoke only French. Even in later life, long after we were married, when excited she had a tendency to break into French.

For many years she hardly saw her father and mother at all, and they were almost total strangers. She lived at Beckington in Somerset where the family owned the abbey, the castle and the rectory, as well as considerable estates in the vicinity. As an only child, rather like myself, she lived largely in her own world and seldom went to children's parties (moreover with a bedridden grandmother, it was not practical to give parties in the house for her). Honor developed rheumatic fever very badly on two occasions. She was not expected to survive, and her parents were told that she could not possibly live beyond the age of fourteen. Accordingly, she never went to school and was educated at home. However, she received a most marvellous education: she read and wrote Latin and Greek and spoke English, French, German and some Spanish. She passed Schools Certificate and Matriculation and was accepted at Cambridge. Honor received a gold medal from the Royal Academy for her painting and drew beautifully. Botany and mathematics presented no problems. Later she was to speak six languages fluently and be able to converse in another four.

I suppose that she too had a rather unusual childhood, despite illness. (In the end it was a cardiac collapse which caused her death.) But I think that she had a happy childhood, going for miles on her bicycle all over Somerset and Wiltshire and from a really very early age running a large house and estate alone and unaided.

I don't think that she ever felt lonely or neglected. In the winter she skated (and skated very well), but that was the only sport in which she was allowed to participate. She took very strongly after the Spanish side of her family (from Avila in Castile), with very white skin, black hair and grey/green eyes. She was very beautiful in a most unusual way, and I have never seen anybody who resembled her.

She had a most remarkable knowledge of herbs, their curative properties and herbal lore, and she had the gift of second sight to a very marked degree. However, this was something that she did not want, and she fought against it all her life.

After her coming-out dance, we met again when my regiment was posted to Marston House near Frome; and she came over for a drinks party given by the officers' mess. The twelfth time that we met was in church when we were married. We were inseparable companions, except for short periods during the war when she could not be with me. Thereafter 'I' became 'we' and we did everything together, travelled together and lived our entire lives together. Whatever I have achieved has been entirely due to her, and when she died in July 1993 I also died – if not in body, alas, then certainly in spirit. My only wish now is to rejoin her as soon as possible.

She had an extraordinary capacity to make friends in whatever company she found herself. Her friends included shop assistants, princes, carpet dealers in the Souk; all manner of people, from dukes to dustmen. When she died, I received cards of sympathy signed by the matron and all the nurses, those who were in the X-ray department, the cleaners who had cleaned her room and those who had brought her food, the sisters and the receptionists, girls in the accounts department and some fifty signatures from all those whom she had met there and made her friends.

She was a splendid shot both with a rifle and a pistol, but disliked killing birds or animals. She could ride well and sail a boat and swam very well. It was largely due to her efforts that the stray cats which live in the ruins of ancient Rome are now classified as an integral part of the ruins and cannot be harmed. She had a very deep sense of compassion for other people and was totally fearless. Perhaps one of her greatest assets was a wonderful sense of humour and a total dislike of pomposity. She was loved by very, very many people and above all by her husband and her children. She radiated a serenity which touched all who ever met her.

Our Wedding

It was at this time that Honor and I were married. We were married in the parish church of Beckington. Honor's family owned the livings of Beckington and also Standerwick and Rhode. They had all been extremely well endowed by the family, as during the Regency period they had been great gamblers, and this was considered to be a sort of insurance policy. The eldest son would become a parson and automatically have a stipend of £6,000 a year (which in those days was a good deal of money), and also money from the estates, even if they had been able to gamble everything else away. With this they were able to employ three wretched curates to do the church work, leaving the eldest son free to run the properties and spend his time shooting, fishing and hunting. The second son would go into the army or navy or take holy orders so as to be able to inherit immediately, should the first son die.

I had not met my prospective father-in-law except very briefly, when Honor and I went down to Thorney Island where he was the RAF station commander. I had a short leave and we drove through an air raid in Southampton to get to an hotel in the nearest village to the base. When we arrived it had been dark for some hours and we found a message waiting for us to say that Honor's father was out at the base seeing off his bomber crews, and that we should start dinner. This we did, only to be interrupted by the entrance of a policeman who wanted to know who was the owner of the car parked outside the hotel. When I said that

I was, he asked me to move it into the car park nearby. During the war we had to have shaded headlights, with which it was almost impossible to see anything. I was manoeuvring the car in the car park when I nearly ran over a large figure, and really all that I could see of it was gold braid and medals.

I followed this shadowy figure into the hotel and saw it go up to the bar and ask for a double brandy. It was a group captain with a whole string of medals. It could only be Honor's father. He downed a second double brandy and remarked to the barman that he needed that as he had to meet his prospective son-in-law.

It was not a very auspicious start to have almost flattened my future father-in-law, but fortunately he did not realise that I was the 'bloody fool' who had nearly run over him, and we got on very well.

The wedding itself presented certain difficulties. As a Catholic I was anxious to have my own priest, and as an Anglican and owning the living, Honor's family wanted it in their church. I discussed the matter with my regimental padre, who was a Catholic as well as a Welsh rugby international. He readily agreed to take part in the ceremony in the Anglican church, and I think that it must have been one of the first ecumenical weddings ever. It had to be arranged when I could get leave, and as I had recently blown up my colonel's car, he was only too happy to get rid of me for a fortnight to get married. I drove down with my best man, Timmy Knott, and we had to borrow some petrol from the carrier platoon and get some more by telling pathetic stories at garages all the way down to the New Forest, where I spent the night with my father. The next day Timmy and I drove over to Beckington. I had asked my padre if he knew anybody down there, and he said that he had lots of friends near Beckington. That became apparent the morning of the wedding, when we found him hungover to the point of being unable to get out of bed. With hot coffee and cold showers, we got him into some state of coherency and mobility, and at 2.15 p.m. I entered him, rather like placing a ferret into a rabbit hole, into the vestry of the church. Honor had her own clerical squad, headed by the Bishop of Bath and Wells, the rural dean and also the local incumbent. Honor's uncle, who was the usual incumbent, had joined the Royal Air Force as a padre and was already serving overseas.

Things did not start very well, as old Freer, the ancient church warden, had insisted on coming out of retirement for Honor's wedding. He came tottering down the aisle, tripped over my sword and knocked himself out on the altar steps. There had to be a bearer party organised to remove him before we could proceed. It was a High Church service, with incense being swung in front of the clergy who now entered headed by the Bishop and followed rather uncertainly by my priest, with his surplice on back to front. He took his place in one of the pews for the clergy and fell fast asleep. The service started and all went well for a bit, but then my man woke with a start and realised that he was in a church and was supposed to do something. Rising to his feet he intoned Gregorian plain chant to the great astonishment of the other clergy and the congregation. After about a minute of this, he realised that it was not going down well, so he suddenly stopped, sat down and went to sleep again. The service continued until my man woke up again and repeated the performance. We were just about to be married when my priest woke for a third time and suddenly remembered what it was all about. Then we were well and truly married by the Bishop and by my priest, who joined with the Bishop, assisted by the rural dean and the incumbent. Honor looked exceptionally lovely and her father, by now an air commodore, was resplendent.

It seems that perhaps one hundred and fifty years before, Honor's ancestor of the time became much enamoured with a gypsy girl, and he gave the gypsies three water meadows in perpetuity. Every year many of them would come and camp in these fields, and Honor used to play with the gypsy children and learnt a good deal of Romany, and a lot of gypsy lore. When they heard that Miss Honor was getting married, some two hundred and fifty of them came from all over the West Country. They had camped in their fields and while we had been in the church, they had garlanded the whole of the churchyard from the church to the lych-gate with swags of wild flowers which many of them had brought with them from Cornwall and Devon, and dressed in all their finery, they lined the pathway from the church to the lych-gate as a guard of honour. This sight caused some consternation between some of the more stuffy members of my family and my great-aunt Anna was heard to remark loudly, 'Oh my God! He has married a gypsy!'

We moved back to Honor's house for the reception. Most of my family hated the rest, and none of them knew any of Honor's family, but there was a great quantity of the most marvellous champagne, and soon there was a certain fraternisation between them. My father was even seen speaking to my great-aunt!

The cake was brought in, and I drew my sword to cut it. Alas, my soldier servant had omitted to clean Excalibur, which had been put away in thick, brown grease for the duration of the war. It was not a pretty sight, and the butler bore it away with obvious distaste to clean it. The reception took place in the dining room, panelled with dark oak and with somewhat grim ancestors looking down from the pictures around the walls. It was a dark room, and my priest had installed himself behind a great oak chest, together with a glass and two bottles of champagne. Here he solemnly poured first from one bottle and then from the other into his glass and drank toasts to both of us, until he suddenly vanished from sight and was not seen again by anybody for three days. He was a marvellous man and won a posthumous DSO at Anzio later in the war.

When my sword was brought back to me, Honor and I tried to cut the cake, but it resisted all our efforts. I said, 'Come on, darling, we'll both try together to drive it in as hard as we can.' We did, and the sword suddenly broke through the icing, cut down through the cake and struck quivering in the table, from which it was removed only with great difficulty, leaving a scar there for ever.

Finally we left on our honeymoon. It was on 10th February, 1941, and the most glorious day of the whole year: the sun shone out of a brilliant and cloudless blue sky. It was really hot, and as we could not go abroad or even very far due to the petrol rationing, we spent our honeymoon at the Branksome Towers Hotel, which only very shortly afterwards was to be destroyed by fire bombs. We were to remain married for fifty-two and a half years, until my darling Honor died of a cardiac collapse in July 1993.

After I returned from honeymoon leave, my colonel arranged for me to go on a chemical warfare course at Winterbourne Gunner. I had a fortnight's leave to get married and another three weeks of the chemical warfare course near Salisbury, which was really a continuation of our honeymoon. When I eventually returned with my bride, I reported to port security, an MI5 branch which was established locally at Temple Ewell just outside Dover. It was run from a charming cottage – Pear Tree Cottage – under Major Thompson, known locally as Gestapo Tom. I had met him on several previous occasions, and apparently he had asked of me. Dover was no place for Honor, and I established her in Canterbury, where she started to work in the radiology department of the Kent and Canterbury

Hospital. Here too she was bombed regularly, and the cross-channel guns targeted the roads between Dover and Canterbury, along which I used to drive furiously and as often as I could.

My father was determined not to be done out of the war, and although he was held together with silver wire and silver plates, he set about forming a local cavalry squadron as soon as the Home Guard was formed. The squadron was mounted on New Forest ponies with the odd hunter, and consisted of estate workers, local farmers and their sons and one or two elderly and local landowners. They were armed with a variety of weapons: pig sticking spears brought back from India, lances, swords and sabres, shotguns, a few sporting rifles and an elephant gun which I contributed – a .600 black powder rifle with a kick like that of the proverbial mule. This was scheduled as the 'anti-tank rifle'.

My father could only ride by balance, as his pelvis had been so badly fractured that he had no grip at all with his knees. This did not deter him in the least. The squadron carried out exercises, and my father even recruited a trumpeter from the local boy scouts. He was taught to sound various calls such as the walk, trot, canter and charge. They exercised in the New Forest and presented a somewhat strange appearance. Some had battle dress, hunting boots and britches with battle dress blouses, while my father, of course, wore his Hussar uniform, sporting First World War ribbons and the wings of the Royal Flying Corps.

The evil day came when they were to be inspected by some local general, and the inspecting officers were grouped on a small knoll facing towards a group of trees some two hundred and fifty yards away to their front. All around was the heather and trees of the New Forest. When all was ready, a trumpet sounded in the wood, and a line of horsemen walked into the open. This was quickly followed by the trot and the canter, and as the line advanced, the charge was sounded and down came the lances and boar spears and the swords and sabres glittering in the sun. The whole squadron came at full gallop towards the general, who hastily took cover behind his car. Suddenly, on the right of the squadron there was a tremendous bang, a flash of flame and a huge cloud of smoke. The 'anti-tank rifle' had been fired. The squadron charged through the small group comprising the general and his staff, who were cowering behind their staff cars, and halted on the far side. My father wheeled with the squadron behind him, trotted up to the general and saluted. The general was visibly shaken and could only say, 'Why are you wearing Royal Flying Corps wings?' To which my father proudly replied, 'Because I won them in the last war.' In fact, he had probably brought down more planes than anybody other than the Red Baron, but unfortunately they were ours rather than the Germans'.

The general mumbled something or other, jumped into his staff car together with his other officers and disappeared over the heath as fast as he could go.

My father was hurt and very much incensed when a few days later there came an order officially disbanding his squadron. After that he took no further part in the war and became largely uninterested in it.

Pear Tree Cottage

At the end of our honeymoon, I reported to Major Thompson and Honor remained in Canterbury. Life at Pear Tree Cottage followed a set pattern. I would open the mail in the morning, go through any reports received during the night and at about 11 a.m. Gestapo Tom would arrive. He was, I think, half German, as he spoke the language flawlessly, as well as a number of other languages.

As a British officer, he had served on the German general staff as a spy in the First World War. He was very reticent about this and did not like talking about it, but I heard that he had done marvellous work. He lived locally in a most beautiful old manor house. Invariably, he would come in and say, 'Good morning, Ronnie. Is there anything in?' I would show him the letters and reports. He would go through them very quickly, throwing some into the waste-paper basket. Others he would pass to me saying, 'Write to them saying that I cannot go.' To others he would say, 'Answer that any way you like. It really only has to be acknowledged.'

The history of the intelligence service can be traced back to Elizabeth I in the sixteenth century, when her foreign secretary, Lord Walsinham, set up a private intelligence service which worked directly under him. The Secret Intelligence Service, or SIS, usually called MI6, still works as a sort of adjunct to the foreign office with a certain degree of autonomy. Military Intelligence which includes the Army, Naval and Air Force Intelligence, work under their respective ministries. MI5 is the security service which works under the Home Secretary and is responsible for internal security and counter espionage, and works with the Special Branch of the police, sometimes with the customs, and also with the service departments. It started as a branch of the army and is of comparatively recent formation (the First World War and shortly before – say the beginning of the century). In war time there is a certain blurring of the roles of MI5 and MI6 and the two services work together in certain fields.

Military Intelligence consists of Air Intelligence, Army Intelligence and Naval Intelligence, each working under their respective ministries. To complicate matters still further, there are the various branches of 'MI' which deal with recruitment, or in certain cases 'assignment'; departments dealing with weapons and the development of enemy weapons; the organisation for assisting prisoner of war escapes (in war time), and very many other aspects of intelligence work. The best-known branch of 'MI' – MI5 – which in fact has a whole number of sub-branches and deals with subversion, counter-intelligence, catching spies and so on. Broadly speaking, the SIS is also MI6 and deals with intelligence gathering abroad, while MI5 deals with counter-intelligence and the security of the state within the United Kingdom, and it works closely with the Special Branch of the Metropolitan Police. There are also various co-ordinating Joint Intelligence Boards and Committees.

This is a gross over-simplification of a rather compli-cated network of intelligence and counter-intelligence organisations which work under different ministries: for example, MI5 comes for the most part under the home office, while MI6, as stated above, comes under the foreign office. The SIS is staffed for the most part with civilians, who may in war time carry a military rank. The MI5 organisation used to be staffed mainly with military officers, but rank meant very little or nothing. There were depart-ments where the head of the department was a captain, and he had colonels and brigadiers working under him. Some, probably most, MI5 officers did not wear uniforms, and in some cases – like that of Mr Knight – military uniforms were sometimes worn to which the wearer was not entitled. It was a complicated system, and in many cases the opera-tions of MI5 and those of MI6 overlapped with MI5 operations taking place abroad (such as the deception organisation, run by XX Committee) and MI6 operations taking place in the United Kingdom. Added to all these there was the Intelligence corps within the army itself, Port Security MI5 (L), regional security officers, SOE and the American organisations. However, there have been many books written about the intelligence services, the various roles they had and the operations which they undertook, together with their organisations. It is an arcane and specialised study, and does not come into this book.

Major Thompson worked for Port Security, which was a branch of MI5 (L). Its function was, in our case, the security of the general area of the south-east coast in the vicinity of Dover-Folkestone and a fairly large surrounding area and coastline. The purpose was to detect or prevent the landing of enemy spies or saboteurs, and to detect their presence in the area as well as any subversive activities intended to help the enemy in any way. Being the area closest to the German-occupied coast of France, only twenty-odd miles across the Channel, it was considered to be especially sensitive.

There were always reports of flashing lights and of people who were convinced that they had seen German agents being dropped by parachute, or that the neighbours next door were in reality German spies. He would deal with it all very quickly and then say, 'Well, that's that. Now I am going off to luncheon' – and off he would go to the Naval mess, where the food was better than in the army messes. After luncheon, he would have one or two glasses of port, put *The Times* over his face and go to sleep until about four in the afternoon. He would reappear at about five and say, 'Good evening, Ronnie. Is there anything in?' I would give him any reports and correspondence which had come in during the day. He would glance at them briefly and then say, 'You had better go out tonight – not too early, say at about ten thirty. Go down Lydden Spout, along the base of the cliffs and then in at the Warren and back again on the top of the cliffs. See if there is anything going on at that pub. You should be back about four thirty. Well, I am going to Canterbury this evening, and I will take your nice wife out to dinner.'

Lydden Spout was a high cliff west of Dover. There had been wooden stairs down it to reach the beach, but these had been blown up to prevent any German landing parties from reaching the top of the cliffs. In order to reach the beach we had to go down on a rope. This was bad enough in the summer, but in the winter, with a gale and sleet blowing down the Channel, it was extremely unpleasant. Even worse was coming in through the Warren. This whole area was a maze of barbed wire and minefields, anti-tank and anti-personnel. Behind it were soldiers with machine guns, ready to open fire on any movement that they saw in the minefields. It was a slow, dangerous and extremely unpleasant performance. The pub on top of the cliffs had attracted Gestapo Tom's attention for some reason, and he always included it in these nightly patrols.

I never really knew what we were supposed to find, and in fact we found nothing. I became convinced that the old man was gaga – until one night we did find something. It was a rubber boat three-quarters buried in the sand. There was very little sand along this beach, which is nearly all chalk, and one of my patrol actually stumbled over it. Clearly an attempt had been made to bury it, and those responsible had very nearly succeeded.

I rushed back as quickly as I could. It was about one in the morning before I reached Gestapo Tom's manor house. I rang the bell and hammered on the door without success. I shouted without response. I knew where his bedroom was, and threw a handful of gravel from the drive up at the window. Almost instantly a head appeared, surmounted by a nightcap. The window flew open and a voice roared, 'Bugger off!' I waited for a few minutes and then tried again, and this time Gestapo Tom shouted at me, 'Bugger off, I tell you. If you do that again I'll shoot you.' There was nothing for it: the window was slammed and I went back to bed.

The next morning at eleven, Gestapo Tom appeared. 'Good morning Ronnie,' he said. 'Is there anything in?' 'Well, sir,' I replied, 'I tried to tell you last night—' I got no further: he whipped round on me and said, 'Don't you ever do that again. Now what was it all about?' I told him about the rubber boat. 'Pull down the wall map,' he said. 'Now, exactly where was it?'

He considered the map for a few minutes and then said, 'There will be four of them. One will have gone into Folkestone, probably to get supplies. He will come back by bus and will get off about here.' He pointed to a point on the map not far from a small wood. 'There will be two more of them in the wood, and they will have a radio transmitter. The fourth man will have gone to the pub – the one on the cliffs you have been keeping an eye on. Now go and get the army.' (He always referred to the army as some extraneous organisation in which he had no part.) 'They must search the wood thoroughly. I want another section hidden close to the bus stop, and take a platoon to the pub and arrest the whole lot.'

'Well,' he said, looking at his watch, 'it is time that I went to luncheon. You had better get on with it immediately. Go to the castle and give the brigadier my compliments, and ask him to let you have the soldiers.' And off he went to luncheon, as usual.

The extraordinary thing was that it turned out exactly as he had said. We found the four men exactly where he said they would be. They even had a radio transmitter in a suitcase, together with English ration books, fairly good English identity cards, four automatic pistols and ammunition, maps, a Leica camera, a code book and field glasses. However, the professional effect was rather spoilt by a half-eaten German sausage and a large Dutch cheese.

They were taken away by the army and locked up in the castle. As usual, Gestapo Tom arrived at five that evening;

and as usual, he said 'Good evening, Ronnie. Anything in?' I told him that we had found the four men where he had said. He expressed no surprise and announced that he was going to dinner.

I said, 'But sir, what about the men who have been arrested?' He replied, 'The trouble with you young chaps is that you are always in a hurry. Let them stew for a bit. Oh, all right. You need not go out tonight. Meet me here at midnight and we will go and talk to them. Now I must be off for dinner.'

At midnight I went with Gestapo Tom up to the castle, and there he gave me a lesson in interrogation that I never forgot. Within a couple of hours, without the use of force or threats, he knew more about the four men than they knew about themselves: how they had been landed, what their mission was, how they were to be picked up and where and when, where they had been trained and, in fact, everything that there was to be known about them. Oddly enough, only one was a German – two others were Dutch, and the fourth a Flamand. I never saw them again or even heard what happened to them.

Gestapo Tom was a most extraordinary man. He taught me a great deal, and I came to respect him very greatly. Life with him was never dull. Now, for the first time, Honor and I were able to work as a team. Her knowledge of languages was extremely useful, and we had various adventures together. Some of these were exciting, and some abortive. On one occasion, a bottle with a message in it was picked up at Herne Bay. The message was written in Hebrew, which Gestapo Tom understood. He told me that it meant nothing but that Hebrew letters had a numerical significance, and Honor and I were sent off to find a rabbi who could put figures under the letters. It was no easy task to find a rabbi at that time, and we scoured the area for hours before we found that there was one at Ramsgate. On arrival there, we were told that he would be found at this late hour at The End of the World. This did not sound promising until it was explained that The End of the World was a pub, and quite close. I drove there, and arrived just after closing time. The rabbi had gone home. We found his home, and he very kindly worked on the message while his wife gave us tea out of a huge silver samovar. They were nice and kind people.

On the way back there was brilliant moonlight, and a German night fighter must have seen our dimmed head-lights on a deserted road. The first thing that we knew about it was when a burst of cannon-gun fire exploded on the road just in front of us. We slammed on the brakes, tumbled into the ditch and switched off all the car lights; then we saw the aircraft turning to come back. It returned along the road and fired again, but this time the bullets impacted just behind the stationary car, which was half in the ditch anyway. Perhaps the pilot thought that he had hit it, because to our great relief, he climbed away and disap-peared.

There were adventures with people who were reported to be signalling with lamps and powerful torches to E-boats and German submarines in the Channel, and on one occasion, we did find a house with a transmitter, with the aerial stuck up the chimney. In point of fact, under a regulation introduced right at the beginning of the war (18B), nearly all enemy agents, together with sympathisers and also a number of totally innocent people, were gathered up and transferred to the Isle of Man, and we had surpris-ingly few enemy agents in Britain during the whole war.

There were the usual anonymous letters accusing neigh-bours, spiteful accusations totally without foundation, and reports of lights which were supposed to be signals to German bombers, but which in reality turned out to be somebody letting their cat out for the night.

Due to the fact that Honor had had two very serious attacks of rheumatic fever as a child and a young girl, which had very seriously affected her heart (in fact she was unlikely to live beyond the age of fourteen, according to the doctors), she had not been called up for war work, drafted into the Women's Auxiliary Air Force, the ATS (the Women's branch of the army), the Women's Naval Service or the land army. However she volunteered immediately war broke out in September 1939 as a VAD (Voluntary Aid Dresser) – in effect a volunteer, auxiliary nurse.

It was then that she discovered that she had healing powers. As a young girl, untrained and under-qualified, she had been sent to sit beside dying men who were beyond any hope of recovery and to comfort them in their last hours. She sat beside them and sometimes held one of their hands, as they drifted in and out of consciousness. The strange thing was that they began to recover.

When this happened several times, the hospital began to think that she had some sort of healing effect. Especially as just sitting beside them, holding a hand in hers, left her totally exhausted after matter of three or four hours. Finally, she could no longer carry on, and the doctor sent her home for a period of complete rest. She herself was completely drained of any vital energy. She never knew what this was, and nether did I, but on two occasions when I was really very seriously ill and thought about dying, I believe that she did it for me.

After we were married and I had gone to work for Gestapo Tom, Honor insisted again on starting work at Kent and Canterbury Hospital. This time she went into X-ray. In fact, she became very good at this, and was able to read X-rays and in emergency to take them. However, I often wondered, many years later, if the cancer which she had, had not had its origins in these X-rays, which in those days were very much less protected than they are today. Thank

God, she died from a cardiac collapse before the cancer became intolerable.

From time to time Honor had a day or two off, and I was able to combine these with chores for Gestapo Tom. I remember one day when I was able to pick her up at the hospital in Canterbury and we went to Herne Bay, on the south side of the Thames Estuary. There had been persistent reports of a 'German' who was a farmer about four miles out of town. He was said to have been flashing lights to German aircraft come in to raid London. This was by no means unusual. We had at least two or three letters every day sent on from the police and accusing neighbours of flashing lights, of being German spies and so on. These were generally just malicious, with absolutely no foundation in fact. However, the German planes raiding London did, quite often, come in up the Thames Estuary; so, no matter how silly these reports were nine times out of the ten, we had to investigate all of them. On the occasion in question, I collected Honor from the hospital, and we went out on the farm. It was quite some way away, and we arrived in the afternoon. The farmer who had been the subject of the accusation was out in the farm, but his wife said that he would be back soon. While we were waiting for him to come back, his wife asked us if we would like some tea. We accepted, and after tea the wife produced a family album of holiday snaps. I was looking vaguely and with little interest through these when I noticed that in 1938 they had both been to Germany and had taken a trip in one of the river boats down the Rhine.

I asked the wife about this and she was enthusiastic. 'We had a lovely time,' she said. 'It was so pretty, and the wine was lovely – and all these marvellous castles perched on crags.'

'How did you get on with the people?' I asked.

'Oh, they were so charming and so friendly. We really loved it.'

'Did you tell your friends about it?' Honor asked.

'Oh, yes. We told them what a wonderful time we had had, and that we really ought to learn some German, as we missed so much not being able to speak the language.'

I asked a few more questions, and just then the farmer returned for his tea. He seemed to be a typical Kentish farmer and quite a nice man. I asked him about his holiday in Germany, and he replied that he had had such a good time there that they hoped that the war would soon be over and they would be able to go back next year.

As Dunkirk had resulted in the German occupation of most of Europe and the virtual destruction of the British Army, I said that I thought that he was being rather optimistic. He replied that perhaps next year was a bit premature, but that he did not believe that that Hitler fellow could last long, and that anyway the RAF was shooting down all the German aircraft.

I asked if he went out at night, and he replied that he did every night to make sure that there was nobody about and that everything was secure.

Later I was to spend two days watching the farm. Before that I discovered that a neighbour, an elderly woman, had written to various people to complain that the farmer, who was 'a German lover' and 'a spy', had tried to poison her drinking water, had set snares to try to kill her cat and had committed various other dastardly acts.

Unfortunately, it was often the case that people denounced their neighbours on no evidence whatsoever. This happened all over Europe, and many people who were totally innocent were seized and often tortured by the Gestapo on the basis of a malicious accusation of a neighbour. This is something to be remembered should we ever have the misfortune to have a police state.

In this case, the man's only crime was that he had been to Germany on a holiday in 1938 and had enjoyed himself and had told the neighbours that they had had a good holiday and would like to go back one day.

The security services had another problem, which was that in the years before the war, very many extremely eminent men, horrified by the ghastly carnage of the First World War had believed that Anglo-German friendship should be fostered to prevent any future conflict between the two countries. To this end, the Link and the Anglo-German Friendship Association had been formed. Amongst the very eminent members of these two organisations were three dukes, a dozen or more peers, the former Director of Naval Intelligence, half a dozen generals, the Governor of the Bank of England, the Chief Advisor to the Foreign Office, goodness knows how many Members of Parliament from both side of the house, and very many extremely important people from all walks of life. All of these were thought to be truly patriotic people, but some believed that we should not be fighting Germany and that to avoid another catastrophic war it might be possible to come to some sort of agreement which would avoid the destruction of most of Europe.

There was also the British Union of Fascists under Sir Oswald Mosley. Although Sir Oswald ordered all the members of this political party on the outbreak of the war to fight for Britain against the Germans (although he deplored the war) and virtually all of them did as ordered, there were some, such as James Joyce (who became 'Lord Haw-Haw', broadcasting anti-British propaganda from Germany) who did not. There were in fact very few. The number of traitors was minuscule. As a precaution, regulation no. 18B was introduced, and all who were suspected of having sympathetic contacts with the Germans and Italians were rounded up and sent off to the Isle of Man – where, in fact, they had a very pleasant life throughout the war, living in considerable comfort and with very much more to eat that we had!

Another danger were the dedicated communists. When Hitler made a pact with Stalin for the division of Poland, there was a very real prospect of British communists organising strikes, possible sabotage and espionage, as well as propaganda, as their ideological home was the Soviet Union, now allied with Germany.

Fortunately for all, Hitler broke the alliance with the Soviets and invaded Russia. As a consequence, overnight we had the British communists wholeheartedly on our side again, as the Soviet Union became an ally of Britain against Germany and Italy.

However, for a short time ideological and fanatical communists were regarded as security risks.

Of course, later on, communist elements within the British services did an immense amount of harm. To mention just a few: Philby, Blunt, Maclean, Blake (whose real name was Behar), and several others who were members of the Intelligence Service or diplomats. There were others who, as military officers, were to change coded messages received from Yugoslavia so as to give credit to the Tito partisans for actions actually performed by the anti-communist guerrillas and partisans, thereby influencing British policy to support Tito and the communist partisans.

I was to meet Blunt in Italy, long after the war. He used to come up to a villa – San Fillipo. This was in the valley below Anticoli Corrado, the village where the British School in Rome had rented a villa from Carbone. A little clique of homosexuals used to come up to San Fillipo most weekends, and on several occasions Blunt, who was on holiday at the British School, came with them. On two or three occasions my mother, who was a rather good artist, hearing that Blunt was at San Fillipo, invited them for tea. I must confess that although the man was absolutely fascinating on his subject – he was a keeper of the Queen's pictures – neither I nor Honor liked him. We thought that there was something vaguely sinister about him.

In fact, during my lifetime I have met a good many people. I suppose that there are few who can say that they have had luncheon with the Pope (when he was a newly-ordained priest at the Seminary in Rome in 1947), tea with Hitler, luncheon with Mussolini, dinner with Franco, luncheon with Salazar, met Churchill and De Gaulle, met (but was not introduced to) Eisenhower (I was far too junior), knew Montgomery rather well and met Alexander – as well as a small army of politicians from all Western European countries and also America.

Army HQ

Finally, I had to leave Gestapo Tom. I was sent to the Army Command Headquarters of the South-Eastern Army in Reigate. Here we had a very strange experience. It was quite impossible to obtain any flat to let anywhere in or near Reigate; but within twenty-four hours I found a house agent with a most charming flat in the centre of the little town. The rent was very reasonable, and I telephoned immediately to Honor to join me there. It was a lovely flat built over an old gate house, and we had the whole of the top floor; there were other tenants below us and on either side, with the great arch in the middle. It was just what we wanted, with two bedrooms, a huge drawing room-cum-dining room, a bathroom and kitchen. It was very well furnished and delightful.

As wives were not allowed to be with their husbands who were at Command Headquarters, we took the flat in my wife's maiden name, and I became her lodger. The first thing that we noticed about the flat was that letters kept arriving there for ten or twelve different people. These letters I duly took to the house agent. The next thing was that it was impossible to keep the front door shut. It had an ordinary Yale-type spring lock and also a chain, but even with the chain on the door kept on opening. I searched the flat thoroughly over and over again, but there was nobody hidden in it. On one occasion, we came back in the evening and I shut the door, locked it and put the chain on (it was of the type which slides into a long slot). I turned round to go up the few steps to our bedroom and heard a loud click behind me. The chain was off and the door was open. I was never able to explain this. I was standing with my back to the door and nobody could possibly have unhooked the chain. There were also footsteps along the corridor, and somebody used to bang very loudly on the door of the drawing room. We heard this very often, and so did guests when they were dining with us. When the door was opened, there would be nobody there. None of this worried us very much except the opening of the front door, which would have meant that anybody could have walked into the flat when we were asleep or out.

As the months went by things became better, and eventually this mysterious phenomenon almost entirely disappeared. However, when we came to leave Reigate, I handed in the keys of the flat to the house agent. He gave me a sort of smirk and asked if we had enjoyed our time there. I said we had, and asked why. Then it came out that in the previous year there had been some fourteen different tenants. Some had stayed only one night and then left. I believe that the place has now been pulled down, but that may well have been for a different reason.

During the time that I was at Reigate I had to ride a motorcycle, to the great peril of myself and other road users. I was never able to be fully in control of this machine, but covered thousands of miles of country on it, becoming familiar with the side roads and by-roads of the whole of the south-east of England. At this time, too, perhaps because I spoke several languages, I was attached to raiding parties across the Channel. These were supposed to keep the Germans on their toes, capture a few prisoners, possibly gain some knowledge of the fortifications being built and to build up an enemy 'order of battle': in short, who was where. I don't remember much about these raids. To begin with, we were all given Benzedrine tablets intended to keep us awake. Alas, on me they had the reverse effect and I fell into a deep sleep, from which I was awakened, only with great difficulty, when we reached the French coast. There, yawning and more than half asleep, I stumbled about in the dark, looking for somebody to kill with a wire garrotte. We were sometimes attacked on the way back by German E-boats and aircraft, but usually I was sound asleep.

For a short time, I was a stand-in ADC to General Sir Bernard Paget, the Army Commander: a most charming man, whom I liked very much. Unfortunately, he was shortly replaced by General Montgomery, later to be Sir Bernard Montgomery, and later still, Viscount Montgomery. One day, very shortly after his arrival, I was summoned by the Brigadier General Staff and told that I had to act as a stand-in for the new general's ADC, who was ill. I protested in vain, and in short order found myself reporting to the general at 'A' Mess. There were those officers who had very great loyalty and unbounded admiration for 'Monty'. I was not amongst them, and I found him to be a most unpleasant man: frequently extremely rude to junior officers, arrogant, utterly lacking in any sense of humour and with an ego complex of monumental proportions.

To give an example. Very shortly after his arrival, I was told the previous evening that the general was to inspect several units on the south coast. My job, therefore, was to prepare a brief for the general, informing him which units he was to inspect and giving their exact positions, together with a profile on the commanding officer, his second-in-command, and the company commanders of each unit. The first of these units was a Territorial Army battalion commanded by a very good officer, whom I will call Colonel Brown. The inspection went off very well – in fact too well, as Monty always liked to find something to criticise, such as crossed boot laces, mess tins without their covers or some other small detail of this sort (including, of course, brasses which had not been polished on both sides). He did not find any and was becoming visibly irritated. The inspection was finally over, and instead of walking back with the battalion commander to the saluting base and taking the salute and the march past of the battalion, he suddenly stopped. Turning to Colonel Brown, he said, 'Can you run five miles?' Colonel Brown smiled and said that he would certainly have a shot at it. Then Monty said, 'Colonel Brown, how old are you?' Of course, Monty knew already, as I had put this in the brief which I had given him (together with other information including that Colonel Brown had got a DSO and MC from the First World War, and had really made the battalion in the twenty-odd intervening years). Colonel Brown replied, 'I am fifty, sir.' 'You are too old. You are relieved of your command,' Monty snapped. Then, turning to me, he said, 'Make a note of it.' He then did not even say goodbye, but turned on his heel and walked off parade without taking the salute and the march past.

Of course, he was right. Fifty was too old for an infantry battalion commander, but it would have been so easy to have gone back to the mess, after taking the march past and the salute, and have said, 'Colonel Brown, you have done a marvellous job with your battalion. It is first class and I congratulate you, but you yourself will realise that fifty is really too old for an infantry battalion commander in war today, and with the very greatest regret I have to tell you that I will have to find you a good job on the staff.'

It was brutal and unnecessary, and my opinion of him was not enhanced on the way back at the end of the day. The Brigadier General Staff was a heavy smoker, and he had not been able to have a cigarette all day, as Monty would not allow any smoking anywhere near him. However, in the staff car there was a glass partition which was wound up. I was in the back with the general, taking notes of the inspection and the brigadier was in front with the driver. He turned and tapped on the glass. I wound down the window. 'Would you mind, sir, if I smoked?' the brigadier asked. 'There is the partition between us.' 'Not at all,' Monty said. I wound up the glass partition and the brigadier got out his cigarette case. He was just about to light a cigarette when Monty rapped on the window and shouted, 'But not in here. Put it out!'

That was the sort of man he was, as I found him. On another occasion, some local admirer sent him a marvellous bottle of old port. In conversation at the dining table with the Brigadier General Staff, he said that somebody had sent him this bottle of port; what should he do with it? The brigadier said that it should be opened, allowed to breathe for a bit, and allowed to become slightly warmer, up to room temperature. Monty turned to the mess sergeant and said, 'Take it out and boil it.' The mess sergeant did not understand, or thought that perhaps Monty had not, and said, 'It should only be brought to room temperature, sir.' Monty snapped back at him, 'You heard me. Take it out and boil it.' Then, turning to the brigadier, he said, 'I hope that you will enjoy it.' There were many such incidents, and the time that I was with him seemed endless, but eventually his own man returned, and I went back to my normal duties. However, it was with him that I went to see De Gaulle. De Gaulle could speak perfectly adequate English, but refused to do so. Monty said, 'Tell the general that I consider that the Free French troops in the command require considerable further training.' I translated and De Gaulle replied briefly, '*Non*.' Monty came out with other demands, and the only reply he ever got from De Gaulle was a simple '*Non*'. The meeting lasted for some time, and frankly it is impossible to translate '*Non*' in a variety of diplomatic ways. Monty got even less change from the Commander of the Canadian Corps. We arrived some ten minutes early for the meeting and inspection, and Monty started in at once with a very rude comment about punctuality. What he got back in reply was infinitely ruder, and he left immediately in a huff.

Not very long after this, there came a directive from the War Office ordering a major security check to be made in the army command area. I was detailed to do this together with a naval officer and an air force officer. For six weeks, we disguised ourselves in different ways, and with false documents we tried to obtain classified information, take photographs of military bases, obtain entry to headquarters, carry out acts of 'sabotage' and so on. It was enormous fun.

On one occasion, I disguised myself as a police inspector and went to a large vehicle park. I explained that there had been a fatal accident the previous day some miles away, in which a military vehicle had been involved, and I requested to be allowed into the vehicle park to inspect the trucks for damage or bloodstains. I was left alone to carry out my police duties; the police identification document was, of course, very badly forged. In the vehicle park, I spent an hour sticking on to vehicles pieces of paper labelled 'Fitted with an incendiary device', 'Hydraulic brakes lines cut', 'Delay action bomb attached to petrol tank', and so on. I then left.

On another occasion, I disguised myself as a Catholic priest (who has ever seen a Catholic priest with a moustache?). Here I obtained the strength of the unit. When left alone for a moment in the operations room, I photographed their maps; but had to beat a hasty retreat when the commanding officer told me that he had five men in his unit who wanted confession. As an engineer officer, I was able to get into a huge ammunition park, and spent some time sticking 'Sabotaged' notices on ammunition dumps. Had they been real sabotage devices, there would have been a bang loud enough to have been heard in France by the Germans.

Meanwhile my accomplices, the naval officer and the air force officer, had been up to the same tricks. We made detection really very easy, but we were never once questioned or suspected. We finally met to discuss what we should do next, and the air force officer wrote himself out a 'pass'. It was headed from the General Headquarters of the Luftwaffe, and read, 'The bearer of this pass is an agent of the Third Reich. All Royal Air Force personnel in the United Kingdom are hereby ordered to give him any information, assistance and entrance to all RAF bases and headquarters'. It was signed 'General von Reichenau, commanding the Third German Air Group, Willhelm-strasse, Berlin'. To make it even better, we put a photograph of the air force officer – in German air force uniform – on it, and stuck a huge swastika rubber stamp on top of it. With this 'pass', he obtained entry to every RAF establishment that he visited in the whole of the south-east of England.

It was a virtual impossibility to teach the troops security. On some occasions, when suitably disguised, I used to chat to troops working on, say, an ammunition depot. They would say, 'You know, sir, this is a security test month, and we are expecting some chap to come along and try to get into the depot.' I would reply, 'Oh yes? and what will you do to him when you catch him?' They replied, 'We'll throw the bugger in the lake and see if he can swim.' 'How will you recognise him?' I would ask. 'Oh, he will have dark glasses, a false beard and speak with a foreign sort of accent,' they said. I did not disillusion them – after all, that was not my job.

At the end, we sent up to the War Office a report detailing our activities and simply stating, 'There is no security in South-Eastern Command'. In due course, a huge military rocket descended from War Office and landed on the desk of the Commander-in-Chief – General Montgomery. It was not long before he discovered who were the authors of this report, and I was once again on my way – as far as he could send me. I reported to Northern Command, and Honor and I moved into a really vile little house in Moorland Road, Fulford, just on the outskirts of York.

Northern Command

It was very dark, very damp and very gloomy. Honor was expecting our first baby. Neither of us enjoyed York. It was cold and there was very little food. I still had my car and some petrol, and I had my soldier servant, Doward, who had come with me from the days in Dover. He was a good cook – when there was anything to cook – and when the baby came, he was marvellous with it, helping Honor enormously.

I set up an intelligence office, and opened a special battle school in part of the grounds of Castle Howard. I had a strange collection of people to train: French, Poles and others who hoped one day to go back into occupied Europe.

We were in York for the Baedecker Raids. The Germans bombed Bath, York and various other towns. They hit the cavalry barracks with several bombs and created some casualties, and did a good deal of destruction in the town, especially in the vicinity of the railway station. On one of these raids a bomb landed just behind our house, blowing off most of the roof. The plane responsible then circled and was very clearly visible. A burst of cannon-fire came through what was left of the roof and landed on our dressing table in the bedroom, blowing it to pieces together with Honor's last bottle of French perfume. Ignoring the shattered window and the glass, she leapt out of bed and, going to where the window had been, she cursed the aircraft and its crew with terrible words. Whether it was due to them or not, within two minutes the plane was shot down by a Z battery (I think that it was the only plane that they ever shot down).

The Z batteries were a form of multiple rocket launcher, with an explosive warhead fitted to a long, iron pipe and, again on the principle that everything that goes up must eventually come down, the rain of these iron pipes descending was infinitely more lethal than the explosive warhead supposed to destroy the enemy aircraft.

The next morning, bright and early, I went out to find the wreck and discovered that it was practically intact, and had made a forced landing in a field. The crew had been hurt but not killed and had been removed to hospital. I put a cordon round the wreck and sent my sergeant back to get a truck with as many forty-five gallon drums in it as he could find. On examination of the aircraft, I came across something labelled 'Pumpe'. I gave it an experimental waggle and out came lovely one hundred-octane aviation fuel. I worked on this most of the day, and this petrol, cut with paraffin, was to last us for the rest of the war. Between working the pump and filling the forty-five gallon drums, I collected maps, the machine guns, the 20 mm cannon, and did the other chores which were expected of me.

I ran a recognition centre for enemy weapons, uniforms, badges, documents and so on, and taught troops how to use enemy weapons. I also ran the battle school, which attracted some attention in higher quarters.

I also managed to get TB. The army doctors were anxious to send me to a TB hospital situated in a marsh from which few emerged alive. I remained at home on sick leave, but we sent Marcus, our son, down to stay with his great-grandmother and his nanny in Somerset. Food was really very scarce, and I think that we were saved by my father, who gave us all that he still had from the gardens of his house in Hampshire – a huge sack of onions, which we had for luncheon and dinner every day. Onions are an old wives cure for TB, and whether it was due to them or not, I recovered fairly quickly. My poor Honor used to walk for miles through the snow to get food, and haul heavy baskets back to Fulford whenever she was able to get any. The walls of our bedroom ran with water, especially after the roof had been blown off, and the damp peeled all the paper off the walls of the sitting room below. Any sort of heating too was in short supply, and it was terribly cold.

Some German prisoners of war escaped from somewhere near York, and everybody was warned to be particularly careful to secure their houses and not to let anybody get in whom they did know. At that time, I had to go off for a three-day exercise with my instructors, and I asked Honor to be particularly careful. On reaching the exercise area that evening, we found that it was already occupied by other troops, so we had to return. It was about 1.30 a.m. before I got back to Moorland Road and banged on the door. There was no answer, and I banged again. Suddenly the door flew open, and something like the Albert Hall fell on my head. I was knocked senseless to the ground, and the door was slammed in my face. When I recovered consciousness, I discovered that my tin hat had a huge dent in it; there is no doubt that had I not been wearing it my brains would have been all over the garden. I set up a very loud howl of protest. Cautiously the door was opened an inch or two, and a voice in the darkness said, 'Oh, it's you. I thought that you were a German.' I still have the tin hat with the dent in it.

It was at about this time that I did a course on explosives and demolition, which I found very interesting indeed. Two of my instructors, Sergeant Major Beckley (formerly of the Scots Guards) and Corporal Horne, were experts in this field. It is fascinating to learn how and where to blow up a bridge and the difference in the amount of explosives required to blow a steel bridge, a stone bridge, a brick bridge or a wooden bridge, and where it should be placed. We worked mainly with plastic gelignite, a gun cotton primer and no. 33 electric detonators, but also with chemical delay detonators and clockwork delay fuses. Then there were the gun cotton necklaces for pylons and telegraph poles and various types of booby trap, ranging from the wire attached to a hand-grenade and stretched across a pathway or in the wood to the pressure switch under a lavatory seat which would cause an immediate movement when sat upon. We also used crooked pictures on walls – the Germans have a great sense of order, and a crooked picture on the wall frequently required to be put straight, with surprising results. In fact the use of booby traps of one sort or another opens the door to inventive imagination which is almost limitless; a wire attached by the bottom of one leg of a chair, through floor boards to a mine underneath could also prove effective.

It was at this time that I met Colonel Elder Wills in the Natural History Museum in London. He was a most remarkable man, and he and his team produced the explosive electric light bulb. This was effective especially if there was to be a meeting of high-level officers. Prior to the meeting, an electrician would come in to check that all the lights worked. Naturally, the meeting had to start in the afternoon in daylight and go on long enough for it to become necessary for the lights to be turned on.

They also invented explosive coal. The trick with this was for a small boy from the Resistance to be seen by a German sentry walking away from a coal dump used for train and factory furnaces and carrying a piece of Elder Wills's coal. The sentry would then order the boy to 'Put that back on the dump'. The boy would do so, and sooner or later, Elder Wills's explosive coal would go into the factory furnace, or the firebox of a train. If the train happened to be an ammunition train, the results would be spectacular!

Wills also invented the explosive dead rat. This, left on the floor of a factory furnace room, would provoke an automatic reaction: somebody would pick it up on a shovel and throw it into the furnace. He invented the explosive dead dog, which would float down a canal until it came up against lock gates. Fitted with sensitive pressure switches, it would blow the gates to bits. He invented explosive goat dung, which was effective in North Africa. A German truck or staff car would pass over it, at least blasting out the tyres. In Burma, he produced explosive elephant dung, which had even more spectacular results. He also produced fish (I suppose they were made of bakelite, as plastics were in their infancy). These were filled with sten-guns, ammunition, explosives, detonators, and so on, and were set to float about a metre or so below the surface of the sea. They were released from submarines off the Brittany coast. The Germans allowed the Breton fishing boats to go out to fish near the coast, guarded by a pack of E-boats. The fishermen would set their nets and trawl up Elder Wills's 'fish', together with other real fish. These were then all landed under German supervision, and the Elder Wills's 'fish' distributed to the Resistance.

To make his fish more realistic, Elder Wills invented a very odoriferous 'fish slime', with which he coated them. Alas, this had some unexpected results, and the Natural History Museum was besieged by literally hundreds of cats attracted by this appetising smell.

I got a bit of shooting round York, which I enjoyed; but on the whole, it was not a very happy time for either of us. It was cold and damp and dreary, and although the countryside round about is beautiful and there are lovely parts of the city, we did not see it under the best conditions, and I was glad when we were moved again. We went down to Grenfell Road on the outskirts of Leicester, and here our second child was born: a daughter this time, and Honor had her with no difficulty, which was not the case with the first child.

Here, I ran a battle school, mainly for people who were to be dropped in behind the German lines. I had a selection of Poles, Czechs, French, Dutch, Belgians, and so on. We made training as realistic as possible. I had done my parachute training when I was with Gestapo Tom. In fact, I had hated every moment of it and was totally terrified. They told me a huge lie when they said that the more one did it, the less frightened one became – I became progressively more frightened. Coming down the inclined wire was just tolerable. The balloon was not. I knew that I would never willingly jump, and I told the sergeant dispatcher so and asked him to push me off, which he obligingly did then and on every subsequent occasion. The jumps from the aircraft were less awful than from the balloon, as it was impossible to measure the distance down; with the balloon, there was the wire reaching to the ground. I never want to jump with a parachute again, and I do not understand those who do it for fun.

As there were plenty of enthusiastic Home Guards about, it was not advisable for Poles, Czechs, Dutch and so on to jump at night, or even during the daytime. We used to take them out by covered truck and dump them somewhere in the dark. We never 'dropped' them in exactly the right place as this very rarely happens in operations; so first of all, they had to find out where they were, come together in operational groups, and then find their way cross-country to a rendezvous at a given map reference, walking for thirty-six hours without food or drink. My instructors were out trying to spot them moving, which was by no means easy for them. At the rendezvous, they had two hours to dig in to a slit trench on the edge of a wood, and at the end of that time they were attacked by the instructors, actually using live ammunition. Provided that the slit trenches were properly dug, there was very little danger and, in fact, we only had one casualty (one of my instructors was hurt by a hand-grenade with too short a fuse).

The trainees were then 'interrogated' non-stop for twelve hours, to see if their cover stories could be broken down, while bombing and battle noises were played fortissimo continually. During the time that they were with us, they were hardened physically with forced marches, rope climbing and river crossing, and taught to use various pieces of equipment. They were taught to move noiselessly at night, to work their way through minefields and also to use push and pull booby trap switches, plastic gelignite, gun cotton primers and detonators. It was very interesting work, and I enjoyed it very much. We also had some Americans to train: they were enormously enthusiastic, but most of them lacked basic fieldcraft, and discipline in the American Army was very different to ours. In some ways it seemed extremely lax and in others very harsh indeed. I remember some wretched lieutenant who was using one of our ranges for heavy machine gun practice. My sergeant major went to ask him to stop as the range was not intended for that weapon, and Lieutenant DiMaggio told him in no uncertain terms to get lost. I reported this to his unit commander. The next day I happened to call there and found to my horror that Lieutenant DiMaggio had become Private DiMaggio. I found the American airborne troops an extremely nice and hospitable lot. Alas, not long afterwards very many were to be killed during the D-Day invasion.

At this time, I also became quite ill. I was sent off to hospital with suspected leukaemia. This was confirmed in the hospital, and I was sent home to die. My wife was told that I should last a fortnight, but probably not more than a month. Knowing that about the only drug I had not been given was whisky, she mobilised friends and tradesmen, who most generously gave me bottles of whisky hoarded up for V-Day. I also went down to London, where leukaemia was confirmed by a battery of Harley Street specialists. Perhaps whisky is a cure for it, because within six weeks I had tested negative.

Italy

Eventually Nemesis caught up with me, and I was told that I was to go to Italy to liaise with the partisans in the north of the country, behind the German lines. I protested violently, saying that I was the person who trained people to do these things and that I should not be expected to do them myself. It was no good, and finally, I found myself packed into the bomb-bay of a Lancaster and on my way to Foggia, where I landed three-quarters frozen stiff and unable to move. Thawed out in the mess, I was sent on my way north, armed with an official letter from the Secretary of State for War requesting all military units to give me assistance, a money belt filled with gold sovereigns, a sub-machine gun and ammunition and my .38 Special Smith and Wesson. I also had a radio, which I was not at all sure how to work, and a Colt Woodsman .22 automatic pistol firing Super X ammunition and fitted with a screw-on silencer.

I will not disclose the names of people who helped me during this time. It may sound ridiculous to be so cautious after fifty years have passed, and those partisans who helped me are probably dead by now. However, *vendetta* is an Italian word and it passes from one generation to the next, and the children of those whom I could trust and who worked with me could still be in danger from an Italian Communist Party which forgets nothing and is very much alive and well, although it has officially changed its name.

Partisan/Resistance Movements

Before I continue recounting my adventures in Italy at this time, I feel it is important to clarify, or even to introduce the reader to, the various resistance movements, and in particular the partisan movement, during the Second World War. Not a great deal was known about them by the general public, and my story would not be complete without the following explanatory notes.

It is a fact that the resistance movements which built up in Western Europe after the German occupation of Holland, Belgium, France, Italy, Poland and Czechoslovakia were formed for the most part by the communists. This is not really applicable to Poland, but in France, for example, the only organised clandestine movement was communist. Those who wished to join a resistance against the Germans found in these communist cells an organised nucleus, with safe houses, facilities for making false documents, a communications network and some arms. They did not have to become communists to join these cells and resist the German occupation, but the majority held left-wing political views of one sort of another. Many, particularly those in France and Belgium, were extremely brave. In Holland, the Germans infiltrated the Resistance at a very early stage – although this was not realised until a good deal later, and a number of agents sent from Britain quite literally fell into the arms of a waiting reception committee of Gestapo.

The Belgian and French Resistance did some excellent work, but in Czechoslovakia the Germans, under Heydrich, carried out a totally ruthless action against the Resistance which, after the assassination of Heydrich, resulted in the massacre of the entire population of Lidice. A certain myth has grown up in Italy regarding the effectiveness of the Italian partisans in their actions against the Germans. Today it is stated by communists and a good many historians, who should know better, that the Italian partisans contributed a very significant part to the Allied victory. Some even claim that it was the Italian partisan movement which was mainly responsible for the German defeat in Italy. This is just not true.

At the time of the invasion of Sicily by the Allies, the Americans struck a deal with the Sicilian Mafia, which resulted in the Mafia playing a significant part in the liberation of the island. This extended into Calabria and Apulia. Italo-Americans, a good many as senior officers in the American Army, landed with the troops in Sicily and soon made contact with their relations in the Mafia. It is also true that the Mafia helped the American Army quite considerably in driving the Germans out of the island, but the price was the release from prison of many thousands of Mafiosi who had been caught and imprisoned by Mussolini for criminal activities, but who now claimed that they were political prisoners. This release of Mafia prisoners was to have serious consequences in the future.

The Gothic Line was collapsing. It had never been a line of continuous fortifications such as the Maginot Line or the Siegfried Line. There were holes in it, and it was possible for a certain traffic in merchandise and the movement of civilians to continue through controlled posts where the degree of security varied; otherwise it would have been impossible for me to have gone through to the north.

The invasion of Italy, which started with the landings in Sicily, took place in stages. After Sicily, there were the Allied landings at Salerno and on the east coast. Then there were lines of fortifications based on Monte Cassino, and after the landings at Anzio, the Germans withdrew again and briefly held a line to the south of Florence, before withdrawing to the Gothic Line far further to the north. Behind the Gothic Line there were German formations, which became more disorganised the further north one travelled.

None of the Mafia were communists. In fact the Mafia lives on a capitalist system and always has done.

The situation in the north of Italy, Reggio Emilia and Tuscany was very different. The partisans were, as in France, built up from clandestine communist or left-wing cells already in existence before the war. They formed, as in France, the nucleus for the Resistance or partisan movement. Again, by no means all who were in the Resistance in northern and central Italy were communists, but found a ready-made structure which they could join, and which again had safe houses, the ability to produce false documents, a communications network and some weapons.

Some of these partisans were extremely brave, and one can have nothing but admiration for their courage and self-sacrifice, but very many were not. My own experience with the partisans with whom I came in contact in northern Italy at this time was that they considered actions against the Germans to be far too dangerous. For the most part they were interested in paying off personal scores and in 'proletarian expropriations', which included robbing banks, torturing those suspected of having money to induce them to part with anything that they had of value, and general banditry. To some extent, this could be explained by the fact that the German Army in this area of Bolzano and Merano consisted of remnants of broken formations which were being regrouped. Most of the solders realised that the war was lost and had poor morale, but were quite ready to vent their bitterness and frustration in acts of great brutality against captured partisans. Moreover, this part of Italy, which up until after the First World War had been a part of Austria, had a majority population of Austrian origin who were generally favourable to the Germans rather than the Italians.

As Mao put it, partisan resistance fighters require water in which the fish can swim. In this part of Italy, which had been Austrian and had become Italian against the wishes of the majority of the population, the water in which the partisan 'fish' had to swim was very definitely muddy, and to a certain degree hostile.

The general command structure, in as much as there was one at all, was centred in Milan, but the partisan groups in the whole of the north of Italy, as well as Liguria, Reggio Emilia, Lombardy, the Alto Adige, Turin, Genoa, Brescia, Udine, Venice and further south into Tuscany, operated very largely as autonomous units, and not infrequently fought amongst themselves.

Mission Impossible?

The purpose of my mission in the Alto Adige was in the first instance to liaise with the partisans in the area, to attempt to get them to fight effectively against the German units in their respective areas. This was, from the outset, extremely difficult. The extreme degree of cruelty and brutality for which all concerned were responsible is not generally appreciated. An attack against a German unit would bring down reprisals on the local people. As a general rule, for every German soldier killed, ten captured partisans would be shot; if there were not enough of them, their families would be shot to make up the numbers, and if that was not sufficient, then people would be taken off the streets and shot, or the inhabitants of nearby farms. After 8th September, 1943, when Italy signed an armistice with the Allies, certain units of the Italian armed forces surrendered. However, before they could do so, German commanders gave order for their troops to open fire on their former allies. Captured Italian officers were shot by the Germans, and a general massacre of Italian troops followed in certain places. Some Italian troops, both officers and men, just went home, and some continued to fight with the Germans, even turning on former Italian comrades. Mussolini, who had been arrested on the order of the King of Italy and held a prisoner in a hotel on top of the Gran Sasso d'Italia, was rescued in a daring operation by German special forces, and taken to Germany. Returning to Italy, he organised a Fascist government at Salo, and there set up a republic. Meanwhile Italian military units were formed fighting against the Germans for the Allies and also against the Italian fascist forces loyal to the Republic of Salo and Mussolini.

It was an impossible situation in which nobody knew who was friend or foe. Within the partisan movement there was also division, the Garibaldi brigades made up of communists fighting against the 'Green Flame' – the non-communist partisans. Irresponsible partisan leaders insisted on attacking German units, and this lead to the massacres of civilians to which I have referred. The most effective actions which the partisans could carry out were those of sabotage: destruction of roads, bridges, the cutting of telephone lines and the general disruption of communications.

The OSS, the American equivalent of the SOE, had in some cases recruited from Italo-Americans with Mafia connections, and this had unfortunate repercussions in Sicily. They sent arms and ammunition in fairly large quantities to the Garibaldi (communist) partisans, as well as to the Green Flames, quite indiscriminately. To make matters even worse – if possible – there was a very legitimate fear that Tito would attempt to seize a large part of the north-east of Italy as soon as Germans withdrew, and in fact De Gaulle did seize the Val d'Aosta and considerable part of north-western Italy in May 1945. There was considerable fear that the Committee of Liberation, a left-wing and communist partisan movement which had been organising the resistance from Milan since 8th September, 1943, would attempt to set up an alternative to the government in Rome.

In short, Italy had become the jam in a sandwich between the Allies and the Germans, between the rump of a fascist government centred at Salo (with fascist troops fighting on the side of the Germans) and Italian troops fighting with the Allies. In the middle of all this there were the communist and non-communist partisans, who frequently fought amongst themselves. In the last stages of the war there were communist Yugoslav troops under Tito trying to seize north-east Italy, and after 2nd May, 1945 French troops under De Gaulle who had been ordered to seize a good part the north-west of Italy. If all this seems very complicated – it was!

A German headquarters had been set up at Bolzano (Bolzen) in the Alto Adige, and a glance at the map will show how strategic this position was. Running north from Trento, the main road runs through Bolzano where two main valleys meet. To the north, the road continues to Bressanone and then to the Brenner Pass into Austria and Innsbruck; to the north-west it runs to Merano, where it divides: one road runs north again to Austria, one west into Switzerland. It was down these roads that German reinforcement came south to Trento, and south again to the Gothic Line; and it was up these roads that withdrawing German troops moved back into Austria. Innsbruck is only a few miles from the German frontier and only around one hundred miles from Munich.

Direct attacks on German troops at any stage were very strongly to be discouraged, and it was part of my mission to dissuade gung-ho partisan groups from carrying out such actions: they brought down terrible reprisals on the civilian population, and in fact achieved very little against well-armed regular troops. At the same time they alienated the civilian population against the partisans, who relied on the former to be the water in which the fish could swim.

Communication was a different matter. Landslides could be started in this very mountainous area which could block roads for hours or even days, and if there was a build-up of German troop vehicles behind the landslide waiting for it to be cleared, they would present a target for Allied aircraft. Avalanches were easy in winter when there was deep snow on the mountains, and at best, the roads were all narrow and twisting in a series of hairpin bends. In the summer, from the mountains (which for the most part are almost bare of vegetation), rockfalls could be started without suspicion of deliberate sabotage, which might bring reprisals.

The Germans were, of course, well aware of this hazard, and established observation posts in strategic places to keep a surveillance on any possible attempts to cause roadblocks.

However, with low cloud, mist, snowstorms, and the cover of night, both rockfalls and avalanches could be started with comparative ease.

Telephone wires also presented a worthwhile target. In many cases, they could be sabotaged in such a way as to make the damage appear due to natural causes. Bridges could be weakened where they were not adequately guarded without blowing them up, and especially with spring floods, they could be effectively sabotaged.

The odd despatch rider also presented a potential target. A wire suddenly stretched across a deserted stretch of road could cause a motorbike and its rider to disappear over the edge of a precipice, and there would be no sign of anything other than an accident.

Wireless communication with the Allies was virtually impossible and also very dangerous, as the Germans were both quick and very efficient at picking up radio transmissions. In the same way communication with other partisan groups was difficult and dangerous, and frequently we had no idea where they were or what they were doing. This made liaison with them almost impossible. Any sort of concerted operation was out of the question.

An important aspect of the mission was to try to discover which units were in the vicinity and what movements they were making, and what reinforcements were coming through from Austria. This was not so difficult, but to get this information back to Allied troops was difficult and usually took too long. The best way was to use the partisans' system of communication. This consisted, for the most part, of messages (usually verbal) being taken by persons having a legitimate reason and permits to travel between Merano, Bolzano and Trento, and from there to Milan, where there was communication between the Committee of Liberation and the Allies.

There were quite a lot of German units in my area: there was a broken German infantry division, a number of SS units, a Jaeger regiment and supply and transport units, as well as forward units from the Gothic Line which had been withdrawn and were being regrouped. There were also a fair number of anti-aircraft units, dispersed up and down the valley to give protection to military convoys coming through the Brenner and other passes and along the mountain roads. There were also Gestapo detachments in the main towns and villages.

I do not propose to say very much about my journey into the area, first from the south, and then up through, or rather around, the Gothic Line. Part of this journey was in a large empty wine barrel, from which I eventually emerged totally drunk on the fumes. My reason for not disclosing more is that I gave my solemn word that I would never, under any circumstances whatever, tell anybody where I had been, who had helped me and how it had been accomplished. It probably would not matter now after so many years, but I gave my word and will not break it. There is also always the possibility of danger to those who helped me. There are still very many communists in Italy, and there is hatred and personal feuds which do not die in a single generation or two. Many of the partisans with whom I came into contact were far more interested in settling old scores than in taking any action against the Germans. Many had the ideological aim of taking over Italy as a soviet socialist republic and distrusted and hated the Allies – 'The Anglo-Americani'. I have considered the option of using false names, places and incidents, but although it is more than fifty years later, some people may still be alive, their children are, and, after all, I had given my word.

Eventually I reached Trento and continued on north to Bolzano. This was a dangerous place, and I was glad to get past it without incident. It was night and I was travelling on a truck going to Merano. Bolzano was the main market town and administrative centre for the district, and I was travelling with a number of local farmers and others who had been to Bolzano to various administrative offices to obtain permits for this and that. It was necessary to get permits to do anything. Suddenly out of the darkness ahead came a flat cart pulled by three horses, harnessed abreast and at full gallop: a sort of Roman chariot! It had no lights, and the truck on which I was travelling had only the dimmest light, as that was all that was allowed. In order to avoid a head-on crash, the driver of the truck pulled it right over into the ditch, where it overturned. The 'chariot', driven by somebody who was clearly a lunatic, continued to gallop madly away into the darkness. The rest of my journey I had to complete on foot and more than somewhat bruised. It was an inglorious end to a rather ghastly journey, initially by British Army transport, then a Jewish Service corps unit which had put me up for a night, and seen me on my way for several miles (I rather think that one of the officers of this unit may have been Moshe Dayan), then in a small boat which threatened to sink at any moment, then by wine barrel, then several days in a hay barn, and finally by truck until ditched by a sort of modern Jehu.

I went to ground in a large castle which, in fact, was more like a rabbit warren than anything else. Between the wars, a considerable number of southern Italians has been moved in to the area to try and balance up the (largely Austrian) population, and to Italianise the whole of the Alto Adige; but German was still widely spoken, and after the Anschluss, in which Austria was forcibly integrated into a Greater Germany, the Germans and the Austrians had their eyes on the Alto Adige. The whole province was taken over after 8th September, when Italy surrendered in the Second World War, and a fascist government continued to fight on from Salo. This was the signal for the Germans to maintain that since the area was once part of Austria and Austria was now part of Germany, therefore Alto Adige was part of Greater Germany, too.

The castle belonged to a former mistress of Franz Josef and had been given to her as a settlement when her services were no longer required. Large parts of it had been let to various people, refugees had occupied other parts of it, and nobody really knew who was there. In fact, I soon heard through the grapevine that there were two German officers in the castle. They had been involved in the bomb plot against Hitler and had managed to escape into Austria. Now they were hiding in the castle, and rather like me, hiding from everybody.

Fortunately, the whole German administration was in very considerable confusion. Experienced and able-bodied officers of the Gestapo and police had been pressed into active military service, and those who remained were anxious for as quiet a life as possible. Virtually everybody knew that it was only a matter of time before Germany lost the war, which at that time was not very far away.

The partisans were not difficult to find. They were a pretty dreadful lot. Their interest in fighting the Germans was minimal, as it was considered to be far too dangerous, and as I have already mentioned they were only interested in collecting 'proletarian taxes', which meant robbing banks and torturing 'fascists' to force them to disgorge any valuables which they might have. 'Fascists' were plentiful, as virtually every professional man before the war had joined, if only in name, the Fascist Party, because this made it very much easier for them to carry on their professional careers as doctors, dentists, engineers, shopkeepers and so on.

There were, of course, a number of honourable exceptions. Very courageous men and women risked their lives and performed acts of great daring: carrying messages, helping Allied airmen who were in hiding in the mountains and shooting up German convoys. For these men and women (and even some children), I can have nothing but admiration and praise, but the bulk of the partisans with whom I came into contact were a murderous crew of thugs and criminals of the most revolting sort, and I can say that they were the only people who very seriously tried to kill me. They knew that I had sovereigns, and they wanted them as well as anything else that they could get: my sub-machine gun, pistol, uniform and papers. They were a constant danger.

For the most part, I lay low in my burrow, protected by a few on whom I could rely – or, at least, hoped that I could. Liaison with the rest was a virtual impossibility, and while it has become a post-war myth that it was the glorious partisans in Italy who, virtually alone and unaided by the Allied armies, 'liberated Italy', to my personal knowledge, this was most definitely not the case.

While I lurked in my cellar, hoping to God that the war would end, the time came when I had to have a bath. It had become a case of imperative necessity, and as there was only one bathroom in the castle, I set off one evening with my towel and piece of ersatz soap – together with some newspaper and sticks, as the hot water geyser was a strange contraption which worked – quite well – if fed with a sufficient quantity of sticks, paper, bits of general rubbish, cardboard and so on. I eventually arrived at the bathroom, and to my surprise, steam and *Deutschland über Alles* issued from under the door. I banged on the door and shouted *Heraus!*

In due course, a German officer in uniform, also with his piece of ersatz soap and towel, came out. We clicked our heels formally to each other, and he came out and I went in. Years later I was to meet him again, and he was to become one of my best friends.

It is probable that my mission in the Alto Adige was largely impossible from the outset. The fact that communications were so difficult both with the Allies and with other partisan groups was a major factor. There was also the fact that the partisans regarded me with suspicion and some hostility. Their dream was to take over Italy as a Marxist republic, and they quite rightly guessed that that was not the intention of the Allies. The groups in my area hardly ever co-operated with each other, but not infrequently they fought against each other and even betrayed each other to the Germans. For many of them the 'Anglo-Americani' were useful only to get rid of the Germans and fascists, so that Italy could become a Soviet-style, Marxist republic when the war ended.

In retrospect, I suppose that we did succeed in some things: we did block some roads, we did start some avalanches and we sabotaged one or two bridges which collapsed under the weight of German tanks. Probably the favourite partisan trick was to kill a German motorcycle despatch rider with a wire across a road, but later the Germans sent motorcycles and sidecars with a machine gun mounted on them, and they were more difficult to 'divert' over a cliff. Possibly some of the information regarding German troop movements and the identity of units got through, but if so it was probably too late for this information to be much use. Our most successful action was to block a mountain road down from the Brenner with a large rockfall. It so happened that a considerable number of German Army vehicles filled with reinforcements and supplies was halted at this block, which took a long time to clear as part of the road had fallen away, smashed down the mountain by the rockfall. By chance, aerial reconnaissance picked this up, and a substantial Allied air strike destroyed a good number of vehicles the following day, shortly after dawn and before the block had been cleared. There were some spectacular explosions, and some of the trucks must have been carrying ammunition. I take no credit for this. I did not know what the build-up behind the blocked road had been, and I certainly had nothing to do with organising the air strike.

I can not praise enough the heroism of some of the partisans, quite extraordinarily brave men and women (and even boys and girls) who risked their lives, and torture. Their courage was humbling and astonishing. Their bravery and cold courage was great or greater than any I have seen in my life.

On the other hand, the majority of the partisans contributed little or nothing to the Allied war effort. They were not motivated by patriotism, although some might say that some were by Marxist ideology. Some of their actions displayed a cruelty and barbarity which could hardly be surpassed.

I have mentioned that the partisans on occasion were known to denounce individuals and other groups to the Germans, and I had one experience of this myself.

Amongst the people I knew there was a rather charming colonel of the Italian artillery, whom I will call Colonel Carlo. He was not a partisan, and after the armistice he came home and was living quietly with his wife not very far from my castle. One day he had to go to Bolzano to get a legal document. He had a permit to travel and went down early one morning, but did not return. Two days later and his wife had heard nothing. She became very worried and went looking for him. Two days later and she had not returned either. Then the following day one of my few reliable partisans, a man whom I trusted, came to me with the news that the bodies of Colonel Carlo and his wife had been found by a shepherd in the mountains, some halfway between Bolzano and Bressanone. They had been both tortured with extreme cruelty and finally killed. It was not known who was responsible. However, about a week later, it was reported to me by one of my men that four men were living in the colonel's house, and that they had a document signed by the colonel selling the house and its contents to them, and that this document had even been witnessed – apparently – by a notary. Further inquiries revealed that the notary was a very frightened man, too frightened to go to his office. More seriously, it was also reported to me that one of the men in the house had obtained from the colonel before he died and under extreme torture a list of persons whom the colonel sus-pected as possibly belonging to the partisans, and that the person who had this list was in the process of trying to arrange a sale of it to the Gestapo. I rather suspected that my name might be on that list, and possibly those of other partisans who worked with me. Something had to be done, and quickly.

That same night I went with three of my partisans, one of whom was only a boy of sixteen, to the colonel's house. It was a very dark night and blowing a gale. There were no lights showing, and the place was in total darkness. We scouted round it very carefully, but there were heavy curtains over the windows, and we could not see or hear anything. There was a window over the kitchen sink at the back, and with some care and under cover of the noise of the gale which was howling down the valley, we broke the window. The boy managed to squeeze through and then open the back door for the rest of us. We moved through the kitchen, through a dining room and into the hall, from which some stairs led to an upper floor. There was another door into what I thought would be the living room. Listening carefully, we could hear quiet words, the chink of glass, and a laugh. I sent the boy back to the kitchen and told him to go into the garden, and if anybody came out, to hit them hard with the rifle butt. I told another of my men to go out of the front door – which was not locked but had a Yale-type spring lock so it could be opened from the inside – and to do the same if anybody came out that way. I also said that they should avoid shooting unless absolutely necessary. When they were in position, I opened the living room door quietly and walked in. I had my .22 Woodsman automatic pistol with me, and it had been tapped to take a screw-on silencer. The advantage of this weapon is that it is really the only pistol which can be silenced effectively. The high-power, hollow-nosed bullet is very deadly fired at close range, and the noise it makes is no more than that of an air pistol.

There were three of them in the room. I shot the first man, who was only some three yards in front of me, through the forehead. The second man was sitting on the sofa with a glass in his hand. I shot him cleanly in the head too. The third man had a bottle in his hand, and he was about to pour some wine into the second man's glass. He dropped the bottle and turned to pick up the Beretta 9 mm sub-machine gun which was on the table beside him. As he turned, I shot him twice through the body. He fell over, knocking over the table with a crash. I shot him again to make certain. Almost immediately there was a tremendous noise from directly above, and then a sound of somebody tearing down the stairs and out of the front door. A split-second later, there was the sound of a heavy blow and then silence. We searched the house but there were no more of them. My man by the front door said that somebody had rushed out; he had neatly tripped him with his rifle barrel and then smashed the man's skull with the rifle butt. It was all over in a matter of fifteen seconds.

There was much to be done. First I collected the empty cartridge cases. The four men were all quite dead, and we searched them very thoroughly. Then the mess had to be cleared up, the broken glass and the wine removed; there had been very little bleeding but what there was had to be cleaned up. It seems that the fourth man had been resting upstairs, and had heard the table crash over. He was fully dressed and, without bothering to find out what had happened, had run for it. We now had to dispose of the bodies, and with this in mind, we had come in a garbage collection truck which belonged to one of my people. He had a contract for the collection of garbage from a German unit down the valley and thus had a permit to use the truck and was given an allowance of petrol. We hauled the bodies out and loaded them into the truck and tastefully arranged a pile of garbage on top of them. I asked the driver and the boy to take it away, drive it down the valley and, when they came to a deserted spot, to put the bodies in the river. The Adige is a flood river which runs very fast with the snow water over large boulders and rocks. It is fairly shallow, and I guessed that within a few miles the bodies would be so battered they would be unrecognisable. Anyway, there were many dead bodies in the river from time to time, and nobody bothered about them very much. If they were stopped on the way by a patrol, the driver had his permit and the truck stank to high heaven, and I did not expect the patrol to search garbage.

The other partisans and I returned to the house and set about a very careful search of it. We went though it meticulously, examining all the papers in the writing desk, clothes and furniture. We also lifted the carpets, but put everything back very tidily. It was dawn before we finished, and we left it as if nobody had been there for many days. We had not found any papers or any lists – other than the 'deed of sale' of the house and contents, signed with a very shaken hand by the colonel, which we took with. Outside, the wind was singing in the telephone wires at the end of the garden. In the distance a dog was barking, and a cock crowed somewhere on a farm. I was glad to get back to my castle and my hiding place there.

There is inevitably a certain reaction to taking a human life. In a battle, when the adrenaline is flowing, the enemy ceases to be a human being and just becomes a target which will kill you if you do not kill him first. To kill in what is virtually cold blood is a different matter, and I have been asked if I did not have any feeling of regret or guilt. I certainly did not. I knew what these four men had done to the colonel and his wife – the revolting tortures which had been inflicted on both of them and the brutal and sadistic way in which they had been killed, not for motive of patriotism or ideology or duty, or indeed for any other reason than personal gain and greed. These four men were not partisans fighting for any cause but just brutal bandits. There was also the factor that they thought to try to provide the Gestapo with the names of suspected partisans in return for money. In this they would have had some difficulty: the Gestapo would probably have extracted any information which they had under rigorous interrogation, without paying a penny. However, had they had time to organise it properly, it was known that the Gestapo did occasionally pay for information if they thought that more could be obtained from the same source later.

In order to protect myself and others in my group, I had to act quickly. I had no regrets whatever. Nevertheless, it seemed prudent to lie low for some days before resuming operations.

When passing through Rome on my way north, I had made contract with Monsignor O'Flaherty at the Vatican. He had been very active in the Red Cross, and also in keeping relatives in Britain informed about the where-abouts and welfare of British prisoners of war. He was a charming man, but I had heard nothing of my mother since the beginning of Italy's entry into the war in 1940. Mussolini had assumed, possibly understandably, that with the collapse of France, Holland and Belgium, and with the Germans at the Channel ports and the British Army evacuated from Dunkirk, that the war was virtually over. There was a good reason for believing this, as we had had to leave all the army's equipment behind, and there was really very little between the Germans and the overthrow of Britain other than the Channel, the Royal Navy and the Royal Air Force. The army had to all intents and purposes been destroyed, and there was only one fully equipped brigade left in Britain. Fearing that he would be excluded from any peace conference, and that he would have to deal with a Germany which had conquered all of Western Europe, Mussolini declared war on Britain and France at the last moment. He was to regret this very bitterly. He sent a number of fighter-bombers up to attack England, to show Hitler that Italy was worth something, but they were all shot down into the Channel. Mussolini was assured that he had a modern and efficient army by his political and military advisers, but the truth was very different: his rifles were 6.5 mm carbines utterly inaccurate at distances over one hundred yards, his artillery lacked shells, and his tanks were worthless. In fact, as a military power, Italy was in very poor way indeed – a fact soon to be demonstrated in the North African desert.

My mother had lived in Italy for very many years, and she never believed that Italy would come into the war against the Allies. She had finally been sent to a forced labour camp near Bolzano, and I was told by Monsignor O'Flaherty that she was still there. There was little that I could do about it when I first arrived in the area. She had been arrested shortly after Italy came into the war, when Mussolini believed that it was all over. She had been taken to Rome and accused of being a British spy. Fortunately our cousin, Prince Fillipo Doria, had been able to get her out, and she went back to her home in the mountains some forty miles to the east of Rome. However, she was subjected to continual persecution by the local people at Anticoli Corrado. She moved with her husband Colonel Cino Bacchiani, a very highly decorated officer of Alpine artillery from the First World War, to be with him near Naples. However, things were made extremely uncomfortable for her there, too, and in spite of her Irish nationality and consequent status as a neutral, the same rumours were circulated that she was a British spy. Finally, she decided to go up to the Alto Adige and try to get into Switzerland. She was unable to do so. Then came 8th September, and the Germans moved in. She was immediately arrested again, and this time charged with listening to British broadcasts on the wireless. She was able to prove that in fact her wireless was broken. She was released, only to be arrested by the Gestapo almost immediately and charged with aiding an Allied airman who had been shot down and was hiding in the mountains. In fact, she had sent blankets and some food out to him. The Gestapo officer tore up her Irish passport, and she was condemned to forced labour. This entailed packing apples into crates from dawn until dusk, pushing empty railway wagons up from the Bolzano marshalling yards, loading them with the crates, and pushing them back to the marshalling yards. The work was just about tolerable in the summer, although it entailed very long hours; but in the winter it was almost impossible, working in the open in temperatures many degrees below zero.

The forced labour was all carried out by women, and each of them had a quota which had to be met each day. If they failed to do this, the first time they were flogged and the second time, they were sent off to Ravensbruch, a death camp from which very few ever returned. My mother was over fifty at the time and she developed terrible arthritis.

She also had pneumonia, for which the German camp doctor gave her three days' sick leave.

With the aid of the partisans, or those few of whom that I could trust, I was able to get her out.

There existed one possibility to do this. The guards were for the most part men who were, either due to wounds or age, unfit for front-line service. There were not very many of them, and the apple-packing station and camp extended over a fairly wide area. There was also the marshalling yards, to which the loaded railway wagons had to be pushed and from which empty wagons were pushed up to the loading area. These were thinly guarded. Most of the women had nowhere to which they could escape, and some were so weak that they could not have run away at all. This presented an opportunity for·a quick action in which the half dozen or so guards would be killed, and my mother extracted and effectively hidden. The marshalling yards were also outside the camp perimeter.

I was able to keep a watch on the daily routine, determine in which shift my mother would be and discover the number of guards who accompanied each party down to the yards and back again. Some, but not all of them had dogs. Morale amongst the guards seemed to be low, and they were not very professional.

The camp was short of transport and there did not appear to be much in the way of men ready and able to go in pursuit of anybody who escaped. The main problem was finding somewhere to hide effectively, with food, water, heat and sanitation, where we could keep my mother safe until the war was over, which appeared to be within the near future.

The 'cut-out' operation went without a hitch. There was a short and half-hearted pursuit, and no serious attempt to find her afterwards.

Again I do not wish to mention names or details, but during this action I had the personal satisfaction of shooting several of the camp guards who had shown sadism which merited no other fate. Here my silenced .22 Woodsman Colt with high-power expanding bullets came in useful.

The problem of where to hide my mother was a very difficult one, as she was very frail indeed. She was virtually a living skeleton, crippled with arthritis and barely able to look after herself. There is no doubt that the camp guards would have killed her in another few weeks, being unable to do any work and of no further use.

The area of the Alto Adige is very beautiful in the summer with glorious, alpine meadows filled with wild flowers and the valleys pink and white with the blossom of the many thousands of apple trees. There were trout in the river, which upstream from Merano was not polluted, and even at this time in the war when food was terribly scarce, it was possible to buy a few eggs, the odd chicken or piece of lamb, as well as other farm produce, from the mountain farms away from town. In the winter it is a horrible place, with the high mountains in deep snow, the river filled with ice and grey snow water, and the glacial wind, sleet and snow howling down the valleys.

The war was coming to an end, and it was becoming easier to move about. Columns of German troops were moving north to the Brenner Pass, and I was able to buy a certain amount of food to build up my mother's health. I was able to hide her not far from where I was, and I will be forever grateful to those people who helped me at that time and took a risk in hiding her. Clearly she could not possibly have survived in the open. While her room was minuscule, dark and cluttered with lumber, at least it provided shelter and warmth.

Possibly she would have been discovered if the war had continued for any great length of time, but there was a great deal of confusion in the area and rumours that the Germans had been trying to arrange an armistice with Allied representatives in Switzerland. The predominately Austrian population in the area was nervous of what might happen when the war was over, and people were inclined to be co-operative.

My mission was pretty well over. I don't think that I had achieved very much. Not long after, the war in Italy ended, and although the Alto Adige was sealed off and not yet occupied by Allied troops, I was able to get my mother down to Rome. But it was a hazardous journey. On three occasions, we were machine-gunned from the hills, probably by partisan groups, and we were held up at a road block by one group of these thugs, whom I shot with my sten gun. My mother was almost totally crippled by arthritis by now and weighed under six stone, although she was a tall woman.

I had to leave her with relatives in Rome, as I was ordered back to England. The night before I was due to fly from Naples, I was told that she had been arrested by some bloody little captain in the Field Security Police, who had accused her of being a German spy. However, I was able to deal with him on the telephone.

I was flown back to London from Naples in a Lancaster Bomber arranged by my father-in-law (by then an air marshal at Bomber Command). I was able to get through the various formalities pretty quickly and caught a train down to London. However, I arrived there too late to make a connection with a train down to Lymington (Honor and the children were in a house which we had taken some miles out of Lyndhurst in the New Forest). Accordingly, I had to go to a hotel, so I went to the Cumberland, near Marble Arch. I was in uniform but had no luggage, but that was by no means unusual. I was terribly tired, but asked to be called very early with some tea in my room, so that I could get the first train down to Hampshire the following morning.

I undressed and got into bed. I put my automatic pistol under my pillow from force of habit and instantly fell asleep. It seemed that I had been asleep barely five minutes before I was woken by a scratching on the door of the bedroom. Still half-asleep but with nerves tingling, I slipped out of bed, jacked a cartridge into the breach of my pistol and, kneeling by the bed, waited for the door to open. I really had no idea where I was and imagined that I was somewhere back in the north of Italy. The door opened, the light was switched on, and the maid appeared with my morning tea – to be confronted by a stark naked man pointing a pistol at her. For a moment, she did not move at all; then, throwing the tray into the air, she vanished down the long corridor, uttering a series of ear-splitting yells. Nobody has ever got dressed faster. I left the hotel by the fire escape and disappeared into the dawn – and I have never been back!

I was looking forward to a period of leave and rest, but only a few days later, I was sent up to Manchester. I went up by car to a large gun park, some miles on the south side of the river, through the tunnel. I was told that some German saboteur, with superhuman cunning, had been setting fire to guns in the gun park and in fact had seriously damaged some twenty or thirty of them. The troops of the unit guarding the depot had been unable to catch him, and the local police had also failed, although they had been trying for weeks. Various men had seen the saboteur and given varying descriptions: a tall dark figure, creeping through the night; a short fat man; an elderly man who walked with a limp. All agreed that he was an extremely expert saboteur, and that he had probably been landed by parachute or by submarine to do his dirty work. There were, in fact, a lot of guns in the gun park: anti-aircraft guns, howitzers, field artillery, Bofors – in fact, guns of almost every sort, covering a large area. Due to good luck, I was able to catch the man the following night. He turned out to be a private from the ordnance depot itself. He was about twenty-two or twenty-three and came from a town not far away. I had him up the following morning and asked him why he had done this. He said, 'It's like this, sir. I've been looking after these bleeding guns for the past three years, cleaning and greasing the buggers, and I'm fed up with it. I thought that perhaps if I burnt 'em up, there would not be any more bleeding guns for me to clean and grease, and I could go home.' The war in Europe was now over, and the poor chap just wanted to go home.

In fact, I felt rather sorry for the young man. He had stuffed cotton waste, soaked in oil and petrol, into the barrels and breeches of the guns and then set fire to them. It was hardly a very professional job but fairly effective, as the grease with which the guns were coated also caught fire. He had really done quite a bit of damage. It was with some reluctance that I handed the poor little man over to the police.

Shortly after, I was detailed to go to Turkey. God only knows why, as I spoke no word of the language. First, I had to have anti-typhus injections, and the first of these had a most catastrophic effect on me. I went home to our house in the New Forest and that night, developed a fever of nearly 105. I remember little or nothing about it but apparently was determined to jump out of the window and had to be forcibly restrained. I was very seriously ill for about a week, and it was decided that I could not have any further typhus injections – and, therefore, I could not go to Turkey!

We were very happy in our little house in the New Forest. I was called in again to deal with the disappearance of highly technical instruments from an ordnance or REME depot, and there again, I was lucky to catch all of the culprits. Again, there was nothing very sinister behind it all: they just hoped to be able to sell the stuff. I caught them red-handed on the railway station with the missing equipment.

This was pretty well my last assignment of this sort. The war in Europe had come to an end, and our main problems were those of demobilising the armed forces, maintaining garrisons in Europe and preparing for a continuation of the war against Japan. However, this was to terminate suddenly with the dropping of the atomic bombs and VJ-Day.

We lived on for a bit at our nice little house in the New Forest, waiting for final demobilisation. It was rather a boring time for everybody. The troops were anxious to get back to civilian life, and there were problems in keeping them occupied and still under discipline. However, for me this did not last very long. I was demobilised, and we moved to a flat in London.

Chapter Four

Peace of a Sort

In London, both Honor and I were seriously ill: she with bronchial asthma, and I with double pneumonia. I was lucky enough to be treated with penicillin, which was just beginning to be used in the old hospital at Hyde Park Corner which is now the Lansborough Hotel.

It was at about this time that I first met Colonel Gilbert Lennox and Dickie Metcalfe, as well as Dusko and Ivan Popov and Lieutenant Colonel Andrew Constable Maxwell. I agreed to join them in Italy and to set up an import-export company with them. The first time that I met Dickie Metcalfe was in the Regent Street offices of TARLAIR, another import-export company which was closely concerned with the deception organisation set up to mislead the Germans as to when and where the invasion of Europe would take place and closely allied with the Yugoslav operations. Andrew Maxwell, the Popov brothers, Freddie Cole and Dickie Metcalfe were all engaged in this. Dusko Popov (now, alas, dead) wrote an amusing book about it and was himself an enormously brave man. Dickie too played a very important part in the deception operations and was personally thanked for his services after the war by the King in a private reception at the Palace. Part of the deception operations were run from the Clock House in Rutland Gate, and part also from TARLAIR. Colonel

Gilbert Lennox and his assistant Giesler were to a great extent the *Deus ex Machina*.

'B' Division of MI5 under Guy Liddell worked closely with Section V of MI6 under Jarvis. Colonel 'TAR' Robertson shared an office with Liddell in the Cromwell Road headquarters of MI5 and was closely concerned with double agents including the Popov brothers, Gisela Ashley, the XX Committee and the Yugoslav Ring of double agents which included Dickie Metcalfe, Friedle Gaertner, the two Popov brothers and others. In fact, TARLAIR, the import-export firm set up in Regent Street as a front operation had been named after Colonel Robertson. The deception operation came to an end in 1943–1944, as its whole purpose was to persuade the Germans that the invasion would come at a different place and at a different time and also to feed them a considerable quantity of information which would mislead their planning strategy, troop movements and so on.

With the end of the war, TARLAIR continued to exist, run largely by Colonel Gilbert Lennox and the super-efficient Gisela Ashley. Freddie Cole and Andrew Maxwell – both of whom had been in Yugoslavia – and Ivan Popov set up an office in Rome, and I was invited to join them.

There was considerable concern, and not without reason, that Italy might become communist, and the intelligence people in London were anxious to obtain more information.

Conditions in Italy were by no means very stable. The Communist Party had emerged from the war with a nationwide organisation, a Stalinist political policy and a considerable number of weapons acquired from both the Allies and the Germans. There were fears that Togliatti, the Communist Party leader, might attempt a coup. I was asked by Gilbert Lennox to keep Dickie Metcalfe informed, and he passed on the information that I was able to obtain.

Andrew Maxwell set up the import-export company in the Via Regina Elena in Rome, and in due course, we all assembled there: Andrew, Freddie Cole, Ivan Popov, Cyril Wiss and myself. I am rather doubtful whether we ever imported or exported anything, although I remember that Ivan Popov filled the whole office with large pieces of statuary which were supposed to be exported somewhere. We were also supposed to export fruit and vegetables to England, and there were large dumps of war surplus material, including some quite good vehicles which could be exported and bought from the depots at knock-down prices. All this gave me and my wife an excellent opportunity to travel around the country and see more or less what was going on.

Ireland

However, before going to Italy, Honor and I went to Ireland. I had finally been able to get my mother out of Italy and she was back, living with us in London, and in a very frail state after all her experiences in the German forced labour camp. Food was scarce in England, rationing was still rigid, and Ireland was a 'land flowing with milk and honey' – or at least with meat, butter, whisky and all the things which one hardly saw in England at that time. As an Irish national, my mother wanted to buy a house in the south-west of the country, and we found a small house on the edge of the sea, some three miles out of Bantry in West Cork. It had probably the most beautiful view that I have ever seen in my life, a garden which ran down to the sea and about ten acres of land. Although it was small and without electric light, it had been very well built and was weatherproof, which was an absolutely vital factor. It had five bedrooms, including a double servants' room, a panelled drawing room with a dining room, a panelled hall, kitchen, bathroom, larder, pantry and storage rooms.

In due course we made the garden very pretty, with ponds and many flowering trees, hundreds of rhododendrons and azaleas and a large herb garden. We also acquired a small boat with an outboard engine, moored right in front of the house. My mother gave this house to Honor and me as a belated wedding present – we had already been married for five years – and she herself bought a farmhouse about half a mile away with another thirty acres which adjoined our property. Honor never liked our house – mainly, I think, because she hated the dark, and having no electric light, we had to light the house with lamps and dozens of candles. She suffered very much from asthma there, and also from the damp – and the west of Ireland is very damp indeed.

The house was also very isolated and approached down a long and dark lane. This ran through the farmyard of O'Leary's farm, past his muck heap, half a mile down to some iron gates, another quarter of a mile to the sea and eventually to the gates leading into our garden. From the house at night, one saw no other light and could look for miles down both sides of Bantry Bay without seeing another house or any light, road or sign of human habitation.

However, I would like to return to Ireland later on, as on this occasion we were only there for a few months before going out to Rome.

Colonel Gilbert Lennox had a lovely flat in Regents Park, and there I was supplied with invisible ink (which did not look like ink at all) for writing messages, special paper which I was told was highly inflammable and could also be swallowed (but which looked very indigestible) and various other James Bond-type of gadgets, and off we went to Rome.

Italy

My mother, who had preceded us, had taken a horrible little house off the Via Nomentana, and we moved in. Right from the first, Honor was enchanted with Rome. Antonietta, who had been my mother's maid before the war, came to cook for us. What we did not know was that the landlord and owner of the house apparently owed money to everybody, and one day, shortly after our arrival, a party of men arrived at the flat. Having presented Honor with a paper she could not read and spoken to her at length in Italian (which at that time she did not understand), they started to remove the furniture. Honor went off to my bedroom and got my pistol, and when the removal men returned for another load, she lined them up against the wall and told them to bring back whatever they had taken and then remove themselves from the premises, and never return. Apparently, the removal men understood the situation very clearly. While one of them brought back the one or two things which they had already removed, the others remained with the tips of their fingers reaching for the ceiling. Then they all removed themselves with the speed of light and were never seen again. However, it was clear that it was inadvisable to remain in that house, and we moved to a lovely place in the Via Donizetti, belonging to the Princess Pio di Savoia. We were very happy there, and all went well. We were joined by our children and their nanny, and life was very good.

There was very little traffic in Rome in those days. There were virtually no buses, and public transport was carried out by *camionetta*, which were small trucks, privately owned and into which as many people as possible were crammed. In fact they ran recognised routes, were fairly regular and, on the whole, worked well. That was more than could be said of my office in the Via Regina Elena, which suffered from a chronic shortage of money to pay the secretaries and meet all other outgoings. There was some wretched little man called Doney, a Yugoslav, who used to be summoned to the office from time to time. Andrew Maxwell somehow managed to extract money from him which kept us afloat. Occasionally, villainous-looking Yugoslavs appeared in the office, and we had visits from Dickie Metcalfe and, occasionally, from Gilbert. There was also a most extraordinary person called 'Professor Parsons'.

Professor Parsons had been born the son of a grocer in the outer reaches of south London. At the age of twelve, his school teachers informed his parents that they could not teach him any more, as he already knew more than they did. In spite of his parents' protests – as they wanted him to work in their grocer's shop – he spent his days in the public library, teaching himself Latin and Greek, and reading Plutarch and the other Greek and Latin classics. Then he went on to higher mathematics, theories on time and relativity, and acquired some eight or nine languages. He wandered about in Europe, backpacking, and then took a job as a tutor to the son of a Dutch family. There he organised the elopement of the son of the house and a girl of whom the son's parents disapproved, and was consequently sacked. He finished up in Venice, not long before the war, where he floated about on the lagoon, played his guitar, sang, wrote poetry and carried on a business selling charms to Africans in West Africa.

These consisted of special pens with which to pass examinations, special ink, special charms to get rid of unwanted crocodiles from local rivers, love potions and so on. It was not long before his name appeared on a 'list of charlatans' which the colonial government had put up in all post offices in West Africa. This brought immediate results, and he received hundreds of letters which started 'dear and most honoured Professor Parsons, We see that you have been recommended by the British government as the greatest charlatan of them all. Now, I have a problem with my examination' – or it could be love-life – 'and I ask you, most honoured professor, to supply me with one of your famous charms…'

He was inundated with these letters, so he used to work one day a week answering them and sending off his charms. All correspondence left over after that one day's work he threw into the canal. This brought him in a good living and a very agreeable way of life. It continued until, to his horror, he received demands for photographs. These became insistent, so he bought several hundred picture postcards of the famous picture in the National Portrait Gallery of Charles Darwin, with white hair, piercing eyes, and enveloped in a black robe. On the back of each he wrote 'With the compliments of Professor Parsons' and sent them off. Even worse was to follow, when he received a cable to the effect that a group of West Africans was about to leave on a pilgrimage to pay homage to the great professor. Perhaps happily, the war broke out, and they were unable to come. Professor Parsons continued his blissful life, disinterested in the war, until the fateful day on which Italy declared war on Britain, in the summer of 1940. Three days later, the Italian secret police arrived and arrested Professor Parsons and threw him into a dungeon below the water level in the old prison of Venice, charged with being a British spy.

From time to time, he was brought up and confronted with a map on which were marked various circles in red ink. Edmund Parsons had never seen it before and had no idea what it was. 'Here are the fortifications guarding Venice,' he was told by the interrogating officer. 'This map has been found in your rooms. Confess that you are a British spy!' He refused, and was promptly beaten up and thrown back into his dungeon. He was there for a year, with periodical interrogations and beatings. Then they put a lunatic in his cell with him, and he himself felt that his mind was going. He decided that he would 'confess', but it was not to be that easy. He was brought up and again confronted with the map. 'What is this?' the interrogating officer asked, pointing to a red circle on the map. Professor Parsons had no idea, so he replied, 'You tell me first.' 'It is an ammunition store for this battery marked here,' the officer said. 'Yes, of course you are right,' Edmund Parsons said. 'And what is this?' the officer said, pointing to another red circle. 'I was never quite sure,' Professor Parsons said, 'but I am sure that you know?' 'Yes, of course! You know as well as I do that it is the eastern battery!' 'I am sure that you are right,' Professor Parsons replied. 'You will sign a full confession in detail?' the interrogator asked. 'Yes,' Edmund said, 'but you write it for me, and I will sign it.' So finally he did and was hustled away, put in a truck and driven for miles out of Venice.

He was quite sure that he was being taken to a place of execution, but was finally removed from the truck and pushed through some iron gates of a most beautiful villa and told to walk up to the house, which he could see about one hundred yards away. He did so, expecting at any moment to be shot in the back. He reached the villa and was received and taken to a bathroom and then to a bedroom, clean and very pleasant. He fell into a deep sleep, to be woken the next morning and told that breakfast was ready downstairs. He went down and found a good breakfast and several other people who seemed to be English, but by this time he was convinced that his mind had finally given way and that at any moment he would come to his senses, back in the dark and damp dungeon in Venice. Finally, after several days, he realised that he was in an internment centre, where the internees were extremely well treated and given the run of the villa and its large and beautiful garden.

Life here was good once again. But one day, the Germans arrived and packed all the internees into trucks and took them off to a camp in Germany. This was very different. There were Tunisians, Channel Islanders and people from various other nations there. The food was meagre and poor, but Professor Parsons gave English lessons to the Arabs (Arabic was one of the languages which he spoke fluently) and acquired a guitar.

He asked the Germans if he could go up to the top of the camp water tower and play his guitar, and the Germans, who had found in Professor Parsons somebody who could translate into very many languages, agreed. He played and sang *Lille Marlene* and other German songs, and they liked it very much; and he played classical music, which they also liked, so he was left alone. In fact, he was quite sorry when he was finally liberated by the Americans and given railway vouchers to go back to Italy, which had been his residence and domicile.

The trains did not work very well, and he finally walked across the frontier from Austria into Italy, wearing a pair of corduroy breeches, a pair of German officers' boots, a Russian greatcoat with a German officer's sword buckled round its waist, a guitar strapped to his back and a rabbit-skin cap.

Walking down a valley into Italy, he stopped at a farm to ask for a drink of water and, if possible, something to eat. A very pretty young girl gave him both. Two years later, he returned to marry her, but then continued on his way south and finished up in Naples. Here he was to work for the Americans, who found him invaluable. He was ordered to go to the Flora Hotel in Rome (one of the best) and book in there to await further orders.

He had a lovely room, and all his meals were paid for. He just had to sign a sheet. No further orders were ever received, and after three months of living in great luxury, the hotel was becoming edgy. Professor Parsons thought it prudent to leave. On return to Naples, he was awarded the American Legion of Merit. He never discovered for what, and shortly afterwards, he came to work with Andrew Maxwell, Freddy Cole, Ivan Popov and me.

He became my secretary and eventually my partner, and a very close friend. When he married his girl from the mountain, the very beautiful and charming Giulietta, I was godfather to his son, and Honor and I took Giulietta through the night to the hospital when she went into labour.

He was a most extraordinary man. He wrote a book on the Nestorian Heresy, and another on the theory of time. He wrote a third, being a commentary on Plutarch, but I don't know if this was ever published. Alas, he died about four years ago.

The great tragedy of his life and in the life of Giulietta was when their son, almost as gifted as his father, died at the age of twenty-two, of a cardiac collapse, on Christmas Eve some twenty years ago. He and his wife left Italy shortly afterwards. They adopted a little daughter and went to live in Grenada, but found this unpleasant and came back to live in Portugal. There Professor Parsons eventually died and his widow still lives.

At the end of 1946 and the beginning of 1947, Italy seemed to be a paradise after the gloom and restrictions of England. There was food, wine, petrol, and all the things which were lacking in England. We had a lovely house and travelled all over the country. The roads were pretty bad, many of the bridges were still down and there were plenty of mines on the verges of the roads, but the country was still beautiful and unspoilt by huge new and hideous towns, suburbs and gigantic motorways down which pour an endless stream of traffic and gigantic trucks. There were still quite a few bandits about, mainly the deserters of different armies, and certain well-known places were dangerous and to be avoided, especially after dark.

Honor and I had been to Switzerland to meet Dickie Metcalfe, and we were returning by way of Venice. Here, many years ago, my family had had a palace. We eventually arrived in Bologna late at night and found that there was no room at the inn. In fact there was no room in any inn or hotel in the town, and we were faced with the choice of sleeping in the car, which was very uncomfortable, or else taking the risk of crossing the Futa Pass between Bologna and Florence at night. This was probably one of the most dangerous roads in Italy. I was driving an old army surplus staff car, of the sort which were called gin palaces during the war. It was a pretty bad vehicle and had brakes which worked on only two wheels, but we decided to take the risk and set off across the mountains. It was a very different road to the autostrada of today.

All the bridges were still down, and the journey meant creeping down a track on one side of the river, fording the river itself and then climbing up the dirt track on the other side. The road had craters in many places, and for much of the way there was a rock wall on one side and a sheer drop several hundred feet down into the valley on the other. It was a brilliant moonlit night, and we crept cautiously along the road. After what seemed like weeks, we emerged at the top of the pass and below us, we could see the lights of Florence. I had just said to Honor, 'Thank God, we have made it all right,' when a man jumped out into the road, some twenty or thirty yards in front of the car, and fired a burst from a sub-machine gun which went just over the top of the windscreen. In an instant, Honor, who was sitting in the front beside me with the window open, leaned out and with a single shot from my long barrelled Browning pistol, which she had been carrying on her lap during the whole journey, knocked the bandit head-over-heels into the ditch. We were travelling at about thirty-five or forty miles per hour, and I had no chance of stopping, even if we had wanted to. There were some scattered shots from further up the hill, and then we were round the next bend. Shortly afterwards we came safely into Florence. It was probably the best shot I have ever seen – but then she was an expert pistol shot.

Many people were killed by bandits on the Futa, and it was not really until a couple of years later that the area was relatively safe to cross at night.

After that, I got rid of the gin palace, and we brought out an Allard from England. This was a close coupled 2/4 seater drop-head, or as the Americans call them, a convertible. It had a big Mercury engine in it and went like the wind. We had it for many years and it gave us wonderful service, although it was a difficult and rather dangerous vehicle to drive, as the power/weight ratio was quite out of proportion, and the car would spin around like a top on ice.

I think that it was in 1947 that Willa came to stay with us in Rome. She was in the process of getting engaged to an old friend and also had been given a small part in a film which was being made at Cinecitta, the Italian studios outside of Rome. Willa was a very pretty girl, and her family had something or other to do with the film industry in America. She had rather nice brown hair, but the part called for a platinum blonde.

The day came when she went off to have her hair dyed or bleached. The same day, a telegram was delivered to say that my great-aunt had died in London. This was not a shock as she was very old, but we had come to look on her as immortal. That evening Honor and I were sitting in our bedroom discussing what I should do. I certainly had to fly to England for the funeral and would be away for several days. We were sitting on the bed talking about the aunt who had played such a great part in my life. It was becoming dusk outside when, looking up, we suddenly saw a white figure reflected in a large cheval mirror. It was totally white, with a long white dress, a white face and long white hair. For a moment we both thought it must be the aunt, or rather her ghost.

I suppose that there was horror written clearly on our faces, and poor Willa – for it was she, and not Aunt's ghost – burst into tears. 'Oh God! Do I look so awful?' she wailed. We tried to comfort her as best we could, but they had made her hair as white as snow, and in the process they had burnt it pretty badly. The next day I went with her to the film studios and saw the director or producer (I have never discovered which does what). I presented myself as Willa's legal advisor and threatened legal action. It must have been a convincing performance as they offered compensation three times more than that which she was going to earn as an actress in the film. Perhaps, though, it was more her family connections in the film industry which induced the producer to pay up.

The next day we left to fly to London.

My great-aunt had left precise instructions for her funeral. These included obtaining a huge lead coffin in which she wanted a number of artefacts placed, together with her body. This in turn was to be enclosed in a massive oak casket. The whole thing was almost incredibly heavy. The funeral was to be in Derbyshire, where we have a family chapel and vault under it. It is rather beautiful, with a huge tomb in the middle of it. It is a Catholic chapel in the middle of a Protestant churchyard, but as the manor originally owned the churchyard it remains there in splendid isolation. There are, or were, stained-glass windows, and all round the tomb there are coats of arms of various quartering of our family. On top of the tomb there is a vast marble slab. To enter the tomb this has to be removed, a certain engineering feat in itself. When the tomb is opened, there is a sharply inclined plane down to the vaults underneath – a sort of chute.

The funeral started off from London at a sedate pace. We reached Derby with plenty of time, the hearse lumbering in front of us as we followed in another car. In Derby, my great-uncle expressed the desire for a quick drink, suggesting that we could easily catch up with the hearse before reaching the chapel. We had a couple of drinks and then drove on. Only too soon we caught up with the hearse. It was broken down on the roadside with a flat tyre. The driver and the funeral director had attempted to change the wheel, but the enormous weight of the coffin in its oak casket buckled the jack put under the axle. We stood about the roadside hoping that a lorry might come past from which we might borrow a jack. It took a very long time, but eventually one did stop for us, and the wheel was finally changed.

We were now very late indeed. The hearse, doing a good seventy-five miles per hour, roared down the road with our car pelting after it. Finally we drew up in a shower of small stones at the entrance to the churchyard. There were quite a lot of people waiting there, and they had been waiting for quite a long time!

A bearer party of eight strong men finally loaded the coffin on to their shoulders and staggered up to the chapel. The lid had been removed from the tomb, and the coffin, with much difficulty, was placed on the slide. Thoughtfully, this had been greased. The coffin was held back by the eight bearers, holding on to green ropes. The service began. Not all the mourners who had come could be accommodated in the chapel, and the majority had to stand outside. At last it was all over. With the words 'Earth to earth and ashes to ashes', the bearers were supposed to slowly pay out their ropes so that the coffin would slide down to the vault. There must have been some misunderstanding about this, or perhaps they did not realise the enormous weight. Seven of the bearers released their ropes simultaneously, and the enormous coffin shot down the chute with the speed of light, landing at the bottom with an earth-shattering crash. Alas, the eighth man did not release his rope but kept holding on to it tightly, and he too disappeared, with a despairing howl, down the chute and into the darkness of the vault.

There was general consternation both inside and outside the chapel. Cries of 'Are you all right down there?' with sounds of anguish and heart-rending groans floating up from the depths. Finally there was a recognisable cry of, 'For gaw'd sake get me out of 'ere!' Unfortunately that was not so easy. The chute was fairly long and steep, and as I have said, it had been greased. There was no way that the wretched man could climb up it.

Some distance from the chapel there were steps leading down into the ground, and the entrance to the vault here was closed by a great iron door. The rector of the Protestant church was supposed to have a key to this, as after the services the bearers would normally go into the vault this way and arrange the coffins on shelves round the walls. However, the rector could not find the key!

The howls and imprecations from the unfortunate man in the vault stumbling about in the dark grew ever louder, but the key could not be found.

The rector gave us tea, while the verger was sent off to the nearest town to try to find a locksmith. However, it was night before the poor fellow in the vault could be liberated, and he appeared to be more than a little mad. He was removed in an ambulance, and we returned to London. It had been a dramatic day, and my great-aunt would have enjoyed it.

The next day we flew back to Rome.

Life in Rome at this time was absolutely delightful. We belonged to a small private club called the San Giorgio, and there we used to have luncheon by the swimming pool in the large garden under the oleanders and meet our friends. These included Maria Lo Bianco and later her husband Professor Pifferi, who remained our very dear friends for nearly fifty years, and with whom we used to stay when we came to Rome whilst we were living in Portugal later. At the club we also used to meet Guido and Eleanor Canaletti, the Princess del Drago and so many others.

There was also, of course, General Cino Bacchiani, whom my mother had married shortly before the war, and his family – in particular his nephew Emilio and later Emilio's wife Elena Fina, who have been our very dear friends ever since and with whom we spent many months every year.

At the weekends, we used to drive up to Anticoli Corrado, just over forty miles from Rome, and up the valley of the Aniene to the villa. There we had wonderful parties in the house and gardens. The house was quite large and had eight bedrooms, of which six were double. There was also a huge drawing room, which was some twenty-eight metres long by eight metres wide and was the whole height of the house. There were three small sitting rooms or writing rooms and a good-sized dining room, seven metres by six. There were also three bathrooms, a kitchen, a laundry and a very large pantry and wood store, and outside there was the gardener's house with another six rooms. In front of the villa, which faced to the south-east, there was a huge terrace garden which fell away down the almost sheer hill through another three terraces to the valley floor some one thousand feet below. There were ponds and fountains and an avenue of cypresses, and at the back of the house another garden filled with roses, vines, pergolas and a kitchen garden.

In all, it covered about three acres, and outside we had fields of corn, olives and vines stretching up the hill to the little copse of oaks perched on a bluff overlooking the valley with an almost sheer drop down to the valley floor in front of it. The villa was largely self-supporting, as we made our own olive oil and wine (which was remarkably nasty), grew corn and, at one end of the kitchen garden, there was an oven for making bread. The kitchen garden itself supplied the house with everything that we needed. From the house and the terrace in front, there was the most spectacular view over the Abruzzi mountains, with Roviano in front and Arsoli, where our friend Prince Massimo had a lovely old castle. It was one of the most beautiful villas I have ever seen in Italy, with hedges of lavender, flowering shrubs, flowering trees, pears, cherries, wonderful table grapes, ancient olives and the tinkling of water from a fountain in front of the dining room, under a weeping willow.

I was largely brought up here as a boy and youth, when I stayed with my mother in Italy. It was an enchanted place on the edge of the village of Anticoli Corrado, famous for its models and for the colony of foreign and Italian artists. The people were for the most part shepherds and were charming, but all that was to change after the war when they became infected with politics. Most of them became communists, and their whole character changed. From being charming, kind and simple people, they became grasping, deceitful, highly dishonest, rude and bloody-minded, filled with envy and hatred against anybody who had anything which they did not. In this, they were encouraged by the communists and left-wing politicians and by a scoundrel priest who was there for very many years, Don Vittorio, a local boy from a neighbouring village who went into the priesthood and in spite of abysmal ignorance, gluttony and stupidity, remained there until his death two or three years ago. He tried to stop the old customs and festivals and encouraged the local boys to burn lizards alive, as they were 'emissaries of the Devil'. He did manage to stop the *Marmotta* as being a pagan rite. The *Marmotta* was in fact a large carnival figure made from wicker-work and dressed in local costumes, inside which a man danced and whirled about. It had been a tradition of the village carnival from time immemorial.

In the days before the war and immediately afterwards, the villagers played the zambonia (a sort of bagpipes), danced in the village square and celebrated the church festivals with colourful processions through the narrow, winding and steep streets of the mountain village. Little by little, this was all to be changed. The festivals were to be replaced by harangues (relayed fortissimo through loud-speakers in the village square) by communist activists imported from Rome and elsewhere in Italy, and a friendly and happy people were to be transformed into greedy, dissatisfied and sullen discontents.

The corruption and dishonesty of the local administration was to become such that it became impossible to live there any longer, and I was forced to sell what remained of the property after a large part of it had been stolen by the local administration and their friends, without any compensation. A court case to obtain redress is still before the courts after a matter of thirty years without any final judgement being given.

Alas, the poison of politics has done very much to destroy Italy, but in the years immediately after the war, living in Rome was easy and very pleasant indeed. We had many friends, travelled the whole country – which was still beautiful and, in spite of the war, largely unspoilt. It was interesting to see that a good many of the former partisans, unable to settle down to normal life and abandon the collection of 'proletarian taxes' in the name of patriotism, had formed themselves into bandit gangs and continued to rob banks, hold up and rob travellers and carry out murders.

It was in fact these people who were to become the terrorist groups of the Sixties, the Seventies and on into the Eighties, organised by such people as Pietro Secchia, who ran the dirty tricks division of the Communist Party 'intelligence', and Gianni Feltrinelli, who organised Potere Operario and through his chain of book shops and publishing houses was to have translated, printed and distributed 'The Mini Manual of the Urban Guerrilla', which became a bestseller to university protesters and students all over Europe, as well as North and South America. He also introduced Baader to Meinhoff in Germany (they were to form the Red Army Faction there), sent ETA terrorists for training in Cuba, printed false identity documents including passports, bought arms and explosives, set up safe houses and organised the international co-operation of terrorist groups and also their training. In fact Feltrinelli was never taken very seriously during his lifetime and was considered to be just a rich playboy with his yacht, his girls and his powder-blue Cadillac. However, he was to become the 'Godfather' of political terrorism in Italy.

Finally, Feltrinelli was to blow himself up with one of his own bombs, but his work was to be continued by the Red Brigades and as many as thirty or forty other terrorist groups in Italy alone; but this all lay in the future.

However, it was at this time that I begun to realise that terrorism represented a new form of warfare. (Not that terrorism itself is not as old as human history.) The Resistance, which had given birth to partisans, had glorified those who carried out attacks on authority. During the war, this had been the authority of the German occupation troops, or the authority of a quisling, Petainist, or fascist government. Those who had carried out acts of sabotage were considered heroes, as were those who had attacked and killed officials of these governments or 'military officials' (soldiers) of the occupying army. In both France and Italy, immediately after the war it was almost impossible to find anybody over the age of five who did not claim to have been in the Resistance.

Now that the war was over, partisans, especially in Italy, found it difficult to settle down to civilian life. They had in many cases got used to collecting 'proletarian taxes', robbing banks, extorting money from 'fascists' (which in practice meant anybody who had money), and committing general acts of banditry carried out in the name of 'partisan actions'. There was another fact, too. Very many of the Italian partisans were communists, anarchists, or left-wing ideologists of one sort or another. They had hoped to take over Italy after the Germans had been defeated, and had been bitterly disappointed when this had not happened.

Apart from the attraction of extortion, robbery, kidnapping and the collection of money given willingly or unwillingly for 'The Cause', there was also the Cause itself. The authority of the German occupation or fascist government might have gone, but authority in the form of a parliamentary, democratic government was now in place, and this was not at all the sort of government or authority which they wanted. It was an authority to be attacked, and all over northern and central Italy in the immediate aftermath of the war, groups of former partisans were being organised to bring about by terror, murder, kidnapping, threat, extortion, sabotage and bombing the desired political change. Officially the Italian Communist Party disapproved of such tactics, but unofficially, and by men such as Pietro Secchia, it was approved and encouraged.

It was to take some time for these small, dispersed and disorganised groups to become a real threat, but already the seeds had been planted and were growing. For myself, I also realised that political terrorism together with organised crime on a large scale could well become the major threat to the free world that it was to become some ten to fifteen years later, and still is.

Over the years, terrorism has changed very much. We have religious terrorism, terrorism to obtain territory, terrorism as an act of hatred, ideological terrorism and various combinations of these objectives, as well as terrorism with no clear objective which constitutes an attempt to burn down the house in the vague belief that something better may arise from the ashes.

Initially, the age-old organisations such as the Mafia and the Cammora which existed on the capitalist system were bitterly opposed to the ideological and communist left. This accounts for the fact that the Red Brigades, Potere Operario and such terrorist groups had no place in Southern Italy and Sicily, which are territories of the Mafia and Cammora.

In my reports to Dickie Metcalfe and Gilbert Lennox, I pointed out the potential dangers of terrorism in Italy starting in 1946–1947, but the real danger was to lie some years in the future. Perhaps I did not realise at the time that terrorism and the fight against it was to be the main interest in my life.

For ourselves, life was very good indeed. We used to go to Fregene to picnic on the sands and bathe in the brilliant moonlight. Then there were perhaps barely a dozen villas there, and it had not been 'developed' in any way. There were the diplomatic parties and those given by the Allied commission, but from time to time there were riots, and immediately following the attempted assassination of the communist leader, Togliatti, there was quite serious trouble for a few days. I had moved from Andrew Maxwell's office in the Via Regina Elena and had taken a small office in the Via Torino. One day, after some trouble in the town, I found a couple of corpses blocking the door into the street.

We had other excitements, too. One day, I received a signal to inform me that Count Ladislaus Almasy would be coming through Rome and that I should meet him at a certain hotel off the Via Sistina. This was followed by a further signal to say that the NKVD were after him and very close behind, and that I had to get him on the first available aircraft for Cairo. Unfortunately, this signal came in when I had already gone out and was picked up by my assistant Deszo de Onody. He went off immediately to the hotel to find that Almasy had just arrived and was in the process of checking in. Deszo told him that he must leave immediately, put him in a taxi and took him to our house in the Via Donizetti.

Count Almasy had been a flying ace in the First World War and had been highly decorated. He had also driven the Austrian Emperor Charles to the outskirts of Budapest in an attempt to regain the throne of Hungary shortly before the Emperor was forced into exile by Clemenceau and Woodrow Wilson.

During the Second World War, Ladislaus Almasy had been the cartographer to Rommel in the Western Desert. Between the wars, he had explored the whole of the Libyan desert, as well as having traversed three or four times the Great Sand Sea in the Sahara. He was a scholar and an archaeologist, and probably knew the deserts of North Africa better than anyone.

As a Hungarian, he was certainly not a Nazi and would probably have served with anybody who would have given him a chance to return to his beloved deserts. There are many stories about him; in fact Jean Howard has written a fascinating book about him.

At the end of the African Campaign, he managed to escape and went to his elder brother's castle at Bernstein in the Burgenland. From there, he unwisely went to Budapest and was arrested by the communists, who threw him into prison and condemned him to death. We wanted him badly, and eventually an escape was arranged. At that time, it was possible to bribe the Hungarian prison guards.

There is good evidence that from Budapest, and for some time before his arrest, he had operated a clandestine radio transmitter to the Allies. Almasy escaped and came to Trieste. From there he travelled to Venice, where he was given a passport, papers, a rail ticket to Rome and also an airline ticket from Rome to Cairo, where he was to be debriefed. These documents, together with a clean shirt and toothbrush; were all put into a small fibre attaché case, which he was given by the British in Venice. However the Soviets were equally keen to get hold of him and were not very far behind.

When I eventually came back to the house where we lived and where Honor was entertaining Almasy and Deszo, I found that, due to some leak somewhere down the line, the Russians knew that Almasy was in Rome and also knew to which hotel he had gone. By this time they were probably already there. The situation was further complicated by the fact that, when Almasy had checked in at the hotel and before he had been given the key to his room, he had handed his attaché case with all his papers in it to the hotel clerk and asked him to keep it for him.

At this moment, Deszo de Onody had arrived and had taken Almasy away immediately. The attaché case had been forgotten. By this time, I thought it too dangerous to go back to the hotel, and we decided to spend the night in the house and leave very early the following morning. In fact, we sat up all night with Deszo and Almasy. The next morning, at about 4.30 a.m., we got into the car.

Honor and I were in the front, and I put Almasy and Deszo with an automatic rifle in the back. I parked the car some fifteen yards beyond the hotel, and Honor went in. We thought that the same clerk who had been on the previous afternoon had probably been replaced by another, and as she walked into the lobby of the hotel, Honor saw two men, semi-asleep and partly concealed behind a potted palm. In those days the Soviets were fairly easy to spot – their Eastern European clothing stood out like a sore thumb.

Honor, who looked like an Italian, walked up to the clerk, who was himself half-asleep, and asked for the key of the room into which Almasy had booked and which, by good chance, he remembered. She then said in Italian, 'Also, please give me the little attaché case which I left with your colleague this afternoon. It is just behind the desk.' The clerk bent down, looked around for a moment, and then handed it up to her. Honor thanked him and also took the key to the room which he gave her. Then, instead of going to the lift, she walked unhurriedly to the door on to the street. As she moved through the lobby, she saw a sudden movement out of the corner of her eye by the two men behind the palm, and once outside the hotel, she ran the fifteen yards to the car and jumped in. As I put the car in gear and started to move away, I saw through my rear mirror the two men come running out and make a dash for a car parked on the other side of the road.

The Allard was fast and was capable of well over one hundred miles per hour, but I had never driven through the streets of Rome at that speed before, nor have I ever tried to do it since! We arrived at Ciampino without incident, and instead of going into the main building, I went to a gate on the perimeter, guarded by the military. I had a pass, and the sentry let us through. I drove right up to the end of the runway. A few minutes later, the aircraft for Cairo rolled out and came to the end of the runway for take-off. When the aircraft turned, I pulled the car in front of it. After some discussion I was able to convince the captain of the aircraft to take Almasy together with his papers and suitcase. We heaved him with some difficulty into the plane. I pulled the car out of the way, and the aircraft took off. We drove back to the gate in the perimeter fence. The Russians must have been watching the whole thing, as we had just got through the gate when they arrived. It was too late: their bird had flown and they could do little other than scowl, but Deszo kept them covered with the automatic rifle just in case they wanted revenge. However, the armed sentry was there too, and they decided that there was nothing that they could do about it. We drove back to Rome at a more sedate pace, keeping a watchful eye open behind us.

But for Honor's courage and coolness, we would never have been able to pull this off. She had quite extraordinary bravery and coolness in the face of danger and she was to demonstrate this time and time again, in Italy, in Ireland, in Africa, in Libya and whenever she was faced with an emergency or a threat. She had perhaps inherited this from her father: it was the same quality which had earned him his place in the Guinness Book of Records for the award of three Air Force Crosses to add to a string of other medals for courage.

Many years later, when she was dying from cancer, she faced this with the same cool courage: never complaining, totally serene, laughing and joking to the end and only once expressing the wish that when the end came, that it would come quickly. Thank God, it did.

Libya – The First Time

I then had to go to Libya. This was one of the very few times that Honor did not come with me. One of the children – our son, Marcus, I think – had black measles and was very definitely ill. I would not have gone myself but had to go with Dickie Metcalfe. Everything had been arranged, and I was not away for long.

Libya was full of mines, and every dawn and dusk, when the temperature changed dramatically, there were explosions all over the desert. We went to Tobruk and went on board the 'unsinkable battleship' – the *San Giorgio*. It was unsinkable for the very good reason that it was fast aground and fixed to the bottom with concrete. The main decks and the armament were all above water, and I took a photograph of Dickie standing under the triple gun turrets of the main armament. He stuck out his chin and gave the fascist salute. In fact, he looked exactly like Mussolini, and I was able to have considerable fun with my friends in Rome by telling them that I was prepared to swear on a stack of Bibles that I had taken the photograph only a matter of a fortnight previously. Everybody thought that it was a photograph of Mussolini, and one could not see that the battleship was partly sunk.

Back to Italy

When we got back to Rome, I took Dickie to Fregene with Honor and the children for an afternoon by the sea. The beach was quite open in those days and there were barely a dozen villas at the beginning of the pine forest. All the rest consisted of sand dunes, pines and long unpolluted beaches. Dickie produced a bathing suit which he must have inherited from his father, with a black top including half sleeves and a bottom piece with black and white stripes which reached down to his knees. As he was as bald as an egg, he kept his black bowler hat firmly on his head to prevent the top of his pate from becoming sunburnt. He entered the sea, where he sat down in the shallows, with barely his head projecting above the water. To a casual observer, he could well be taken for the top of a post. When he had enough, he got up and turned towards the beach.

As I have previously written, he really looked very much like Mussolini. With the black top of his bathing suit out of the water and his black bowler hat which could easily be mistaken for the black fascist cap which Mussolini used to wear, he stuck his chin out and gave the fascist salute. Some idiot on the beach shouted '*Viva il Duce*', and in an instant the beach was cleared, with people running in helpless panic for the pines. I had given the photograph taken on the deck of the 'unsinkable battleship', *San Giorgio*, to a friend of mine in the press, and he had published it with a caption to the effect that the photograph had been taken only a few days previously, and it could be true that il Duce still lived. The appearance of the man himself emerging, or at least half-emerging from the waves was too much for the bathers on the beach at Fregene.

A while later, we had 'The Case of the Defecting General'. There were very many cocktail parties, receptions and so on going on in Rome at that time, and members of the embassies and the Allied Control Commission were usually there. It was at one of these that Honor met a Polish general, who clearly was very much taken with her. He invited her to show him the sights of Rome, and she was to be seen driving about with him in his official car with a large red flag flying, much to the astonishment of our many friends. He was well escorted with minders – grim-looking men with unsmiling faces and bulges under their left armpits. They were clearly suspicious, but as the weeks passed and Honor showed the general more and more of the almost endless sights of Rome, they became somewhat relaxed and visibly bored.

Finally, he told her that he wanted to get to America. We informed our American 'cousins' of this fact. They were interested because he apparently did have access to useful information. Honor told the general that he would have to pay for his passage with whatever information or documents the Americans wanted, and he said that he was willing to do this. Very shortly afterwards he told her that he was being recalled to Poland, and arrangements had to be made quickly. It was decided that he should actually escape during the night stopover in Paris, where he would express a wish to go to the Lido (or some similar place of entertainment, I forget which now). During the interval he would go to the lavatory and disappear, taking the information and documents with him. He would be met in the lavatory by an American agent, who would identify himself in a certain way and would then get the general out and away safely.

In fact it all worked according to plan, and we heard later that the general had reached America safely. By now he must be long dead; we neither heard from him again nor expected to do so.

Not all our ploys were so successful. I made a contact with a Hungarian diplomat, and it seemed that he too was anxious to remain in the fleshpots of Rome – or preferably further away, in America or Britain. He had a good deal to say and agreed to an interview with me, on the basis of which it would be decided if he had sufficient of interest to make it worthwhile getting him out.

His English was virtually non-existent, but he spoke some Italian and German. I asked for instructions, and in due course I was told by Gilbert Lennox that a wire recorder was being sent to me via the embassy. This duly arrived with a lieutenant commander who was to teach me how to use it. The wire recorder was the forerunner of the tape recorder. It turned out to be an enormous machine, the size of a large television and about as heavy. It was also immensely complicated and ran with a wire between the two spools. This wire frequently broke and then had to be tied together. I have always been exceedingly stupid about gadgets, and after forty-eight hours, the lieutenant commander was desperate.

'You *must* know now how the bloody thing works,' he insisted. 'I have to go back to London this evening. Now try it again.'

I did, and it seemed to work. Rather like Professor Higgins, he said, 'I think that you've got it. I really think that you've got it. Now try it again.' I did, and after several more trials, the commander was satisfied. He handed the huge machine over to me and said goodbye. I took the thing home and finally got it up to our penthouse flat at Lungotevere delle Nave, a beautiful flat with a marvellous view down the Tiber and with the great dome of St Peter's in the background.

The commander had told me to play with the machine until I was certain that I had completely mastered it, and so we did. I got the children to sing into it. The only song that they knew was 'Bandiera Rossa' – 'The Red Flag' in Italian, which they had been taught by our cook. They sang this with much gusto. I then got my wife to recite a poem, and Honor duly delivered *The Owl and the Pussycat*.

I then gave a rendering of Bruce Belfridge reading the news, and how a gigantic anti-cyclone was rapidly approaching from Iceland. Also, how there had been a serious accident that day in Downing Street, where the Prime Minister had swallowed his false teeth. We finished the tape and I rewound it most carefully, ready for the recorded interview with the Hungarian, which was to take place the next day. I concealed the microphone in the approved manner in a large bowl of flowers and arranged to receive a telephone call some three minutes after the arrival of the Hungarian. The telephone was in the hall and the enormous wire recorder in the dining room, so that when the telephone rang, I could excuse myself for a moment, pass through the dining room and at the same time, switch on the wire recorder.

Everything worked as planned. The Hungarian arrived, suspicious and jumpy. I gave him a drink, and then the telephone rang. I excused myself, switched on the wire recorder in the dining room and then, very audibly, answered the telephone. I then returned. The interview went off all right in a mixture of Italian, German and the few words of Hungarian which I then spoke. My interlocutor left after about an hour. I stopped and carefully rewound the spool and in some triumph took it to the embassy, where I arranged with the air attaché to have it sent on immediately and delivered in London. Honor and I waited for the congratulations, but instead another message arrived. It seems that deep in the bowels of some high security building, top brass switched on my wire recording and out came the piping voices of children singing 'The Red Flag', followed by a woman reciting a poem about a cat and a bird who had gone to sea in a boat to the land where the Bong Tree grows, and this followed by a man stating that the Prime Minister had swallowed his false teeth. The message we received was an instruction to forward immediately the key to the code.

Eventually, we had to repeat the interview, and the second time it was much more difficult. I have never liked gadgets and usually manage to break them.

Often in those days, we used to drive up through Italy and France to London. It was a marvellous time. There was very little traffic on the roads and for many miles on end none at all. The small hotels in the villages where we stayed were clean, the food was delicious and they were incredibly cheap. However, we did have two disagreeable experiences. The first was at some place just to the north of Paris, where we spent the night. There were bed bugs, and when she discovered this, Honor spent the night standing in a large basin of water in the middle of the floor. They have a disagreeable smell, and I recognised it at once when we went into the room but said nothing, hoping that it was a hangover from a past infestation. Unfortunately it was not. The second was at the Roi René, at Aix en Provence. We had had a fairly long drive and had dinner and went to bed very early. Some time after midnight there was a very clearly audible shot from the room next door, followed by three more shots and a loud groan. Later I heard footsteps, voices and more footsteps. I got up shortly after 5 a.m. and went into the corridor. There I found an hotel servant and asked what had happened. 'Oh, Monsieur,' he said, 'there was a terrible thing in the night! A man has been murdered in one of the rooms. He had a woman with him, who it seems was not his wife. She was wounded too and has been taken away by the police. They will be back here directly and will want to interview all the hotel guests.'

I feigned great surprise, went back to our room and got Honor up and dressed as quickly as possible. We had left the luggage on the car (you could in those days) and had only an overnight bag with us. We left the hotel by the back stairs, slipped into the garage and departed as quickly as possible, before we could be held – perhaps for days – by the *judge d'instruction*, as we were in the room next door. We passed into Italy the same day and were well down on our way back to Rome by that evening.

Austria

At this time, we also spent a wonderful month in Austria. Ladislaus Almasy had returned from Egypt and was staying in Carinthia. As I could not go into the Russian Zone where the beautiful castle of Bernstein (which belonged to his brother, Count Janos Almasy) is located, Janos took a huge semi-derelict castle for us near Klagenfurt and organised one of the most amusing house parties to which we ever went.

The Moosburg Castle was enormous and overlooked a lake, and here we all stayed: Prince Franz Auersperg, Count Draskovich, Countess Nostitz, Countess Pacetta Kuefstein, Janos Almasy, Bubi Hoeffer and Count Mathias Thurn-Salm-Hohenstein. Ladislaus Almasy had a villa by the lake some miles away, and the party was joined by Alaeddin Bey Mohtar, a Turk whose aunt had been married to King Fuad and who had the most marvellous estate at El Marg, outside Cairo. It was a wonderful month, and we sailed on the lake and bathed, had picnics in forest clearings in the evening and visited Hoch Austerwitz, the home of Prince Khavenhulle, and also the castle of Count Goëss. Later we went to the Tyrol, where we stayed with Count and Countess Trautmannsdorff at Mayerhoffen and had some chamois shooting, which was very exciting. Both Honor and I climbed the Zillerthaller Alp, on top of which I shot two chamois.

It was a month which neither Honor nor I ever forgot, and we formed friendships with other members of the party there which were to endure for the rest of our lives. This led to many visits in the future to Austria to stay with the Auerspergs, the Stubenbergs at Gutenberg (a marvellous medieval fortress which belongs to Count Stubenberg, who married Cara Nostitz) and also to Bernstein, and to stay with Count and Countess Draskovich at Güssing, where they have thousands of acres of boar shooting in their forests.

We were the guests of Janos Almasy and his brother: I think this was their way of saying thank you for our efforts in getting Ladislaus Almasy out of Europe and away to Cairo. If so, it was a most generous and wonderful holiday. We also visited the fascinating site of one of the great cities

of the early Celts, which had been discovered by Prince
Khevenhuller's brother. Like all good things, it had to come
to an end, and we left sadly, driving over the Brenner and
down into Italy to Porto Fino, where we met Dickie
Metcalfe and his wife, Evelyn, and then on back down to
Rome.

Libya – the Second Time

I took Honor to Libya for the first time, and she was
enchanted with the beauty of Cyrenaica. We stayed in
Benghasi, but I took her to see Derna and the site of the
ruins of the city of Cyrene. I had arranged that we would
arrive there just as the moon was up, and the ancient ruins
of this wonderful Greco-Roman city, set in its natural
amphitheatre on the top of the escarpment, was bathed in
moonlight. It was a sight never to be forgotten. Indeed the
whole of Cyrenaica was lovely.

There was Derna, which used to be called 'The Pearl of
the Mediterranean', with its white walls, little courtyards
and bougainvillaea climbing everywhere in a riot of mauve,
red, yellow and white. There was the Wadi Kuff, a great
gorge in the mountains filled with trees and honey-coloured rocks, and Ras el Hallal, where the Italians had
submarine bases under the western cliffs and where only a
few hundred metres offshore there was the ancient Greek
city sunk beneath the sea during a violent earthquake nearly
two millennia ago and which was clearly visible through the
gin-clear water.

It was a place of enchantment, with the turquoise sea
breaking on the beach of white sand, then blood-red earth
running inland, covered with flowers and low green bushes
up to the honey-coloured rocks of the escarpment, which
rose dramatically almost sheer to the top, itself crowned
with pines and Mediterranean heaths and scattered with the

white columns of ruined, marble Greco-Roman temples. It must be one of the most lovely places on Earth, and in those days it was quite untouched and unspoiled.

Italy

We returned to Italy and made one more trip to England by car. Curry was unknown in Italy in those days, and before we left to go back to Rome, we bought two large screw-top jars of very special Indian curry powder, which Honor loved. We crossed the frontier at Monte Cenisio, and to our surprise, the customs guards there pounced on us and started to take the car almost to pieces. Amongst the luggage, they found the curry. I asked them what it was all about and what they expected to find, but they remained tight-lipped and refused to give me any information. However, when they found the curry powder, the chief customs officer, an officious little rat of a man, grinned like a hyena. Watching me carefully, he unscrewed the top of one of the jars and, burying his nose in it, inhaled deeply. For a moment nothing happened; then he rushed into his customs hut, and the walls almost bulged with the explosions. I had done my best to explain that it was a sort of herbal condiment which was eaten in India with food, but they clearly thought that it was some sort of a drug. It was clear that the chief customs officer at the post was not popular with his men, who fell about laughing. They then told me that they had a tip-off that two cars carrying cocaine or some other drug were expected to try to get through the frontier that day, and in fact, they had caught one with a tin of drugs strapped to the back axle. They thought that we must be the second car.

I remember that we gave one of the customs officers there a lift down to Turin, but the chief customs officer I never saw again.

The time had come for us to leave Italy for a while. I had applied for a visa to go to Czechoslovakia, and this had been refused. My informant, who met me at Doney's in the Via Veneto, asked me what I had done to upset the Soviets. He told me that a directive had come from Moscow to all the satellite embassies and consulates that under no circumstances was I, or Honor, to be granted a visa to go to any of the Soviet Bloc countries. Well, it was much better that way than to be allowed in but not allowed out!

There was one incident before we left Rome which caused a bit of a stir. I have already said that I am no good at gadgets, and when the lights fused in our penthouse on the Tiber, I pulled down the master switch to cut off the electricity, but could not find any fuse wire. It had a somewhat old-fashioned system, and I was able to jam a pair of scissors into the fuse box before pushing up the main switch. There was a tremendous flash and I was thrown right across the room, and all the lights went out in the entire quarter of Rome. I retired to bed to lick my wounds, while jeeps filled with armed men of the Reparto Celere arrived and rushed into the flat believing that there had been some sort of a terrorist attack or start of a revolution. I don't know how they located the flat, and I left Honor to deal with them, which she did most admirably.

Before leaving Italy, I had set up a re-insurance business with a Genoese, and for some years, we re-insured the Italian Air Line Alitalia. I had met another very old, dear friend, David Craig and his wife Betty immediately after the war. He was the British Director for Alitalia and has remained a friend all our lives. In Italy, I had also set up a company of international insurance adjusters with Professor Parsons, and this continued long after we left Italy and until Edmund Parsons and his wife Giulietta left Italy in about 1968.

We left Rome very sadly. I think that the years there were amongst the happiest of our lives, and living in Rome with weekends at the villa in the mountains, the parties and the excitement of it all was a wonderful chapter in our life together. We went to London and from there back to the isolated house on the edge of the sea in the west of Ireland.

Ireland

Our children had grown up speaking Italian, and Marcus, our son, had been to an Italian school run by the church. He and his sister, Juanita, talked and played together in Italian; so coming to Ireland, where they both attended the local school at Bantry and learnt English with a West Cork accent and Irish, must have been something of a shock for them. But in many other ways, the place and the years spent in Ireland were ideal for children.

The country was beautiful and wild. They went for miles over the mountains on their bicycles and came shooting and fishing with us on the bogs and on the mountain loughs. There were glorious days in the boat, fishing, and when they were running, we could catch up to one hundred mackerel or more in an afternoon. We would land on one of the many uninhabited islands, build a fire from driftwood and cook up sausages, eggs and bacon in my mess tins, or split and cover the mackerel in oatmeal and fry them with bacon.

We walked for miles through the mountains, and I had eight thousand acres of deer stalking at Muckross, on the other side of the Kerry mountains. I would shoot a stag and drag it down to the car, then we would have roast venison, boiled venison, venison pie, venison hamburgers, venison cooked with beer and honey, hot venison, cold venison – until neither of my children nor Honor could ever eat any venison again. Actually, I still love it!

We would shoot woodcock in the gullies and amongst the gorse bushes on the mountains, and fish in remote lakes hidden right up in the hills. We acquired a larger boat, a Redwing, and there is undoubtedly some special deity who looks after the fools who, knowing nothing about sailing or boats, used to go out in the teeth of a full gale and huge waves. How we were not drowned a hundred times over, I do not know, but I can also remember the many nights when we would come back under the moon on a calm sea with the phosphorescent wake behind us, dolphins playing around us as we sang and laughed.

There is a sort of magical madness about life in Ireland, certainly as it was in those days. Things happen there which do not happen elsewhere in the world. Our friends came to stay – friends from Austria, from France and Italy, from Spain and England, from America and elsewhere.

My lifelong friend, John Scott, who was also our children's legal guardian and my lawyer, often came to stay. On one occasion he appeared in a gent's blue suit and had apparently no other suitable clothes; so the next day, he came shooting up on the mountain dressed as he was. Within a few minutes, he had fallen into a bog and emerged as the original Mud Man. We shot for the rest of the day and came back with some snipe, woodcock and a hare. After a hot bath and a couple of strong whiskies, he clearly felt better.

Dinner had just finished when Justin McCarthy appeared. Justin was the butcher in Bantry and my good friend. He told us that two Spanish trawlers had come into the bay, and that one of them carried a cargo of Spanish brandy for him. He asked if we would like to go out to the trawler with him to collect it. John and I agreed, but Honor said that she was tired after all day on the mountain and would stay at home. We went down to the harbour, where there was a rowing boat with one of Justin's men to row it.

The trawler was a good mile and a half down the bay, and we reached it without incident. We were welcomed aboard with aguadente and rough Spanish red wine. There seemed to be an inexhaustible supply of both, and before long John was speaking fluent Spanish, which he had no idea previously that he knew. We were there for quite a long time and were surprised to note when the time came for us to leave that quite a considerable storm had arisen, with a strong wind and high waves with spume blowing off the top of them.

The rowing boat was brought up alongside, and cases of brandy lowered with some difficulty into it. Justin's man stowed the brandy in the boat, and then I climbed over the rail. The next time the boat came up on a wave, I dropped into it. By this time, John had established a brotherly friendship with the captain of the trawler, who presented him with an enormous pink fish as a mark of esteem.

With some difficulty, John and his fish were lowered into the rowing boat. Then the Spanish sailor who was holding the painter let it go, and the dinghy went astern. With each wave it came crashing up under the counter of the trawler. We were filling with water and in danger of sinking. We shouted as loud as we could to tell them to bring the rowing boat alongside the trawler again before we were all killed or thrown into the sea. Eventually this was done, and we were able to bail out most of the water.

Justin, by this time, had come on deck. His hat blew off, and as he got over the rail, he suddenly realised that there was a critical moment in which the rowing boat would come up on a wave, but then it would go astern again. He was a pitiful figure, hanging to the rail and declaring to Mary, Joseph and Jesus that he was drowned.

'Jump!' we yelled, but he couldn't. 'Jump!' we shouted again, but he was clinging to the rail of the trawler with great desperation. The captain realised the situation. The next time we shouted 'Jump!' he hit Justin smartly over the knuckles with a piece of wood, and with a despairing howl of anguish, he luckily fell into the boat. We went rapidly astern. Soon the trawler's riding lights were out of sight, and Justin's man appeared to be rowing towards a light on the distant quay. Justin meanwhile had burst into song. 'I want to go to Heaven,' he bellowed, 'I want to go to Heaven on rollerskates, I want to roll just through those Pearly Gates.'

He varied this with another song: 'All the little angels arse end up on high. Which end up? Arse end up! All the little angels arse end up on high.'

I asked Justin's man what was the light towards which we were making unsteady progress. 'Sure, it's the customs house jetty,' he replied. 'Might it not be better to land the brandy elsewhere?' I asked, but Justin reassured me by saying, 'And haven't I told the customs man to go to the cinema tonight and not to come out again until I come to fetch him?' he asked.

So it was that we landed the brandy at the customs house, and from there transferred it into Justin's car – and some into mine. John, still with his large pink fish, drove home. It was fairly late, and we were met by a furious Honor, who had become very worried indeed when the storm blew up and was not best pleased when John lurched forward and said, 'Dearest Honor. I have brought him specially for you!' and pressed the large, pink, slimy fish into her arms.

The following morning she had her revenge. Our children arrived fairly early, and Honor told them to go to the larder and get the hare which we had shot the previous day and insert it into John's bed, with the bloody face as close to his face as possible. Stentorian snores assured us that John was sound asleep, and the mission was accomplished successfully. Nothing happened for at least an hour, and then John woke, feeling distinctly unwell. He opened his bleary eyes and saw the hare. There was a terrible yell of terror, and John leapt into the corridor with his hair on end and stark naked. The children were much amused.

Every New Year's Eve, we drove over to Colonel Knowles's house at Reen-na-faraha in Kerry, where he and his wife, Olga, gave a huge New Year's Eve party and dance. It was always great fun and lasted until dawn. He had one of the most beautiful gardens in the west of Ireland, with more than one hundred acres of rhododendrons of various species, azaleas, specimen trees from all over the world (I remember a Chinese 'pocket handkerchief tree' in particular). The whole garden was made round a series of small creeks and little spurs of rocky land running out into the bay. It was lovely all the year round, but when the rhododendrons and azaleas were out, it was a fairyland of indescribable beauty.

Traditionally there was a shoot on New Year's Day, and on one occasion, the MacGillicuddy of the Reeks, who was staying in an hotel nearby as not everybody could be accommodated in the house, refused to get out of bed unless he could come shooting as he was. We agreed to this, and he shot all day in bedroom slippers, pyjamas and dressing gown. It also transpired at the same shoot that Colonel Craig Wilson, who had a lovely house over the mountains near Killarney, had omitted to pack a suitcase. Having changed the previous evening into a dinner jacket, that was all he had. So he shot all day in a dinner jacket and black bow tie. We were a motley collection of guns, and the bag at the end of the day contained more liver spots than woodcock.

Our cook's father, who lived some miles away, used to give us a barrel of poteen each year for Christmas, and this we used to bury in the garden to age it for two or three years. Poteen – a home-made Irish whiskey – is colourless, and if it is well made and well aged, it is good. If it is badly made and not aged, it is lethal. We used this as a basis for cocktails and a fruit cup which we gave our guests when we gave parties. It induced almost instant hilarity, and we used to station our gardener, Jackie, at the bottom of the drive with his horse and a drag line, as at the bottom of the drive, there was a very sharp left-hand turn, and if a driver did not make it, the car went on to the beach – and if the tide was in, into the sea. His services were generally required by some of the guests.

O'Leary, who lived in the farm at the top of the lane leading down to our house, I suspected of stealing my coal. When I used to hear noises from the coal shed at the top of the garden at night, I would go out and fire a couple of bursts from a sub-machine gun. I could then hear sounds of rapid withdrawal. Anyway, he complained to Sergeant McDonald of the Garda, who asked me to come in and see him. I explained my reasons, and the police sergeant was very understanding. 'Well, it is all right for you to fire your little gun,' he said. 'But please make sure you don't hit him.'

It may have been O'Leary who started the rumour that I had a huge collection of modern weapons – 'Hundreds of machine guns and rifles, you know'. Whoever it was, the rumour reached the IRA, and through the grapevine, I heard that they were coming to raid the house and make a collection of my arsenal. In fact I did have shotguns, sporting rifles, some modern pistols and so on. This was long before the beginning of the terrible terrorism which was to plague Ireland some years later. The bulk of my collection – eighty-five per cent of it or more – consisted of flint locks, early cap-fire muzzle loading guns and pistols between one hundred and two hundred years old.

However, on the basis of this rumour I consulted my keeper, Dinny-Joe, whom I knew was the head of the local

IRA. He was highly indignant. 'I've heard nothing of it at all,' he said. 'It would not be any of the boys from around here. None of them would ever touch you. No,' he concluded, 'it'll be some of those from Dublin or up near the border. But I'll hear of it, never doubt, and then won't I and some of my boys come into your house, and won't we give those buggers from Dublin a hot reception!' In spite of the assurance we kept a close watch, but nothing happened and the weeks passed. Eventually, I had to go up to Dublin, several hundred miles away. The day that I left, Honor got word that the IRA would be coming that same night. She could not get hold of me as I was travelling on the long road and could not be there before the late evening, and certainly could not get back in time. She told the servants to go to the cinema in Bantry that evening and then loaded my .38 Special Smith Wesson and sat up to wait for them.

They came at about 10.30 that night, three car loads of them. First they tried to break down the front door; then they fired a shotgun against it, but it was made of heavy oak and secured by a huge steel chain. So then they went to the back door, which was much more flimsy, and started to break that down. The downstairs lavatory and bathroom window opened to give an excellent view of the back door at a distance of only about ten yards. Honor opened the window silently (we had Crittal steel window frames, and they did not make a sound). She steadied the big gun.

Bang! The man who was attacking the door saw his hat sail off the top of his head, and there was a sound like a heard of elephants in full stampede. The car engines roared, and they were away. Honor waited up for them for the rest of the night, but they did not return. In fact, we saw and heard nothing more of them until some three or four weeks later.

We were in the little town of Bantry. It was in fact really a village, and everybody knew everybody else. A man whom neither Honor nor I had ever seen before came up to Honor and said in a bitterly aggrieved tone, 'You're a terrible dangerous woman! Look at this, will you?' He took off his hat and poked his fingers through two holes in the top. Honor looked at it and said calmly, 'You're a lucky man. The next time, it'll be your head.' We never saw nor heard of them ever again, but Dinny-Joe was disappointed that he had not been told so that 'I and the boys could have had a bit of fun'. Such is Ireland – or rather was, in those happy days.

There were odd incidents from time to time. A man was found up on top of the mountain by the tunnel. He was stone dead, and in his hand was clutched a whiskey bottle. The label had been partly scraped off, and a white label stuck on with a rather badly drawn skull and crossbones and in huge capital letters the word 'POISON' written underneath. The fact that the poor fellow had a couple of bullets in him rather discounted the suggestion of suicide.

Perhaps a year later, I had to go to Dublin again. Honor could not come with me as she was having an attack of bronchial asthma. I wanted to go and return the same day, as I knew that the following day we had to drive up to Shannon Airport. Cork Airport did not exist in those days. I started before dawn and drove fast. However, it was in the late evening before I was able to start back again. I had 'flame throwers' mounted on the front of the car, which lit up the road for a good mile ahead. Past Cork, and at one in the morning there was no traffic on the road to the west at all, and I switched on the flame throwers. The brilliant tunnel of light bored down the long, empty road ahead, and I was driving fast (at over ninety miles per hour). I saw some movement in the hedge in front, and just as I reached it, a fox dashed out on to the road and under the wheels of the car. I stopped and went back. The poor animal was still alive, but its back was broken and it was unable to move. I went back to the car and got my pistol. I had taken to carrying one in the car ever since the IRA raid. I shot the fox twice through the head, killing it instantly, to prevent its further suffering. I then picked it up and threw it into the boot of the car, intending to bury it the following day.

I got home to find that Honor was much better. The following morning, we had to make an early start at 8.00 a.m. to get to Shannon in time. Honor came with me, and we drove over the mountains into Kerry and up through Tralee. Not far from Limerick, we ran into the South Limerick Hunt, and I pulled into the side of the road to let them pass. Suddenly, the hounds went mad round the car. I had been very tired the previous night and had forgotten all about the fox. To have produced a fox which had very obviously been shot would have invited my own death or dreadful curses from the huntsmen and women, so I engaged the gears, and we shot off through the hunt with their blasphemies and curses ringing in our ears and the hounds in full cry after the car. I drove some five miles up the road, until all sounds of the hunt had long vanished. Then I stopped the car and opened the boot. Grabbing the fox by its tail, I heaved it over the hedge into the nearest field. I then jumped into the car, and we continued on our way.

Amongst many other guests, we had Peter and Dorothy Baden-Powell, our Austrian friends from the Moosburg, and also Alaeddin Mohtar, who each year nearly killed my head keeper at Muckross. He was enormously fit, and Mat Leahy had a job to keep up with him as they went for many miles over the mountains, stalking.

The last time he came, he brought a friend of his, Esnaud de Maillard, with him – a French minister of (I think) defence, and a charming man. As we could not all get into the Allard, I hired a car for Alaeddin from the local man, and Alaeddin drove this with great enthusiasm and in all directions at once.

It was on the last day of their visit. We got back to the Muckross Arms Hotel, where we had an arrangement to change and have a bath, before starting back on the sixty-mile drive to our home. Alaeddin was in tremendous spirits, as he had shot a royal stag which he had been stalking for a week. We all had champagne in the bar, and Mat Leahy and his assistant, Joey, who preferred whiskey, consumed a bottle between them.

We were all wet and tired, but Esnaud had shot a buck and Alaeddin had a really spectacular trophy (the best stag ever shot off the forest). We eventually set off home; Alaeddin was filled with Turkish delight and champagne. He drove like the wind, and Esnaud remarked gloomily, 'You see – he is mad, that Alaeddin. *Complètement fou!* *Regardez*, 'e now drives off the road and across the mountain so as to take a short cut, rather than the road round that bend. Ah, *voilà!* 'e 'as 'it a rock.'

I could not bear to watch this, and I thought that if I passed him – and I had by far the faster car – he would slow down. This I devoutly hoped, as my darling Honor was driving with him.

I picked a straight stretch of road up a hill and was able to pass them. Alaeddin was laughing madly, and I drove on fast, so that he could see that it was useless to try to catch me and would come on at a safer and more sedate pace.

Apparently, as I learnt afterwards, he didn't. He hit a wall, and then another, and finally turned into O'Leary's farmyard and went straight into O'Leary's muck-heap at forty miles an hour. He emerged the other side with the muck-heap adhering to the car – or what remained of it.

He arrived back at the house still in excellent spirits, and for our last evening it was decided that each of our guests would cook a speciality for dinner. Esnaud retreated into the kitchen to prepare moules marinière, and Alaeddin seated himself in front of the fire in the drawing room to cook kebabs on two swords, which he had taken off the wall. My mother, who liked Alaeddin very much, was seated on the floor beside him, with a bottle of whiskey and two glasses. Honor had laid the table, and dinner was nearly ready when the wretched owner of the hired car appeared to reclaim his property.

When he came into the house, it was to be met by Esnaud, babbling in French and carrying a large pot of steaming moules. When he went into the drawing room to get the papers for the car, he found the Turk seated crosslegged in front of the fire, cooking on two swords, and my mother clutching a bottle of whiskey.

The car owner showed a strong desire to be gone, and I took him outside to introduce him to the remnants of his car. At first he did not see it, as he mistook it for a huge heap of manure. He looked at it in silence for a moment. Then, with a loud cry of 'You're all mad, you are! Mad, mad, mad!', he jumped into the pile of manure, managed to get it started, and drove it away as fast as he could. Subsequently, Alaeddin had to buy him a new car.

Pamela Morsome lived some miles away at Durrus Court. This was a vaguely sinister house, which had been a courthouse. Outside was the hanging tree, on which condemned criminals were instantly hanged. Both our children disliked it intensely, and even Honor found it eerie, especially the landing upon which accused men used to stand to hear their sentence. Pamela did not seem to mind it in the least, and any local ghosts were certainly more frightened of her than she was of them. Eventually, for financial reasons, she had to leave it and went to live in a bungalow down by the sea, not very far away from us. There she invited several of her friends for luncheon one day. She put the roast in the oven and then thought that she would walk down the drive to have a drink before luncheon at the local pub. She was on her second gin and tonic when a countryman came in and said, 'Good day to all here.'

Pamela, who knew the man slightly, asked him if he would care for a drink, which he accepted with alacrity. They chatted about this and that, and when he had finished his drink, he thanked her and said, 'I suppose that you know that your house is on fire?' Pamela rushed out, but it was much too late. Perhaps due to some electrical fault, the house had caught fire, and by the time that she reached it, it was little more than a large pile of ashes.

Pamela walked down to the end of the drive, and as her guests arrived, she greeted them and said, 'I am afraid that we will have to go out to luncheon in the pub, as the joint which I was cooking for our luncheon is rather overdone.' It was a couple of days before any of her guests realised what had happened.

My mother, who spent part of the summers with us, had for some years fought a losing battle with her false teeth. Due to her experiences during the war, she had lost her teeth early and had a number of pairs made, none of which fitted her and all of which seemed to have been imbued with a sort of life of their own. She hated them all, and on occasions, they flew out.

It happened that once we all went into Cork and found that both the restaurant and the hotel where we normally had luncheon had been fully booked. We were reduced to going to the Metropole, a temperance hotel from which the demon drink was expressly excluded. Honor and I arrived first and sat down at a table, and my mother arrived shortly afterwards, in a hurry. She always walked in a very determined way and held herself very straight. She was marching towards our table when her false teeth flew out and fell to the ground, just as one of her shoes was coming forward. The teeth struck the moving shoe and flew upwards, landing in a plate of tomato soup which one of the other guests in the dining room was just about to eat. The poor man, clearly from the colour of his nose a reformed drunk who had taken the pledge, stared at the set of uppers and lowers in his soup in total disbelief. My mother bent over and said, 'Excuse me. Those are mine.' She then picked them out of the soup and carried them over to our table. The man looked at his tomato soup and then, rising unsteadily, groped his way to the door and out of the hotel. After that, I wonder if he went back on the bottle again.

Those days in Ireland were wonderful. We stalked on the mountains overlooking the Killarney lakes, and I have to admit that there was something really rather strange about them. Virtually all our friends who shot there with us felt it, and some were unashamedly frightened. Below the mountains and running down the shores of the lakes there were ancient forests of oak interspersed amongst the boulders and rocks covered with moss, while lichen hung in grey veils from the trees. There little streams of crystal water gurgled into pools in the shadows of the trees. Great masses of bracken filled the glades. It was a silent place, and I never heard a bird or even saw a rabbit there. People said that there was an air of silent menace, but I myself never felt it. For me, the mountain and the forests were friendly, and even a part of my being. Esnaud de Maillard was not an imaginative man, and as a French politician, he was not given to illusions. When staying with us, he cut the top of his eye on the telescopic sight of his rifle when shooting at a buck. It bled profusely, and I asked Honor to take him down the mountain to where the boy waited near the road with the pony to bring down any buck or stag that we had shot. When they got into the wood, Honor stopped by a pool to wash the blood off his face and bathe his eye. She then said, 'Look here. You stay here, and I will go on down through the wood and bring the boy with the pony up for you.' Esnaud was frankly terrified, and said, 'Oh no, Madame, please do not leave me here alone. I am frightened of this place.'

A strange thing happened to me too one day. I was high up on the mountain and had shot a stag. It was getting towards evening and when we had grolloched the stag, Mat Leahy said to me, 'It's getting late. We had best be off the mountain before dark. I'll go down now and get the pony.' He asked me if I would be all right. Surprised, I said, 'Yes, of course! Why?' 'It's a strange place, this,' he said. 'We should be away before nightfall. I'll not be on the mountain here after dark.' With that, he stumped off down the mountainside.

I lay back in the heather and watched a hawk high above me in the evening sky. A little chill wind was coming up the draw, whimpering through the thin grass and the low, scrubby gorse and heather. The evening was coming on, and already the little creatures of the night were beginning to move. A hawk circled and screamed in the sky and then slanted away over the top of the mountain. I noticed for the first time some stones and what might have been the ruins of a house some thirty or forty yards away and then several others, covering perhaps an acre or more. There had once been a track there too, and it had come up the draw beside the stream and through what I now saw was a ruined village and out the other side and up the shoulder of the mountain towards Kenmare, some twenty miles away.

It was then that I noticed voices. At first I mistook them for the noise of the little brook tumbling down the hill, but then it seemed to me that they were clearly human voices, and I wondered who could be hiding amongst these ruined stone walls. Whoever it was, they had certainly seen Matt Leahy walking down the mountain and had probably not seen me lying down in the heather. I decided to investigate. I used to be a pretty good stalker, and I wormed my way down the hill, using the ground and the heather as good cover. I came up level with the village and went down through the brook and up the other side. A few yards further on there was a bit of a wall still standing, and I took cover there.

Now, away from the brook there was no possibility of mistaking the human voices, and there were two: unquestionably women arguing. My left ear was damaged by an enthusiastic German with a machine gun, and I have ever since had difficulty in locating sound, but it seemed to me that they were straight in front of me and probably about twenty yards away. I started to creep towards the voices. Although now nearer, and very clearly audible, they were not clearly distinguishable, and I could not understand what was being said. Another few yards and I could hear that they were speaking half in Irish Gaelic and half in English. I had learnt quite a lot of Gaelic, enough for simple conversation and even to reply to simple letters from 'The Devil in Dublin' asking for tax. 'They'll never come back,' one said. 'Oh, you're a stupid old woman!' the other replied. 'Of course they'll be back – any day now. You'll see.' 'No, they won't,' said the first voice. 'They will have taken ship by now, and they'll never come back again.'

I started to work my way even closer, as I had not been able to see the speakers or even be quite sure where they were, but then the voices stopped. A few minutes later, I heard the hooves of the pony and the sounds of Matt and his boy coming back up the hill.

We loaded the stag and started down the mountain. It was beginning to get dark, and Matt and the boy were clearly in a hurry. As we were walking back, I told Matt what I had heard. He gave me a very queer look and told me the following story.

The great famine of 1846–1848 was very bad in these parts, and whole communities emigrated to America. (The population of Ireland, which had been nearly eight million, was reduced to about 1.5 million over this period.) There had been a small village up the draw, although there were no signs whatever of any cultivated land there now. Finally, the whole village decided that they would all leave together and go to Kenmare and there try to get a ship to America, or perhaps to Limerick or Cork and from there to America. All of them agreed except two elderly women who were determined to stay, and no amount of pleading or argument would move them. One day the whole population of the village, carrying their few possessions, did leave. The two elderly women came to the edge of the village to see them go out along the track over the shoulder of the mountain towards Kenmare. A last attempt was made to make them go too, but they remained adamant, and their last words were, 'You'll be back soon, and you'll find us waiting for you here.'

It is a strange story, and it certainly was no dream. It seems that they had been heard many times before, and that the local people would never be near the place after dark.

Even Alaeddin found the mountain eerie, as did our Austrian friends who had high lonely forests and mountains of their own.

I often think of it and of the happy days there with Honor and of the breathtaking view over the lakes from Torc and Mangerton mountains.

It was at about this time that a radical change came in our lives. We had had a cat, Adrian, for several years. A rather uninteresting and unfriendly cat, but now my mother gave us two blue Siamese kittens, and for the rest of our lives our cats were to have a very great influence. We called the new arrivals Tripitaka and Kai Lung. To begin with they looked like little white rats, but soon they grew into the most beautiful big cats. Tripitaka in particular became enormous, like one of the old-fashioned royal cats which were kept to guard the palaces in Thailand. He was enormous and, in his prime, weighed just under twenty-eight pounds. He used to come shooting with me and would actually retrieve snipe. He had an excellent nose and would find snipe very quickly and pick it up and bring it towards me, but when he saw that I had seen that he had found it, he would put it down and let me go to pick it up for myself.

He did not mind the water in the bogs in the least, but after a few miles he would get tired and would climb up on my shoulder and want to be carried for a bit, before getting down and walking with me again.

We used to take the two cats everywhere with us, out shooting and also fishing, and this they enjoyed very much indeed. However, we made a bad mistake once. We took them to the sand dunes at the Mizzen Head and they vanished. Finally, towards evening, Kai appeared, but there was no sign of Tripi. We called and called, and it was becoming quite dark. At last, he emerged from a rabbit hole. It seemed that he had found a nest of young rabbits down there and had eaten them all and then gone to sleep.

The cats were excellent guards, and when strangers came to the house, we had to introduce them. On one occasion, David Pigot, a very good friend and our lawyer in Ireland, drove down to spend the weekend with us. He came from Dublin, and it was very late when he arrived. He came into the drawing room, but the cats had already gone to bed in the kitchen. We had no electric light in the house, but we did have a telephone. Almost as soon as David arrived, the telephone rang in the small sitting room off the dining room. I asked David what he wanted to drink, and he said that he was thirsty and would like a beer. I asked him to go along the corridor, through the kitchen and into the pantry, where we had a paraffin refrigerator. In there, he would find some bottles of beer. I excused myself and went to answer the telephone. A minute or two later, there was a dreadful crash and a yell, and David burst into the drawing room with both cats hanging by their claws from his neck, which was pouring with blood.

They had apparently been asleep, and were woken by a stranger groping his way through the kitchen towards the pantry. They waited for him, lying in wait on top of the door into the corridor, and when he came back with the beer, they both dropped on to his shoulders and went for his jugular. They appeared very pleased with themselves having, as they thought, caught a burglar. David was by no means pleased, and was less so the following morning when they accompanied one of the maids upstairs to David's bedroom with his breakfast. When she had left, they both jumped on to the end of his bed and came crawling towards him with blazing blue eyes. He was terrified and too frightened to call out or to try to get out of bed. They ate his breakfast – all of it, including things which they would not normally touch.

The cats had a much exaggerated idea of their own size and were convinced that they could kill a cow. We often used to watch them stalking the cattle in the fields, just like little leopards, and in the evenings, when the cattle were driven up the lane towards my mother's farm, they would wait for them. There were a few large oak trees up the lane, and their boughs spread out over the lane. The cats would wait there on the boughs until the cattle passed underneath and then drop on them, trying to get them by their throats. Even Tripi could not manage this, and the cows shook them off and went on their way, but the cats persisted, and were clearly convinced that one day, they would be successful.

They were beautiful little wild animals, extremely affectionate with us but not overly friendly with strangers except certain of our friends whom they liked – and, of course, with our children. The sheepdogs were frightened of them, including my Irish Setter, Fan. Sometimes she would be asleep on a sofa in the drawing room, and one or both of the cats would wish to get on the sofa themselves. They would sit and look at Fan, unblinking. She would become more and more uncomfortable and finally get off, and the cats would jump on and curl up there themselves.

When we were away, they would go down to the big stone gateposts at the entrance to the drive up to the house. A cat would sit on each until we returned. Sometimes, they would be there all day, oblivious to the rain and wind.

We took them with us almost everywhere, except in the boat, which they did not like. But when we got back from a fishing trip round the islands, they would always rush down to the beach to meet us to see what we had caught.

We used to take them to Lough Brin. There was supposed to be a monster in Lough Brin, and it is a strange fact that there are very many stories of monsters in the Irish loughs. It is a curious fact too that on many of the ancient Celtic crosses there are depicted very large snakes. There is the legend that Saint Patrick drove the snakes out of Ireland, and while this may well refer to the saint having driven some sort of *worship* of the snake out of Ireland, I am convinced that at one time there were large water snakes in the country, possibly similar to the anacondas of South America. The monster of Lough Brin, if it exists, is entirely different. We first heard about this old legend more than forty years ago. It seems that the legendary hero, Finn McCool, with his Fianna or hunting party was pursuing a deer near the lough when, to escape the hounds (led by Finn McCool's great Irish Wolfhound, Brin or Bron), it plunged into the lough and swam across. Only Brin or Bron followed, and somewhere in the middle of the lough, while still swimming strongly, the hound gave a great howl and disappeared, having seemingly been dragged down.

Lough Brin is in Kerry and is very isolated. It is connected by underground rivers to two other smaller loughs, and when we first went there, the three or four farms near the loughs were the only habitations for many miles. Surprisingly, the farmers were anything but friendly and seemed to be highly suspicious of us.

Little by little, as we returned over the years, they changed their attitude and finally admitted they had at first thought we might be excise men, as they distilled poteen on the mountain behind. Finally, they became very friendly, although for obvious reasons, they discouraged tourists and fishermen. They told us that they had all seen the monster on many occasions. They described it as being like a giant newt, with four short stubby legs and a crest on the top of its back, and said that sometimes it would come out of the water, although on land it was ungainly and unable to run very fast. It was a vegetarian and lived on water plants at the bottom of the loughs, but there were stories that sometimes it took lambs and occasionally tried to chase the farmers' dogs, although it could certainly never catch them.

One of the farmers told me that during a particularly hot summer, he had been bathing in the lough, when the monster attacked him and bit him. As he could not swim, he was still in the shallow water near the edge of the lough, and he managed to get back to the shore. Honor was some way away fishing, and the farmer took down his trousers and showed me. Something certainly had bitten him! It was no dog and no pike. He was missing a good two pounds of flesh taken out of his upper leg below one of his buttocks.

There was no reason for the local people to invent this story, as the very last thing that they wanted was any sort of publicity or tourist attraction in their area. Something had certainly taken a huge lump of flesh out of the man's leg. There was the legend, and in those days, there was also a rather crude stone at the end of the lough by some stepping stones, which had once been carved in the shape of a huge newt with a crest on its back.

Honor and I and the children and the cats used to go there very often, and I always took a camera and a rifle with me, but we never saw the monster, and the nearest to any evidence that I could get was that sometimes water weeds were floating on the surface which looked as if they had been cut near their roots at the bottom of the lake.

It was a lovely place, and I will always remember our picnics there. The children used to pick mushrooms, and we had bacon and eggs and sausages and mushrooms cooked in my mess tins over a fire of dry heather stems. Sometimes, if we were lucky, we had little pink trout, caught from the lake. The mountains were full of lakes: the Yellow Lake, the Lake of the Red Trout, Lough Beg (where Juanita, our daughter caught her first trout), and one hundred others. In the summer evenings, when it was getting dark, Honor and I would go to a silent pool deep in the wood behind Glengarrif and fish for the sea trout with a lure moved slowly along the bottom and a couple of maggots on the hooks.

Up at the farm outbuildings, I had set up a small factory with a friend of mine from the army days who had fallen on hard times. He was something of a chemist, and we made industrial soap, anti-freeze (which we used to sell to Ford's in Cork), and also disinfectant, shampoo and window cleaner, as well as perfume (which was really very good). Alas, we were too far away from the possible centres of consumption, and the transport costs killed the business.

Egypt and Libya

I adored our life in Ireland. We had had my father to stay with us and very many friends. Gilbert Lennox and Dickie Metcalfe never came, but one winter, Alaeddin invited us to stay with him in Egypt in the spring, and so we went. Alas, the climate in the west of Ireland did not suit Honor at all, and she had recurrent attacks of bronchial asthma and also pneumonia and rheumatic fever once again. The two or three months that we spent in Egypt were unforgettable. Alaeddin had a huge property at El Marg. The garden of some two hundred acres was surrounded by a high wall, and the house where we stayed was approached by a quarter-mile long tunnel of different coloured bougainvillaea trained over large iron hoops to form a kaleidoscopic tunnel from the main gates to the house. There we were introduced to our chauffeur Vasfe, our cook, the butler, the valet and the other servants, none of whom spoke anything other than Turkish or Arabic.

It was explained to us that this was our house and these were our servants, but that Honor had to run the whole establishment – which meant that she had to learn Turkish in a hurry, which she did. By the end of our stay in Egypt, she could carry on a conversation in Turkish with some fluency.

Egypt was for us a sort of Thousand and One Nights brought to life. There were the most fabulous receptions given by the Egyptian princes, with the servants all in marvellous uniforms, and gigantic gold and silver platters groaning with food flown in, in many cases, from Paris. There were visits to the Pyramids, the Step Pyramid and Sakara; to Memphis; and a private viewing of the Cairo Museum and the treasure of Tutankhamun. There were visits to the Souk and to the Gaziera Club to watch the polo, dinner at the Semaramis and the Automobile Club, concerts, and the most marvellous dances.

I got some quail shooting on the several thousand acres of Alaeddin's farms. We took trips into the desert and to Alexandria, had incredible buffet luncheons in Alaeddin's huge garden kept in perfect order by over one hundred gardeners and, of course, took many meals with Alaeddin at his house, which was some three hundred yards away from ours in the huge garden.

Although he was his first cousin, Alaeddin disliked Farouk intensely, and the feeling was mutual. We saw Farouk on many occasions, but Alaeddin made a point of never introducing us to him or even of speaking to him himself. I met Colonel Nasser at one of the receptions but exchanged only a few words with him. The Egyptian royal family were nearly all Turks; Alaeddin's father had been a pasha and army commander and an almost legendary hero of the Turkish Army against the Bulgarians, while his grandfather had been Pasha of Albania. Alaeddin's aunt was Farouk's mother, so there was a close family connection in spite of mutual antipathy. We visited the Baktashi Monastery outside Cairo and were going to go to Luxor, but alas, I became ill with some form of enteritis, and this had to be cancelled.

There were plans for us all to make an expedition to the desert beyond the Quttara Depression, where it is believed that the army of Cambyses (who was the son of Cyrus the Great and conquered Egypt in 525 BC) was lost in the sands together with the King himself in about 522 BC. Ladislaus Almasy said that he thought that he knew where this was, and also spoke of his discovery of a lost city further to the south-west.

This was a major project, and it would have entailed making petrol and possibly water dumps in the desert and a good deal of preparation. It was planned for the following year, but in the meanwhile Ladislaus became ill in Salzburg and died.

Eventually the time came for us to leave Egypt. The dry atmosphere had done Honor a great deal of good, and she was very well again. We spent a month with my mother up at the villa at Anticoli before returning to Ireland, and there

Pietro Gaudenzi painted his wonderful portrait of Honor, which when it was framed and put on show, stopped the traffic in the Via Margutta in Rome.

Libya Again

Some two years afterwards, Dickie Metcalfe became ill, and Honor and I were asked to take over for some months in Benghasi. It was another chance to get warm, dry weather for Honor, and we jumped at the chance. The journey there was not without incident. We flew from Rome, and shortly before coming in to land at Tripoli, a vile, small boy, who had been an infernal nuisance during the whole flight, running up and down the aisle and making a noise, was firmly strapped into his seat by his mother who said loudly in Italian, 'Now be good! Very soon we will be landing, and you will see Papa!' To which the horrid child replied loudly and for all to hear, 'Which papa?' It made our trip, except at that moment one of the aircraft engines caught on fire, rapidly followed by a second. We did not quite make it to the runway, and had a forced landing about one hundred yards short of it. Surrounded by fire engines and ambulances (for which, thank God, there was no need), we never got to see which papa!

We put up in the officers' club in Benghasi, which had been the former building of the Bank of Italy and was very splendid, with marble columns and floor. The food, however, was not so good. When we were faced with a temperature of over one hundred in the shade and roast beef and Yorkshire pudding, followed by plum duff, we decided that we must do something about it. Vegetables well peeled and salads washed in permanganate of potash became our daily diet, and we were the only people there who never had any trouble with 'Libyan tummy'.

Dickie Metcalfe had an office in Benghasi, a garage and the agency for Austin cars, amongst other things. He was also running an agent into Egypt, where things had become very critical with the rise to power of Colonel Nasser. Farouk had been deposed in 1952, and Nasser had become premier in 1954. Alaeddin was forced to leave Egypt. They had shot his dogs and seized everything that he had, and he was graciously permitted to leave the country with just one suitcase. All this happened only a few months after we had been staying with him.

We enjoyed ourselves greatly in Benghasi and Cyrenaica. We made expeditions into the desert, and I managed to borrow a dreadful old gun from an Arab. It had once been a Browning semi-automatic, seven-shot twelve-bore, but the Arab had filed the seer, so that when the trigger was pulled, it went off like a machine gun. The first time I fired it, it knocked me flat on my back. However, with a bit of practice we had some excellent shooting on the Djebel Akdar, and also in the Wadi Kuff and the marshes leading up to the Tokra Pass. I have kept a game book for most of my life, and see that on one day we had a wonderfully varied bag of twelve partridges, four snipe, a golden plover, a snake, a desert wolf and ten rock pigeons.

We bathed in the harbour at Benghasi, and with Carlo Forni we swam out to look at the drowned city of Appolonia off the Bay of Ras el Hellal. We very nearly came to grief there.

It was fascinating floating over the city, which could be seen quite clearly below the water. I myself cannot dive, as I have a damaged left eardrum. However, Carlo Forni could. He brought up an exquisite little bronze oil lamp from one of the ruined houses.

We were so fascinated that we did not notice the off-shore current, which was sweeping us steadily out to sea. When we did we were some three miles offshore. With the current against us, even with fins on our feet we barely made it back to the shore. We were so exhausted that we had to lie on the sand for more than an hour to recover.

I used to go to have tea with King Sayaed Idris at his palace at Lete. There is a huge hole there which goes down into the earth. It is very deep indeed, and at the bottom there is an underground river, which – so it is said – contains white snakes and white crocodiles, which live in the dark. The King was charming, but I had to drink three cups of ceremonial tea – never less and never more. The first was ordinary tea, the second had mint in it, which was not too bad, but the third had peanuts in it and was revolting. Lete was one of the classical Entrances to the Underworld, and I suppose that one entered down the hole and along the river. I had no desire to explore!

However, there are a number of such underground rivers in Cyrenaica, and also strange holes with sheer sides which are usually circular and can vary from a few yards across to two or three hundred yards across.

A team of British Army engineers, all expert divers with proper diving gear, tried to explore one of these rivers to try to find irrigation water for the desert. They were never seen again.

Thousands of rock pigeons live in the holes, nesting on ledges down their sheer sides. There are snakes too. Every morning the pigeons come swirling out of the holes to fly off into the Djebel and feed, and every evening they come swirling back, circle, fold their wings and dive straight in. They make very good shooting: the trick is to get them when they are away from the actual hole, as it is impossible to retrieve them from there. They are also excellent to eat.

The army had cleared a lot of the mines, but one still had to be very careful in the desert. On one occasion we heard that there was a desert war going on, so we took the office car and went to look. It was a wonderful sight, straight out of Beau Geste, with horsemen galloping about firing off their guns into the air and waving swords. However, some of them had modern rifles, and when bullets started to kick up the sand on the dune where we were lying watching it all, Honor and I thought it a prudent moment at which to make our withdrawal.

On another occasion, Honor was invited to watch a Senussi circumcision ceremony. By that time, she spoke quite a lot of Arabic and more than sufficient to carry on a conversation. Lots of fat women dressed in their best clothes danced about and sang very lewd songs. There was an enormous amount to eat, and Honor enjoyed it all greatly.

Amongst Dickie's activities was the admiralty contract for the clearance of mines, torpedoes, bombs, shells and other explosives from the bottom of the harbours of Benghasi and Tobruk. There was an enormous amount to be recovered as well as ships of all sizes – over one hundred in Benghasi and, I think, rather more in Tobruk – including the 'unsinkable' battleship *San Giorgio*.

One day we had a big explosion on the harbour wall at Benghasi. Vast dumps of torpedoes, shells, gun ammunition, bombs and other explosives including mines had been brought up by Carlo Forni and his divers, and one day the Arabs were unloading a lighter which had been re-floated and which was filled with Bofors ammunition. This has a tricky fuse at the best of times, and long immersion in the sea had not improved matters. They had nearly unloaded the boat and were doing what they had been forbidden to do a hundred times – throwing the shells in a chain, one to the other. Alas, the man nearest the dump on the harbour wall was a butter-fingers, and there was an explosion which I should think could have been heard in Europe across the Mediterranean. It blew up a huge section of the harbour wall, and a good many people as well. It was also the signal for many of the local inhabitants of Benghasi to cut their wives' faces with broken glass, of which there was more than a sufficiency, and then besiege the office with loud demands for compensation.

Honor and I explored deep into the desert, and on one occasion we had an experience which could have turned out badly. I had discovered that the local partridges could run much faster than I, so I asked Honor to get out of the car, get a stick, look out for mines and snakes and give me fifteen minutes to get in position a mile or two ahead, and then beat the camel thorn towards me. With luck, we might have roasted partridges for dinner. She did as I asked and I drove on and waited. Honor meanwhile had started to beat the camel thorn and shout 'Hi cock', as one does in Ireland. At this moment, a party of twelve Senussi horsemen came over the top of the dunes and saw a woman, miles from anywhere, beating the bushes and shouting and heading into the deep desert towards Kufra some three hundred miles away.

They rode up to her and then round her in a circle – and closed in. The Arabs are kind to mad people, whom they believe have been touched by Allah. This woman was clearly mad, and ignoring her completely they held a conversation between themselves. 'The woman is, of course, mad, my brothers. What shall we do? Shall we take her to our tents?' 'No, our wives would not like that.' 'Shall we then take her to the coast?' 'No, that is too far away. But we should not let her walk on into the desert. She will die of thirst and that would be cruel.' Honor tried to explain that her husband was just over there, but that only strengthened their conviction that she was mad. 'There is, of course, no husband – she is clearly mad.' Honor tried to break through the circle, but they would not let her. It was just as well that I got tired of waiting for partridges which did not come and drove back over the dunes to see this tableau below me. I got out of the car and, holding my gun ready, approached.

The Senussi were clearly very surprised to see me, and their leader said, 'Saida! Is this your woman?' I said, 'Saida! Yes, she is!' Honor was then ceremoniously handed over to me, and they mounted their horses. As they rode away, their leader said, 'Take better care of your woman!' I decided that I most certainly would.

On another of our desert explorations, I managed to break some vital part of the car. It was, after all, just the old office Austin saloon, and not really suitable for desert exploration. Luckily we had enough water, and we travelled at about three miles an hour for three days before reaching the coast road.

On another occasion we had quite a bad sandstorm and then had to dig the car out of the drifts. It was extremely interesting in the interior of the country. During the time of the Romans, Cyrenaica grew the wheat for Rome and much of Italy. Even deep down into the desert there were the remains of what had been terraced fields, and clearly there had been water and cultivated land.

I had a good deal to do with the Senussi of Cyrenaica. They are a very different people to the Tripolitanians and the people of the Fasan. They were a proud, warrior people with many admirable qualities.

Unfortunately, I became very ill with gall-bladder trouble. I had had this for some time and had postponed having the operation for too long. There was some talk of performing an emergency operation in Benghasi, but the excellent Indian surgeon there told me that although he could do it (the operation was in its infancy in those days), he certainly did not have the equipment, and there would be a very good chance that I would not survive. Luckily, I got better, but it was clear that I would have to have the operation as soon as I could get back to London.

We left Cyrenaica and flew to Tripoli, and then to Malta. At Benghasi airport, Carlo Forni, who was coming with us to Italy on leave, was arrested. He had been denounced by some Libyan whom he had discharged some weeks previously. In spite of all our efforts, we had to leave him behind, and it was several weeks before he could get matters straightened out and fly on to Italy. For our part, we had a somewhat dramatic flight. When we took off from Malta for Rome, we had to make an emergency landing almost immediately we became airborne. We transferred to a second aircraft, and that caught fire in the air on approach to Catania; so we had to transfer to yet a third aeroplane to get back to Rome.

We stayed with my mother at the villa at Anticoli for some weeks and then flew to London, where I had my gall-bladder and a lot of ulcerated tissue round it removed. They filled a couple of kilner jars up with the bits that they removed, and Mr Guardham, my surgeon, used to lecture to students about it. It looked very disgusting!

Ireland Again

We returned to Ireland to recuperate and carried on with what for me was an almost ideal life there. Alas, it was not for Honor – she developed bronchial asthma again, heart troubles due to the old rheumatic fever and (also once again) pneumonia in the winter. We had X-rays taken in Cork which looked like a black cat in a dark room, so we decided to go to London again for a thorough investigation. Her lungs were badly scarred, and we were told to leave the damp climate of the west of Ireland and never return.

Before doing so, we had to get rid of my mother's farm. This was not easy, as it had a reputation for being badly haunted – and, in fact, it was. There were interesting but disconcerting events there: heavy objects, such as a huge roll of barbed wire which took two strong men to lift with a pole through the centre, were thrown down a corridor, down the stairs and into the living room. A filled forty-five gallon oil drum was hurled from an outhouse into the garden some forty yards away, and there used to be a rather strange phenomenon in the living room at nights.

We used to take guests who had come to dinner up to the farm to see this as a sort of cabaret turn. There was, of course, no electric light at the farm, and the house was lit with pressure lamps, oil lamps and candles. Usually between 11.00 p.m. and 1.00 or 1.30 a.m., the same thing frequently happened. We would go up to the farm, light the fire in the living room, light the oil lamps and the pressure lamp, light the candles and wait. Sometimes the strange events happened and sometimes they did not; but frequently they did. First there would be a feeling of cold which would become more intense; then the fire would die down, the lamps and the pressure lamp would die down to a faint glow and the candles would dwindle to bare pinpoints of light. This would last for five to ten minutes. Then the lamps would light up again, the candle flames burn up and the fire, which had been reduced to a dull glow, would also burn up again.

It was interesting but a nuisance. As nobody would live in the farm, I could not let it or sell it. In desperation I went to Dublin to consult the Dominicans and the Jesuits, but they both told me that they had full order books for exorcisms for the next year or more. This was too long to wait, and I persuaded the local church of Ireland parson to do his stuff. He and his wife and Honor and I repaired to the farm. The parson drew a circle on the floor and a pentacle and put various bit and pieces which he had brought with him on the points of the pentacle. We were all seated back-to-back in the centre of the circle and told that under no circumstances should we leave it. Ian Connor began to intone in Latin. He had told me previously that he had taken a course in exorcism and knew what he was doing. He said that he intended to call the spirit or whatever it was and then get rid of it. There was brilliant moonlight outside and flooding in through the windows. As I had no idea what, if anything, would appear and believed that somehow there could be a human origin to all this, I had slipped a .38 Special into a shoulder holster, unknown to Ian Connor.

After a bit, I began to sense that something was approaching, closer and closer. Then, against the moonlight, there began to appear the top of a head. I got out my .38 Special. Almost as if it was growing out of the ground outside, more and more of the head came into view – until I saw that it was Jory, the mentally retarded son of a local farmer, who used to be let out at night. Hearing the chanting from the house which he knew to be empty, he had come to make a cautious investigation. I am afraid that Honor and I burst out laughing and were immediately expelled from the house by Ian, who was furious with us. He and his wife restarted the ritual, and oddly enough, it did have some effect – sufficient at least to allow me to sell the house and farm to a Mexican.

Eventually, the time came for us to go. For the last three or four weeks before we left, we had a string of visitors: friends who came to say goodbye and also people whom I hardly knew. One man had come on a pony and travelled from some thirty miles away, spending a night with friends on the way. He came in and told me that some three years previously, I had been shooting over his land up on the mountain, and he had invited me in for some tea. I had forgotten all about it. 'I heard that you were going,' he said, 'so I thought that I would come over to say goodbye to you and your missus and bring you a little farewell present.' He gave me a packet of twenty cigarettes. When we eventually left, there were many of the local people standing along the roadside to wave us goodbye. I confess that I was in tears, but we never went back again.

The cats had gone on to Italy by air with my mother, and by this time, our two children were at school. Our son, Marcus, was at Headford in County Meath, and our daughter, Juanita, at the Hall School in Dublin.

It had been a wonderful place to bring up children. They had a good life in West Cork, shooting, fishing, sailing and having picnics by the mountain loughs. They had developed enormous self-reliance and physical stamina. Even our daughter, who had been small and very young, used to go for miles and miles over the mountains – as much as ten to fifteen miles a day over the bogs and up the glens. They would both swim out to the boat in the icy cold water of late autumn and thought nothing of it.

I think that for both of them, it was the happiest time of their lives. Today, it has all changed. There is a rash of small bungalows along the coast and an oil refinery in the bay; the beauty has gone, and hordes of tourists have arrived. In those days, though, it was a wonderful wild and isolated place, where nobody would ever dream of harming a child, and where one could go where one liked in complete safety.

Honor and I had planted some ten thousand trees, but I have been told that much of the land has been sold off for building plots. I do not ever want to see it again.

We drove first to London and then to Rome. I had the Allard repaired, but it had done many thousands of miles and was becoming elderly.

There is one more incident that I want to recount before I leave this subject. It happened when we were packing up the house at Brughad-na-Geallaigh. We realised that we certainly could not take everything with us, and at the same time, the cost of storage was high. There were quite a few things in the house which we thought we should sell, and when the children went back to their respective schools, Honor and I started going through everything, making piles of items which could be sold locally. These included a number of paperback books, pots and pans which were nearly worn out, clothes and a whole mass of things which one collects but, when going abroad for ever, has to sell.

The house was not very big, and when we had first come to Ireland all those years ago, we had brought everything, including a collection of artefacts which had been made by one of my great-uncles who had been an explorer in the 1860s and 1870s. He had his own yacht and had spent some time in New Guinea, Samoa, and the Western Pacific Islands at a time when they were still, to some extent, unknown. There were sharks' teeth weapons, tappa from New Zealand, bows, arrows, stone and wood implements, a chief's ceremonial spear or stick from New Zealand, a sacrificial bowl and many other things. Honor did not like these things, and together with a good deal of furniture which would not fit into our house, we had them stored at a large mansion, Bantry House, which belonged to friends of ours and was some miles away. It was a big place, and the owners very kindly stored these things of ours for us in three or four rooms in one of the outhouses near the stables.

When we had to leave Ireland, we had all these things brought back to our house and went through them to see if there was anything that we wanted to go into store or that could be sold. After the elimination of some furniture, we had the whole lot put into Juanita's bedroom, which was a large room immediately over ours. The things arrived in the morning, and we spent all day going through them, keeping some and taking others to the garage where we were making a collection of those things which we would send to the local auctioneer in Bantry. We spent all day doing this and were exhausted that night, so we went to bed early. Some time in the middle of the night there was a loud crash from upstairs. This woke us both up and was followed by several more.

Honor and I got up and with our torches we went upstairs to see what was going on. Halfway up the stairs, the noises stopped. We went into Juanita's bedroom and searched, but nothing appeared to have fallen over or to have been moved. There were no more noises and we went back to bed and to sleep.

The following day was a repetition of the day before. We slowly worked our way through everything and again removed a great many things to the garage. Again we went to bed very tired. We were woken up some hours later by some really tremendous crashes, like somebody throwing furniture about – and heavy furniture at that. We rushed up the stairs, and once again, the noises stopped halfway up the stairs and before we could get into the room. Again, nothing had been moved and there was no sign of anything which could possibly account for the noises. They were far too loud to be occasioned by a rat or other animal. I searched the room very thoroughly and looked out of the windows to see if there was anybody outside, although the windows were all locked on the inside. We went to bed very much mystified.

The third day, we worked all day and finished the job. Honor and I discussed what might be the cause of these noises, and we finally decided that it could possibly be a sacrificial bowl (I think from New Guinea) or the chief's stick from New Zealand. We cleared everything out of Juanita's bedroom, leaving only the bowl in the centre of the floor, and we took the chief's stick and propped it up by the fire in our bedroom, where we could see it. We made sure that all the windows of Juanita's room and also the door were locked when we left. There was nothing at all left in the room except the bowl.

We went to bed, and in the middle of the night, there was a most monumental crash – again, as if somebody had picked up a large and heavy piece of furniture and hurled it against the wall. This was followed by other noises, even louder, and by distant screams from the maids' rooms. In fact, the whole house seemed to be shaking with the noise. Again, we went upstairs. The noise stopped as we went into the room. There was nothing and nobody in it, except the bowl. The windows were all locked, as had been the door. There was no way that anybody could possibly have got out. There was nothing behind the walls, no secret passages or anything of that sort. We went back to bed, and the next day Con O'Leary came to collect all the things for the auction. He took the sacrificial bowl with him.

That night we slept soundly, and there were no more noises. Two days later, I telephoned to ask Con O'Leary how the auction had gone, and he said, 'You're a terrible lucky man, so you are!' I asked him why and he said, 'Last night, some fellow got into the auction rooms, but God knows what he might have been doing there. Whoever he was, he was kicking up a tremendous row, so that I heard it up the street from my house, but when I got there he must have heard me coming, because there was nobody at all about. He was making such a row that I thought that he must have been smashing up all the furniture, but I could not find any damage done and nothing at all had been moved.' I asked him if the bowl had been sold. He had to look through his papers and said, 'That would be Lot 97, would it? A wooden sort of washing bowl made of some foreign wood.' I said that would be it. 'Well, it did not fetch much,' Con said, 'it went for five shillings to some fellow from Goughane Barra way.'

I have often wondered since whether he had any trouble with it. Oddly enough, it used to be in the long passage from the drawing room to the ballroom at Morley Manor. Quite frequently, people who used to sleep in the 'Empire Room' (so-called because it had French Empire furniture in it) used to complain that they had been woken up by loud crashes and noises in the night coming from the direction of the ballroom, which in fact was quite some way away and on a lower floor.

Italy and the Balearic Islands

We spent that Christmas up at Anticoli, and it was terribly cold. The villa stood at between two thousand and three thousand feet and we had deep snow. We even saw wolves in the garden. We were near the National Park of the Abruzzi, and there are, and were, quite a few wolves there. The cats were asleep by the big stove in the dining room and did not like the wolves snuffling under the big wooden doors which opened out on to the garden. The house was much too big to keep fully heated, and we were all glad when the spring came.

Anticoli was still a pleasant place but slowly became less so, as the virus of politics began to infect the people.

The children came out for Christmas. By then Marcus was already at Stowe, and Juanita went to Chatelard in Switzerland. We decided to move on in May and look for another home for ourselves. To begin with we decided to try Majorca. I had been there very many years before with my father. In those days it was a marvellous island. There was about one kilometre of tarmac road (in Palma) and about two hotels on the island. We had stayed at the Mediterraneo Hotel, where my father experienced a very bad attack of gout, so a three-week holiday became three months long. I explored the island as best I could, but there were very few roads and almost no public transport. I think that there were two taxis on the island. It was incredibly beautiful.

Now we found that it had changed completely and there were many roads. Palma had become quite a large city, and there were thousands of tourists – although, in fact, they were merely the vanguard of what was to come later. We were there for a month and then decided to move on to look at Ibiza, which was at that time completely unspoilt. The armies of yobbos and lager louts were still things of the future, and we spent a glorious summer there. The only problem was how to get the children to the island and back again at the end of the holidays, as there was only one boat a week from and to Palma, and that was always fully booked. I solved the problem only by chartering a yacht, the *Solita del Mar* – a beautiful big sailing yacht on which we had a great deal of fun, visiting the bays all round Ibiza and Formentera.

When we left Italy to go to Majorca, we travelled from Naples on a Turkish ship, the *Adana*. She took only a very few passengers, and I fear that their accommodation could not have been very good. However, we had the suite reserved for the directors of the line, and it was very comfortable and spacious indeed.

The *Adana* was painted bright green – 'a beautiful pea-green boat'. She was loading onions in Naples, and I imagine that we could have been smelt a good mile away. The food and everything else smelt and tasted of onions. Fortunately, both Honor and I liked onions. There was also an abundance of raki, which drunk 'on the rocks' can be rather good.

The Allard was lashed to the deck (and stank of onions for weeks afterwards), but only after a furious row which I had with the customs officials at the port of embarkation. They wanted to charge me some exorbitant sum of money for which there was no legal requirement or justification and which was really intended as a simple but expensive bribe.

We set sail up the coast of Italy in a miasma of onion, and eventually reached Genoa, where we had a day in the port. Our good friend Carlo Forni lived with his wife in Genoa, and they came to meet us at the boat. Things between them were clearly going very badly indeed, and it seemed that Angela, Carlo's wife, blamed us.

'He has become a *bevone*,' she said. (A *bevone* is a drunkard.) 'It is all your fault! When he was in Benghasi you taught him to drink whisky, and now he drinks it every evening. It is disgusting!'

It was a dreadful day, as the two bickered incessantly. They took us to luncheon and snarled at each other over the meal. They then took us on a sightseeing tour of Genoa and offered to take us to tea, but by then we had enough and said that we had to get back to the boat. As a courtesy, I invited them on board and was rather surprised when they accepted. Having had a tour and inspected our palatial cabin, I offered them a drink. Angela whipped round on me and said, 'There you go again – encouraging Carlo to drink.' I replied, 'Angela, you know this is a Turkish ship and the Turks are strict Moslems. They maintain that alcohol is forbidden by Allah.'

With some reluctance, she came with us to the bar. There was nobody there except the barman, and I said that the best thing that they had – no whisky of course – was a Turkish drink which was very cooling when drunk on ice. She agreed to try one and in a matter of seconds had swallowed it and asked for another. I saw Carlo's eyes open wider and wider, as she said, 'This is absolutely delicious. I think that I would like another, please.' Eventually the bell rang for the passengers ashore. After six large rakis, Angela was most reluctant to leave and announced to the world that she wished to travel round and round the world on this delightful ship.

'But Angela,' Honor said, 'what about your children?' 'To hell with children,' Angela replied. 'I've had children for years and years and years, and now I want to travel for the rest of my life on this lovely ship.' She was by now incapable of standing, and so we had to carry her off and down the gangway. Carlo's chauffeur at first thought that she had had an accident but soon realised to his intense surprise that Angela was totally, and happily, drunk. We waved them goodbye. When we docked at Marseilles, some little time later, there was a cable sent to the ship from Carlo. It read, 'Thank you, dear friends, you have saved our marriage. Now Angela has her raki every evening and I have my whisky and soda.' It is nice to have done something good in our lives!

The summer that we spent in Majorca and Ibiza was wonderful. Honor and I and the children explored the islands, swam for miles in warm, clear, calm water, looked down on sunken ports, recovered pieces of Phoenician pottery and Roman amphorae, fished, lay in the sun and walked for miles along deserted beaches and through lovely pine woods. Honor discovered a cousin, Captain Don Diego de Alcazar y la Vittoria, who was serving in the garrison on Ibiza. His mother and sister had been raped and killed by the Republican communists during the Spanish Civil War, and his father had raised his own regiment from their estates but had been killed fighting together with his elder son. Diego, who had been sent to school in Portugal, ran away and joined the nationalists and fought with them throughout the rest of the war, seeking a terrible revenge. With the war over, he had been sent to North Africa to fight against the Riffs. As an officer in a parachute unit, he had been told to take a Riff village. He had done so and came on the radio to report to his colonel. The colonel told him to assemble all the head men of the village in the village square, and the colonel would come up to speak to them. Diego had said, 'My colonel, I cannot obey this order.' The colonel snapped, 'Why not?' Diego replied, 'Because I have already hanged all of them.'

To settle down to peacetime soldiering was not easy for Diego, and he was always in trouble.

Ibiza was a paradise in those days. For several months we swam in a limpid sea and at night danced on the sands in the moonlight. Thank God, we never went back to see what happened to it later.

It was in Ibiza that we first met Sibille and Karl Herzog. He was a brilliant economist, and she was on her honeymoon with him. She was a remarkably pretty girl of about eighteen. We went with them to Valencia and on to Ifach when we left Ibiza. They returned to Paris, and we went on towards the Portuguese frontier.

Some friends of ours had a disagreeable experience in Ifach some years later. They were staying in an hotel near there – in those days, there were not many. Amongst the other guests there was an elderly English woman, with whom they became friendly. They used to take her out with them in their car, and she would sit in it when they went bathing. One afternoon, they went to the beach as usual, but when they returned to their car they found that the elderly lady was dead. She had apparently suffered a stroke or something of the sort while they had been bathing. They drove back immediately to the hotel, where the manager, in considerable consternation, told them that the best thing that they could do would be to go immediately, together with the corpse, to the nearest British consul – then in Barcelona. He warned them that if they reported the matter to the local police, they could be held as material witnesses for several months. They left immediately and managed to arrive in Barcelona just before the consulate closed. However, the consul told them that it would be very much better to go immediately, together with the corpse, to Madrid and report the whole matter to the embassy there and to the consul general.

By driving all night over the mountain roads, they arrived exhausted at the embassy the following morning, a couple of hours or so before it opened. By this time it was midsummer, and it was clear that the elderly lady was very obviously dead. She also looked very dead, and they decided that rather than leave her in the back seat of the car, they had better put her in the boot. With some difficulty, and choosing a moment when there was nobody about, this they did. They then went into the embassy and eventually told their story. The embassy people were not at all pleased to see them and said that they had better go back to Ifach and report the matter to the local police. However, they said that carrying a corpse round Spain in the summer heat was not very advisable, and they blankly refused to go.

'Oh well,' said the embassy man, 'I suppose that we had better go and get the old girl in here and then get the embassy doctor and deal with the officials. I'll come out and give you a hand.' They went out to the car but found that it had gone. While they had been in the embassy, some thief had stolen their car. He would certainly have got a surprise when he opened the boot, but neither the car nor the elderly lady were ever seen again.

Honor and I loved Spain, and we both spoke Spanish. We decided that we would travel about in the country and then find somewhere there to make our home. Ibiza was not practical owing to the very great difficulty in getting on and off the island. In those days there was no airfield and in the winter no boats either.

We had to get out of Spain in order to renew the triptique on our car, which was a necessity. We decided to make for the Portuguese frontier, mainly because neither of us had ever been to Portugal. We drove to Madrid and from Madrid to Merida. Here there was one of the first paradors, but we found that not only could we not get in, but they would not even let us spend the night on chairs in the sitting room.

We slept in the car. During the night, strange men appeared from time to time to peer at us and to feel the luggage on the boot rack. The next day, I demanded that we be allowed to wash and given breakfast. I then discovered that Franco had been staying there during the night, and the parador had been reserved for him and his entourage.

Portugal

We drove on to Lisbon and stayed at an hotel overlooking Edward VII Park. We knew nobody in Portugal other than Nicky Horthy, the son of the admiral who had been Regent of Hungary. Nicky had been a good friend of ours in Rome and had been up to the villa on several occasions. I had taken a staff car filled with food up to his parents in 1947, when they were interned in a villa by the Americans at Weilheim, south of Munich, and had had almost nothing to eat.

We telephoned Nicky, who subsequently came in from Estoril to see us. Two days later he invited us to a party, where I met the SHAPE mission officer, a Lieutenant Colonel Montgomery. He introduced me to several other people, and I woke the next morning with the uncomfortable feeling that I had agreed to do something or other – but what?

An hour later, Pat Montgomery telephoned to say that he would pick me up in an hour's time. By some judicious questioning, I discovered that I had agreed to meet the Chief of Staff of the Army, General Pina, with a view to becoming an instructor at the Portuguese Institute for Advanced Military Studies.

General Pina was a most charming man who spoke excellent English. I told him that the previous evening, in some sort of drunken frenzy, I had agreed to discuss this matter with him, but that I had long forgotten anything that I had ever known and that in any event I did not intend to stay in Portugal and was there just to renew the triptique on the car. I was unqualified to teach anything and did not want to.

General Pina explained to me that the teaching at the Institute was almost entirely theoretical, but that he was anxious to get somebody who had actually seen warfare to explain to the students that things never worked in war as they were meant to: the field telephone and radio often failed to work, messages did not always get through and if they did were generally garbled, and so on. He wanted to impart that a battlefield was as remote from the theoretical instruction of a sand table or an operations planning room as was the Earth from outer space.

He asked me to give it a try. I said that I could not speak Portuguese, but he said that did not matter as I could speak Spanish and that I could also speak English to the officers, who ought to learn it anyway. I finally ran out of arguments and agreed that we would give it a trial for a month. At the end of that time, if I did not like it or if they did not like me, we would call it a day.

Thus I became an instructor at the Institute for Advanced Military Studies at Pedroucos, outside Lisbon, and in fact remained there for nearly nineteen years.

As Britain's oldest ally and a member of NATO, the Instituto de Altos Estudios Militares received fairly frequent visits from American and other military personnel, but we also had a few students there from countries outside

NATO such as Spain – which at that time was not in NATO – and Brazil.

For the first few years the Instituto was in an ancient palace about halfway between Lisbon and Estoril. It was a rather beautiful building, but totally unsuited for use as a military training school. Various courses were held there. A senior course for colonels, which they had to pass for promotion to the rank of brigadier; a staff course for officers from captain to major, with a few lieutenant colonels; and also a course for junior officers, a company commanders' course. My duties consisted of lecturing to the staff course. Over the years, I got to know very many Portuguese Army officers, who were to go on to become generals. I made a great number of friends there who later became chiefs of staff of the army, army commanders, and ministers for the army. Now, very many years later, many still remain my friends, although all have now retired.

One of the first things that I did was to write a book on the Mau Mau rebellion in Kenya, and this was translated into Portuguese. I finished up by suggesting that much the same thing was almost certain to happen to the Portuguese in Angola, Mozambique and Guinea. This amused the Portuguese very much, and they assured me that there could never be any sort of a rebellion in Portuguese Africa, as they had been there for four hundred years, and there was a completely different relationship between the Portuguese and the Africans: there was no racial discrimination, and in fact, nobody knew how many blacks there were in the Portuguese 'overseas provinces', or how many whites, as it was questionable how black one had to be to be classified as a black, or how white to be classified as a white. In fact, very many Angolans and Mozambicans were of mixed blood. Portuguese was the language which everybody spoke (and for that matter they still do), and although there were some thirty-five native languages in Angola alone, Portuguese was the language of trade and the only common language between them all. They certainly thought that I was crazy when I continued to maintain that sooner or later what had happened in Kenya would also happen in Angola, Mozambique and Guinea. This was in 1958 and 1959. In 1961, it did.

Honor and I took a horrible little house in Estoril, Villa Chiquita. It was small and really rather beastly, but it served our purpose while we looked around for something more permanent. That summer we were lent a most lovely house: the Quinta de Capella, out beyond Sintra. It had been rented on a long lease by friends of ours (Bertie Landsberg and his wife) from the Marquesa de Cadaval, to whom it belonged. Bertie had another wonderful villa on the Brenta Canal in Italy, perhaps the most beautiful of all the great Palladian villas there. As he and his wife spent the whole summer there, they let us have their house near Sintra for five months.

The children came out for their holidays, and we spent a very happy time there, especially as the Instituto closed down for three months in the summer.

The Allard had become very elderly and unreliable, and I bought a 4.25 litre Bentley 'razor-edge' saloon from a friend. It had been built shortly before the war but was in good condition and lasted us for the whole time that we were in Portugal. It was a fast car, capable of over one hundred miles per hour, very solid and built like a tank. It was also incredibly heavy to drive, but in it we explored Portugal and also Spain. We drove many thousands of miles to Seville, to Madrid, to Granada, and even to see my father at Cannes, where he had moved in about 1957.

At that time too, Karl Herzog came to see us from Vienna. He was attached to one of the United Nations organisations – UNESCO, or something of the sort. Sadly, he and his wife Sibille had split up. It was Karl who introduced me to the European Centre for Documentation and Information, of which the president was the Archduke Otto von Habsburg. The CEDI met annually in Spain, nearly always at the Escurial. They also had meetings in Britain, France and elsewhere, and through it I was able to meet ministers from most of the Western European countries.

Nor was it long before Gilbert Lennox and Dickie Metcalfe reappeared in our lives and came to stay with us. On one occasion we took Gilbert for a picnic and had our luncheon in a wood not far from Obidos. I took a photograph of him then, sitting surrounded by bushes. I entitled it 'Spy Caught in a Thicket' and sent it to him. He was much amused and kept it for years in his house at Lymington.

When we left the Quinta de Capella, we moved to a house in Cascais. It was called Villa Madrid, in the Rua Marques Leal Pancada. Cascais was then an undeveloped fishing village, and the fishermen used to land their catches on the beach about forty yards away from our house. Villa Madrid was small, but it had a pretty garden and an old pepper tree in it, and across the road, there were the walls and battlements of the old castle.

Alas, one of our cats, Kai Lung, had died of a sort of feline enteritis up at the villa in Anticoli Corrado while we were in Ibiza, and he was replaced by Kai II. Both Tripitaka and Kai II enjoyed the Quinta de Capella enormously as it had a huge garden surrounded by a high wall, and they were quite safe there. This was not the case with Villa Madrid, and one day, Tripitaka was stolen.

He was in the habit of lying asleep on top of the wall overlooking the road, and one day he disappeared. The Bentley was parked in the road, and on top of the roof, I found footprints. Somebody had climbed up on the car, grabbed Tripi while he was asleep, and thrust him into a bag. I alerted the police, the traffic police on the roads going into Lisbon and staff at the airport in Lisbon. I even enlisted the army in a search for anybody who could find him or give information as to his whereabouts. Soon the whole village of Cascais was looking for him.

Two days went by, and then a small girl arrived at the house to say that Tripi was in a large pile of bricks and masonry not far away. He had been seen making his way home, and some thirty or forty people had tried to catch him in order to claim the reward. Tripi had taken fright and fled into the pile of bricks and building materials, which the local populace was even then dismantling. We ran down the road, got rid of the crowd and called Tripi out.

He had clearly been locked up somewhere. He was covered in oil, and it was clear that he had torn his way out of the door of his prison as his claws were broken, and he had splinters in his paws. He also had a good deal of blood on him, which was not his blood. The small girl who had the good sense to come to us received the reward, and the police caught the catnapper. He was a local man who had been suspected for some time of stealing cats from people and then either selling them or killing them and selling their skins. It seems that he had tried to kill Tripi, who had then attacked the man and torn his face and hands very badly indeed. The man had escaped from the shed and had gone to the local hospital for treatment. While he was away, Tripi had torn a hole in the door of the shed and started to return home. The man received a stiff prison sentence. We were just happy to have our cat back.

Spain

One day, we made the first of many trips to Cordoba and Granada. Cordoba is a fascinating city, but for us, even more fascinating were the ruins of Al Zahra, some miles outside Cordoba and at the foot of the Sierra Morena. It was here that Al Mansour, the great Arab emir, built a city for his favourite wife, Al Zahra (The Flower), and called the city by her name. Unlike the Alhambra at Granada, which is built and decorated with plaster, Al Zahra was built with white marble imported from Italy. It must have been of incredible beauty, and craftsmen came from all over the Mediterranean to build it.

Ships brought blocks of pure white marble from Carara in Italy, and little by little, a marvellous city arose. The white marble was cut and pierced and worked into a lacy tracery. Great marble basins flanked by colonnades and avenues of cypresses adorned the palace. Fountains of white marble played in the palace courts and in the city which, set against the background of the mountain and surrounded by forests, must have been like a white jewel glittering in its emerald cup.

This pure white city of Al Zahra was to have a short life. Only a few years after it was completed, the wild Berber horsemen crossed over from North Africa. Under their black banners, and in the name of Allah, they burnt it, sacked it and burnt it again and yet again. In their frenzy of religious hatred of what they thought to be a heresy of Islam, they systematically set to work to smash up everything in the city, until there was nothing left larger than a man's fist.

Al Mansour was driven north, but Al Zahra perished in the flames of the city. Later he was to return to take a terrible revenge, but his love, like the city, was gone for ever.

Yet it is still there, in mounds, under the soil. Where once the Moorish Hispanic princes rode and hunted in the cool glens, and amongst the walnut and chestnut forests, the remnants of the city sleeps. A little has now been excavated – sufficient for one to be able to imagine what it must once have been, but the rest lies covered under grassy mounds and the wild flowers of the mountain.

We drove on to the other great Moorish city of Granada and stayed at the Alhambra Hotel, a modern red-brick building which by any standards could not be called beautiful. We had just parked the Bentley when an American couple arrived in their car. They got out and stared at the hotel. 'Is that the Alhambra?' the man asked us. 'Yes,' I replied. Clearly bitterly disappointed, the man said, 'Is that so? Well, it does not look very old to me.'

Both Honor and I loved Granada, the Alhambra (not the hotel), the gardens of the Generaliffe and the great mountain of the Sierra Nevada behind. We were to return here many times, but the last time was with a man called Poulson, an architect who was to get into serious trouble with the law and spend some years in prison.

We went there with a friend of ours, Leslie Pollard, who was the managing director of Construction Promotion Ltd, a firm based in London. Poulson had ideas about building an hotel and setting up a ski resort on the mountain, and Leslie Pollard came with him, as he was to organise the building works. Honor and I flew down to Faro from Lisbon and met Pollard and Poulson there, where we hired a self-drive car and drove to Granada. It was a ghastly few days. Poulson found fault with everything. Like some people from the north of England, he took great pride in being blunt, which in his case amounted to intolerable rudeness.

One day – and he had been particularly obnoxious that morning – a telegram arrived while we were having luncheon, recalling him urgently to London. As he spoke no Spanish, he asked Honor to arrange for a taxi to take him to the nearest airport at Malaga. Honor, who not only looked Spanish but spoke beautiful Castillian fluently, found a taxi driver willing to take Poulson to the airport, which was a long way away over precipitous mountains. Honor explained to the driver that this Englishman was in a very great hurry and that he was a very unpleasant man, who hated Spain and Spaniards. She suggested that if he were to be given a good fright, it would be only a proper revenge for the nasty things that he had been saying about Spain. The driver understood perfectly, and a one thousand peseta note only made him happier. Poulson disappeared in a cloud of dust and, as we heard later, had to go into hospital for several days on his return to London, to recover from nervous shock!

Other people have since built a hotel and ski resort there, which I have been told is very good.

Every year, Honor and I used to drive up to Madrid in the Bentley and go to the CEDI meetings. We were usually lodged in the Victoria Hotel in the town of Escorial, but on one occasion we were put up in the actual monastery of the Val de los Caidos. Here a huge basilica has been driven into the mountains of the Sierra Guardarama. We were there for its official opening, and it really is one of the wonders of the world today.

We arrived on a night of storm. To reach the church and the monastery, there is a long road which winds up a wild and rocky valley through the forest. There was thunder and continual lightning, and low scudding clouds raced over the top of the mountain. Against these storm clouds, there was projected from the lights at its base a gigantic cross which surmounts the mountain under which the church is built. It was a weird and eerie sight, and one which we never forgot. The church itself is like a vast tunnel, driven into the heart of the mountain. When we first saw it, there were no pews or seats, and it was quite bare except for the wonderful tapestries on the walls. At the far end, under an enormous dome only one metre lower than that of St Peter's in Rome, there is the altar, and on it is the crucified

Christ, carved out of olive wood and horrifyingly lifelike. The dome itself is all mosaic and depicts the figures of soldiers, sailors, airmen, civilians, nuns, priests and a vast host of people killed in the Spanish Civil War from both sides. They are all rising in a swirling movement upwards to the great central figure at the top, of God the Father.

It is an extraordinary and wonderful thing, and I am not in the least surprised that the architect and artist who created it went mad. It is a work of genius. In the dome there is a tiny opening, and at the moment of the elevation of the Host, a ray of sunlight comes down and illuminates the figure of the crucified Christ on the altar. Further back into the mountain, there are buried all together those who fell on both sides in the civil war.

The meetings of the European Centre for Documentation and Information lasted for three days. On this occasion, it was remarkable for the fact that an Italian woman delegate found herself trapped in her room. She had locked herself in and could not get out. She banged on the door, yelled, went to the windows and shouted herself hoarse, but nobody heard her. She was there all day and became desperate, until finally, she got out of the window and climbed down the wall of the monastery. How she did it, I will never know.

We met a lot of interesting people there: Michel Debré, Count de la Noe, Habib Deloncle and Jean-Claude Prost, all from Paris; Martin Artajo, the Spanish foreign minister, who was called by the nickname 'The Sacred Elephant'; also Fraga Iribarne, and many others from Spain, including Franco. From England, there was Caufield, Sir John Rogers and Sir John Biggs-Davison; and from Germany, the minister von Merkats, Prince Waldburg-Zeil and his brother, Colonel George von Gaupp. The Archduke Otto von Habsburg was there also. I met again Ewald von Kleist, whom I had last seen coming out of the bathroom in the castle at Merano during the war. We did not recognise each other, and it was only years later that we did.

Either on the way to these meetings in Madrid or on the way back, Honor and I used to spend a week fishing on the Tormes river in the Gredos and visiting castles which had belonged to her Spanish family. I was very much tempted to buy the Torejon de los Guzmannes in Avila, a wonderful building owned by the Count de la Vega. It was Honor who pointed out that as it had no heating we would freeze to death in the winter and that as it apparently did not have any bathroom or lavatory we would not find it very comfortable at any time of the year. She also noted that we certainly could not afford to make it habitable, and even if we could, we could never get servants to run it. Women are more practical than men!

I tried to buy the castle at the Barco de Avila, and we had plans to build it up. The owners agreed. The only snag was that there were some seventeen bodies buried in the courtyard; in order to get them moved to the cemetery, we had to have permission from the bishop. This I obtained. I was also able to trace twelve of the people buried there, and get permission from their relatives; the others I could not find, and nobody knew who they were.

We could have gone ahead and built, but at any time somebody might have turned up and demanded that we dig up the dining room floor and return the corpse of his grandfather. There were five unidentified bodies, and we thought that the risk was too great that as soon as we built and moved in we would have to dismantle the house again to recover the long-lost relatives of some claimant, so we had to abandon the idea.

The Gredos are beautiful, and the Tormes is a lovely river, full of trout. Sometimes, we would get twenty-five or thirty in a day's fishing, and they would cook them for us at the Parador de los Gredos, where we stayed.

Another place where we always stayed on our way from Estoril to Madrid (and also on the return journeys) was the parador, built in the castle of Oropressa. It is a lovely parador, and we stayed there for New Year's Eve in 1974–1975.

We arrived on this occasion to find that a group of French people had taken the whole castle for themselves and their guests. They were shooting nearby and had reserved the whole place for a week. However, we knew the manager (Señor Diaz), and his wife well, and they were able to find us a room. We changed, had our baths and came down for dinner. It had been explained to us that the French group had arranged a huge table in the centre of the dining room and that we were invited to sit with Mr and Mrs Diaz and their staff at a small side-table.

When we came down and had a drink at the bar, we realised at once that something was very wrong. There was distant shouting, and discreet enquiries revealed that a French ambassador, who had been one of the guests of the shooting party, had shot another guest, with both barrels, in the backside. The host, a well-known and immensely rich manufacturer of perfume and women's cosmetics, M. Oreal, had ordered the French ambassador to return to the parador immediately, while the wounded man was removed to hospital. It seemed that the French ambassador had had his pride pricked, and while less painful than what he had done to his victim, he had announced in a huff that he would return to Paris immediately and had ordered a car to take him to Madrid (about one hundred miles away). He had then locked himself in his room and would not come out until the car arrived to take him away.

The dining room was beautifully decorated with streamers, paper decorations of every sort, holly and balloons. The enormous central table was covered with flowers, and the French and their guests arrived to celebrate the New Year

Above: Honor and I driving our old Bentley on a visit to England – in Hyde Park. It was the most beautiful car we ever owned.

Below: The tower above the watergate at the Castle of Ninfa where my ancestor Count Robert de Varingeville trained his condotta in 1489, having borrowed it from our kinsman Prince Gaetani. It is on an island in the Pontine Marshes and was even then partly ruined, having been burnt about a hundred years previously.

Above: Killronan Castle where my mother spent most of her childhood and youth – now an abandoned ruin.

Below: A part of the North Wall of the sinister fortress in Tuscany but near Umbria, which we built in 1493–1494 and which we owned for some 450 years.

The Castle of Gutenberg in the Steirmark where we stayed and shot many times with our friends Count and Countess Stubenberg. It was from here that I nearly fell out of the top of an immensely tall tree when shooting a wonderful roebuck.

Above: Morley Manor, Derbyshire, where I spent much of my childhood. Only about one fifth of the house is shown in the photograph and there were forty acres of gardens. The place belonged to my Great Aunt.
Below: The Castle of Bernstein on the Hungarian frontier, once the property of Prince Battyany (a distant cousin), then owned by Count Almassy and where we went shooting many times when staying with Countess Pacetta Kueffstein-Almassy. It was from here that we launched Honor's birthday balloon over the Hungarian frontier.

Honor – Duchess of Valderano, Duchess of Castel di Spano, Marquesa de Rio Castel, Countess de Varingeville, Dame Grand Cross of the Order of Saint George, Dame Grand Cross of the Order of Saint Ignatius of Antioch.

The Pussycat as a young officer at the beginning of the Second World War.

Pietro Gaudenzi's wonderful portrait in charcoal and pastel of Honor, then aged about thirty. Her mother's family is descended on one side from the noble Spanish families of Leon and Alcazar and on the other side from John of Gaunt and the Plantagenets.

The author shooting in Ireland, 1953. I am in the woods below Muckross with 9.5 mm Mannlicher and am hoping to stalk a stag to feed the ravening family.

Honor at dawn, shooting in the woods of the Alentejo in Portugal.

Our son, Marcus, dei Duchi de Valderano, Ph.D., MA

Dickie Metcalfe. This photograph was taken when he was still the
Deputy Director of Foreign Office 'Positive Vetting'. He had previously
been in both MI5 and MI6.

Honor and I at Juanita's flat in London.

Our Golden Wedding dinner party, 10th February, 1991. It was freezing cold, the country was covered with 'the wrong kind of snow', the airports were closed, the roads were closed, the trains did not run and the guests whom we had invited for a big party could not get to London. Dianne gave us a splendid dinner at an Italian restaurant to which as many as could slid!

Left to right: Nicholas Elliot CBE, (a former Director of MI6), Jean Howard (the whiz-kid who ran the Enigma machine at Bletchley Park during the war), myself, Dianne, Honor, Roger Howard (a former bomb disposal officer and explosives expert), Elizabeth Elliott, Charles Du Cane, Juanita (our daughter).

Myself, all dressed up ready to go to a Livery Dinner in the City – at which I was poisoned. I even look a bit apprehensive in the photograph.

Honor and our daughter, Juanita.

Honor and I at our Golden Wedding dinner, 10th February, 1991.

in style. Honor and I joined our table in the corner and had an excellent dinner.

At the end of the dinner, the *Pièce de Résistance* was brought in with a fanfare. It consisted of a model in cake and icing sugar of the castle. It must have been about two metres long and a metre wide, and it was really spectacular! The rather awful French party applauded loudly, and indeed they should have done so. It was placed on a table at the end of the room, and then brandy was poured over it, and this was lit. The manager of the parador announced that this was made in honour of the French party and represented '*Le château en flammes*'. There was even more applause, but then the flames from the brandy poured over this wonderful piece of confectionery caught on to a trailing paper decoration, and this on to another. Soon, there was quite a fire at the end of the room. One of the waiters, losing his head, seized a bottle of what I suppose he thought was water, but which was in fact anise, and poured this over the *château en flammes*. It went up with a whoosh and so did the decorations. In fact, the real castle was on fire.

The French party, with screams from the women and oaths from the men, expressed their concern. It was not really going to be their day! Two more waiters rushed in with foam extinguishers, and soon the fire was put out, but so was the *château en flammes*. There was a moment of total silence, and then Honor said in perfect French, '*Alors, maintenant c'est le château sous la neige.*' ('So, now it is the castle under snow.') With the distorted sense of humour which we both had, we thought this very funny. So did the Spaniards, but the French were not amused.

Later in the evening, the French had moved into another room, where their hostess was giving out presents from underneath a tree. We were kindly invited in by the manager and his charming wife, the chef and other members of the staff of the hotel. When Madame had distributed all the presents there was one left over: a pigskin briefcase, clearly intended for the ambassador who by this time was probably at Madrid Airport waiting for his flight back to Paris. For a moment Madame hesitated; then, coming up to me, she said, 'Well, at least you look like an ambassador, so you had better have this.' I have still got it, although one of our cats peed in it, I don't think that he approved.

All this, though, was to lie in the future. I have only mentioned it now as I was writing about the Castello de Oropressa.

On four or five occasions we went fishing on the Eo river between Las Asturias and Galicia in the north-west of Spain. This was a most beautiful river which ran through pine forests and into a series of huge rock pools on its way into the flat, marshy ground and finally to the sea. Honor and I went there by ourselves two or three times, but once our old friend John Scott joined us there and also our son, Marcus. We always had the same ghillie, whose name was, rather surprisingly, Mr Chamberlaine. Every year we caught five or six salmon during the week. Honor had the job of catching our dinner for every evening, and she never failed to bring back between a dozen or two dozen good trout. It was a most beautiful place and one to which we often dreamed of returning once we had left Portugal. Alas, we never did.

Portugal

In those days there used to be excellent shooting in Portugal. The rice fields were filled with snipe, and the wood and fields of the Alentejo were alive with partridges. Honor accompanied me when I used to go shooting at Melides and up the Tagus at Abrantes. After the revolution in 1974, all the shooting reserves were declared illegal. Enormous parties of people from the towns came by bus, and in an orgy of destruction they killed nearly everything. The communist thugs from Setubal and other towns shot the partridges in their nests in the breeding season with Kalashnikov automatic assault rifles; they burnt large areas of woodland and systematically killed everything that moved in the way of wild game. Now, more than twenty years later, it has only just begun to recover in a few isolated pockets.

However, then it was quite different; with a group of friends we took a little syndicate shoot down near Ourique in the Alentejo. It was quite small, but it was full of partridges, as well as rabbits, some woodcock and pigeons. It had one major disadvantage: to reach it we had to cross a river, either on slippery stepping stones (which when there was much water coming down the river could not be seen), or alternatively in a mule cart. It was totally informal and enormous fun. We used to have our luncheon in the little farmhouse on the property; this invariably consisted of scrawny chickens which had been atomised. I do not know how they did this, but it looked as if a hand-grenade had been placed in them, as there were splinters of bone and shreds of meat all mixed up with a glutinous rice. It looked – and was – really rather nasty, but we all enjoyed it, and the many days we spent there were amongst the happiest of our lives.

My father died in 1961, so I went to Cannes where he was then living to bring him to England. He was desperately ill with arteriosclerosis, and I was told by the doctors in France that it was a hopeless case and that nothing could be done. Certainly, they did nothing. He was in an extremely expensive nursing home. Every morning the professor would come on his rounds and say, 'Well, how are we today?' My father, who had by this time developed gangrene in his feet, used to say, 'I am in a good deal of pain.' The professor, accompanied by a gaggle of junior doctors and nurses would then say, 'Well, perhaps you should take two more aspirins.' He would then leave. Each visit would be billed to my father, costing fifty pounds a day for a two-minute visit. Fifty pounds in those days is the equivalent of at least four hundred or five hundred pounds today.

The problem that I had was getting my father back to London. He could not walk at all, and I had to make special arrangements when I discovered that the aircraft were pressurised at six thousand feet. At that height the blood would rush into my father's eyes and blind him, and I was not sure that his heart would stand it either. The airline was extremely reluctant to take him, but eventually I was able to persuade them to do so. We left the nursing home in a French ambulance driven by a homicidal maniac, who with flags flying and siren blasting drove to the airport at Nice at the speed of light. I managed to get my father on to the aircraft, and we took off. It was a brilliantly sunny day, and as we climbed up over the French Alps, we were greeted by the wonderful sight of the snow fields below and the mountains glistening in the sun.

My father was enchanted, as he had not flown since the First World War. Alas, it did not last very long before he began to have trouble with his eyes and had to have oxygen. I was thankful when we landed in London and were able to get him into a hospital. There, I think they did what they could for him. Once again, various specialists at astronomical expense gave him what treatment they could, but he was seventy-three and had miraculously lived for more than fifty years since the terrible accident he had as a young man. Ever since then he had been in pain, sometimes intense, but he retained his spirit until the end. I miss him greatly.

I inherited what remained of his money and possessions as well as his titles. Shortly before he became terminally ill, he had made a sentimental journey to see the castle of our ancestors in Tuscany. He had gone by car, but once in Italy the Italian driving had so alarmed him that he had driven into a field; then from a telephone in a house nearby he had called for a taxi from Cannes to pick him up and drive him on to Florence and for another driver to take his car back to Cannes. He travelled with a special suitcase containing one hundred thousand Swiss francs, a litre bottle of liquid paraffin to keep his bowels open, a small bag of gold sovereigns to bribe the natives if necessary and a .45 service revolver to shoot them if all else failed. He put up at the Excelsior Hotel in Florence. Alas, the luggage porter who had carried this suitcase up to his room must have dropped it, as the bottle of liquid paraffin had broken and soaked the roll of Swiss bank notes, reducing them to an oily, mushy ball. The following day he had the very greatest difficulty in changing some of this money into Italian currency at the bank.

He wrote to me about this and to complain that the Italians drove up on to the pavements in the narrow streets, and that anyway Florence was 'full of Italians'. I do not know who else he expected to find there, and as he was himself partly Italian, I always found his xenophobia rather strange.

Honor and I moved into a charming house in Monte Estoril. It was quite a big house, with a drawing room over twelve metres by eight metres, a large dining room and a hall with a pretty spiral staircase leading up from it. Upstairs there was our bedroom, a big landing, another bedroom, a bathroom and outside an enormous terrace. The kitchen and downstairs cloakroom led out of the hall, and on the ground floor there were another three bedrooms, a huge hall, a cupboard room for glass, china and so on, a wine cellar and a large store room, as well as another bathroom. Outside there was a laundry and further store rooms for wood and so on. There was a nice garden and a beautiful view of the sea. With the furniture from Ireland and the furniture which I had inherited from my great-uncle and my father, we furnished the house very well. We had some nice pictures: two Constables, a Van Husum, a rather doubtful Vandyck, a Springer, a Westerbeck, a beautiful Verschuur, the Gaudenzi portrait of Honor, a Bonington, a Maltese still-life in the dining room, some portraits of my ancestors and various other pictures.

It was really a very pretty house, and Honor furnished it and decorated it beautifully. In fact, it was one of the prettiest houses I have ever seen. In our bedroom we had furniture which had once belonged to the Princess Pauline Borghese. There was my collection of antique firearms, another of Samurai swords, a collection of some twenty-four eighteenth century fans, and some very beautiful furniture – English, Dutch, French and Italian, but which all went together very well indeed.

We were very happy at Avenida Sanfre in Monte Estoril, and there we were able to entertain our friends and to live a very good life indeed.

Honor told me that she would like her own car, so I bought for her a 3.5 litre drop-head Bentley which I found in a garage in Lisbon, abandoned and in poor condition. I had it largely rebuilt, and in it we travelled all over Europe for very many years. It never gave us any trouble at all. It had belonged to a friend of mine, Harry Ruggeroni, and it had been the car which brought out from France a quantity of platinum bars which were eventually sold and which financed, from Britain, the beginning of the Free French Air Force. It was, I think, the most beautiful car I have ever seen, and it gave us infinite pleasure. Alas, it was rather too heavy for Honor to drive herself, so I drove it for her.

When we came to leave Portugal after the revolution, the new authorities did not want the car to leave the country. Honor went to the Automobile Club and they asked her what it was worth. She replied, 'Well, it is not going at the moment and it requires a number of spares before it will. These are not available in Portugal, and the new government has, quite rightly, forbidden money to be sent abroad to buy inessential things such as spare parts for old cars. What would you give me a the car which will not go more than a few yards and for which spare parts are unavailable and cannot be bought from abroad?' The official replied briefly, 'I would not buy it.' Honor persisted, 'But if you did, what would you give me for it?' The official replied, 'Nothing!' Honor then said, 'Well, you have answered your own question. It is worth nothing.' The official said, 'But if you want to take it to England, and I have to give a permit, I must put in some value.' Honor suggested two hundred pounds, and the official agreed and issued the permit.

Two days later, we went to the docks in Lisbon with the car. On the steering wheel there was an instrument with which it was possible to advance or retard the ignition. We put it right back and advanced into the customs area with a succession of backfires and loud chug-chugging noises. I stopped the car and rushed into the customs office. I got hold of the senior customs officer there and insisted that he should come and have a look at the car. 'It is extremely interesting,' I chattered. 'You see, it has two carburettors, two magnetos, and this is a really fascinating engine. Of course it does not go at the moment, but it is really a most interesting car for people who are interested in old cars.' The customs officer was not. He made that quite clear, but I would not let him go. 'No, don't go,' I said. 'You really must see this, it has a one-shot lubrication system.' The man wanted his luncheon, and he wanted to get away early as there was some communist celebration that he wanted to attend. 'To hell with your old junk,' he said, and marked it all over with chalk to indicate that it had been inspected and cleared together with its contents.

A few minutes later a couple of really nasty-looking men appeared and wanted to inspect the car. I told them that it had been inspected and cleared by the head of the customs and pointed to the chalk marks. Reluctantly they withdrew, and with the ignition still right back, we proceeded in a series of leaps and bounds accompanied by backfires up the ramp and into the car ferry bound for England. In it there were all Honor's jewels and my matched pair of shotguns and also my son's, together with many other goodies. This was in 1975, and very many years into the future.

Kai II did not have a long life. He died of some sort of tuberculosis. He was an immensely brave and delightful cat, and we missed him greatly. He was replaced by Tao, a Siamese who had been abandoned by his owners when he was just a kitten. He came to live with us and remained with us for twenty-three years. Eventually he earned the title of 'The Venerable Tao'.

While we were still living in Cascais, we had made contact with Sibille again. Karl Herzog had gone off to Burma and had been murdered by bandits in the Shan States. Sibille had remarried, and she and her husband, Dieter Sturken, came to live in Cascais, by chance taking an apartment over the garage where I kept my old Allard. It was certainly the only one in Portugal, and Sibille recognised it immediately. Through the owner of the garage, Senhor Marques, she got in touch with us again and was to remain one of our closest friends for the rest of our lives. Alas, her marriage to Dieter Sturken was not to last very long. They had a son, Nico, but there were to be many terrible rows between them, and while we tried to lend a sympathetic ear to both sides, it was soon clear that this union would not last. Sibille then married Kiko Costa Lobo; he too was to become a very close friend, a companion on most of our shooting expeditions and the organiser of the syndicate shoots in which we as well as Sibille and Kiko were to participate. We were a group of very good friends: Léon Paumier, a Frenchman who was one of the most amusing men I have ever known, Tony and Anne Ruggeroni, one of the Salema Reis brothers, Ione and Bill Tanton, Jorge Goncalves Pereira and Julio Bastos, who had a marvellous property near Elvas where we went very many times. There was also Nuno Brito Aranha, Joao Mexia, and we were joined by guests such as the Count of Galveas, the Count of Barcelona, John Scott and Bob Lee.

There were others, too, and as I have kept a game book all my life, I look back on those days with very great nostalgia. Honor was my constant companion. Later, when I once caught my loader sticking the barrels of one of my guns into the mud before handing it, reloaded, back to me, I got rid of the loader, and thereafter Honor always loaded for me.

Chapter Five

War in Africa

Angola

In 1961 war broke out in Angola. This was to open a new chapter in our lives. As I have mentioned, I had written a book on the Mau Mau rebellion in Kenya, and when in March 1961 the same thing did in fact happen to the Portuguese in Africa, Salazar (the prime minister, who apparently read everything), asked me to go to see him. I did, and he said, 'I have read your book on the Mau Mau. Will you go to Angola now and report back to me personally what you think will happen there, and also what is actually happening now?' I consented to this, but only if Honor could accompany me. This was agreed, so one day we found ourselves together with a lot of troops in a Lockheed four-engine aircraft on our way to Luanda.

We stayed at the Inter-Continental Hotel in Luanda, and I cannot say that it was anything very wonderful. There was an all-pervading smell of drains, it was grubby and the food was more or less inedible. However, it was the best that there was, as Luanda was a city under siege, with some fighting in the former Belgian Congo and in Katanga still going on. Holden Roberto and his largely Marxist guerrillas had started burning down farms, massacring blacks and whites and attacking villages and small towns all over the north of Angola. Much of the country there is covered with thick elephant grass, providing ideal cover for guerrillas to move about, lay ambushes and hide. They had penetrated as far south as the outskirts of Luanda, and it was even dangerous to move more than three or four miles from the centre of the town. Hashish, which grows well in much of the frontier area with the Congo, was liberally used by the guerrillas. Only that can explain the incredibly bestial tortures and murders which they inflicted on the farmers, both white and black, and all those who stayed loyal to them. I myself saw pregnant young white women who, having been raped nearly to death, were slit open and hanged with their own guts from trees, and there were other obscenities even more horrible.

On arrival in Luanda, we went to see the General Officer Commanding in Chief, a most charming man called General Andrade e Silva. He was probably one of the best officers in the Portuguese Army, and I found him extremely well informed, highly intelligent and doing what he could to protect the country. Alas, the Portuguese were totally unprepared and never believed that what had happened in other parts of Africa could ever happen to them.

He arranged for me to fly out on a general reconnaissance of the north, and I landed first at Maquella do Zombo near the border with the Congo. It was impossible to move out of Luanda without a major escort of troops, even though they were stretched very thinly on the ground. The airstrip at Maquella do Zombo had been cut out of the elephant grass and resembled more a switch-back railway on a fairground than any landing ground for aircraft. We bounded up and down, coming to rest at the far end with the propellers of the Nord Atlas twin-engine plane churning in the elephant grass.

The town had been attacked but comparatively little damage done. There were many refugees from the fighting in the Congo and a splendid Franciscan priest, who seemed to be running everything at once. To my very great surprise, some six months later when I was on a short visit to England I came across an old newspaper with a date-line of Maquella do Zombo and the dates when I was there myself. This described in some detail a massacre carried out by Portuguese troops at that time and in Maquella do Zombo itself. It certainly never happened. It was backed up by photographs, which I eventually identified as having been taken months previously in Katanga. There were no foreign journalists in Maquella do Zombo, nor could they possibly have got there.

I went out several times with army patrols. On one occasion we ran into an ambush. The elephant grass grew right up to the dirt tracks, and ambushes were only too easy. There was firing ahead. My jeep stopped, and I got out to get under cover as quickly as possible, as I presented a most tempting target sitting in the vehicle. As I ran past the side of the car, there was a tremendous bang and a large quantity of old iron slammed into the side of the jeep just beside me. I was very much surprised, but eventually saw my would-be assassin in the elephant grass about fifteen feet away. I considered this a most unfriendly act, so I shot him with my .45 Colt and took away his gun. It was what was called on the west coast of Africa a 'Dane Gun'. I don't know why. It was a muzzle loader, cap-fire of some considerable age, loaded with black powder, screws, bolts, nails, and so on. It was really quite a dangerous weapon, and had the man been further away, he would almost certainly have got me. I have kept it as a memento ever since.

On the following day, on another patrol, we ran into another ambush. This time a terrorist came rushing out of the elephant grass, and with a machete he chopped the head of a Portuguese soldier clean off. The soldier was standing next to me, and he had started firing his sub-machine gun as soon as he saw the terrorist running at him. I could actually see the 9 mm bullets hitting the terrorist as he came on, but they seemed to have no effect on him whatever. He rushed across the track and into the elephant grass on the far side. I took a snap shot at him as he vanished. When the action was over, we searched the areas and found the man with nineteen 9 mm bullets in him; he had been so high on *bhang* (unrefined hashish) that he had not felt a thing. On occasions, the terrorists would be up the trees when we went into a wooded area, and I later recommended at least one pump-action shotgun using SSG to be used by each section. I know that this had been used successfully against the Mau Mau, but when I got back to Lisbon I was unable to convince the army staff that a 'sporting gun' would be useful in Angola.

The Portuguese Army had little experience or training in this sort of war. For hundreds of years they had been in Angola and Mozambique, and they had little or no experience of any sort of serious fighting. Virtually none of the officers or men had ever seen a shot fired in anger before, and we took unnecessary casualties due to their inexperience. On the other hand they were very brave and also had the ability to live and fight under conditions which would have been intolerable to other European troops. They would go for days on a bag of dried beans, which they soaked in water contaminated with bilharzia. At night they would tie themselves up into the trees and sleep like that. They were capable of covering on foot and through the elephant grass and thick bush distances of over one hundred miles on a three-day patrol. They would then have two days rest and go out again.

Casualties were buried where they fell, but only too frequently terrorist groups which came on the scene several days later would dig up the bodies and eat the hands and fingers, being the tastiest parts. The troops had no comforts of any sort, no books to read when off duty, no footballs, nothing to entertain them in any way. This was another recommendation that I was able to make to Salazar when we got back to Lisbon, and the situation gradually improved.

The vehicles were for the most part unsuitable for this sort of warfare. There were a few Panhard armoured personnel carriers, but these had difficulty in getting through the elephant grass; made a very great deal of noise and were insufficiently armed and armoured. There were some light reconnaissance scout cars which were useful. The troop-carrying trucks might have been suitable for carrying troops and also military equipment on manoeuvres in Portugal in peacetime, but they were totally unsuited to a country where ambushes could be round every corner. First the tailboard had to be let down; then the troops had to jump out, all bunched together and presenting a perfect target for an enemy machine-gunner. The tanks were totally useless in the elephant grass, in any sort of marshy ground and on steep, rocky mountains, as well as in the rains when the unmade earth, laterite tracks turned to seas of mud. There were very few radios; those that existed were of Second World War vintage and in many cases completely useless. I was able to prevent troops in contact with the enemy from washing much and above all from using soap. The terrorists, as we had discovered in Kenya, were capable of smelling soap up to one hundred metres away – also cigarette smoke could be smelt a long way away.

I suggested the use and training of pseudo gangs, which had proven to be invaluable in Kenya, and the Portuguese began the training and use of the Flechas, native Angolans, usually under their own officers, who fought very well. Unfortunately, the actual use of the pseudo gangs had to be abandoned after two or three groups of Angolan Portuguese were shot up by their own troops, who mistook them for terrorists. Most of the small towns and villages in the north of Angola at this time were under constant attack, isolated and surrounded. They could only be reached by air, and on a number of occasions the aircraft could not land to let reinforcements disembark. In desperation the Nord Atlas would touch down, brake sharply, and the troops would throw themselves out of the rear end of the plane when it was still travelling at thirty to forty miles per hour. The aircraft would then roar off at full power and become airborne again. There were a few broken arms and legs, but surprisingly few, and the reinforcements were able to help beat off the attackers until more substantial help arrived.

On another occasion we flew over Nambongongo, which was held by the terrorists. Between there and Bembe we saw a homestead being attacked. The Nord Atlas was unarmed, and we could do nothing to assist, but some twenty miles away there was a military garrison actually at Bembe. We decided to throw a message down to the people in the farmhouse that we would fly on to Bembe and get a patrol sent out to rescue them. An empty lemonade bottle was found, and the pilot scribbled the message. He then asked me to take over the controls of the aircraft, bring it in as low over the tops of the trees as possible and straight over the farmhouse, and then pull it up so as to miss the trees on the other side of the clearing. The people in the farm had put out a large SOS in white stones, and it was clear that they were in a very bad position.

I had taken flying lessons at Brooklands before the war, but had not got my pilot's licence. I had flown aircraft once or twice since in emergencies, but I had never flown a twin-engine aircraft or anything of that size. However, the pilot said that he needed to be able to lean out of the side window to drop the bottle as near the farmhouse as possible, as otherwise the people would never be able to get it and get back again inside the house. We circled and the pilot said, 'Now, take her.' I missed the tops of the trees coming in – I don't know by how much. The pilot leant out and threw the bottle, which landed almost on the doorstep of the house, and I pulled the machine up steeply with the engines at full power. I think that we were lucky to have missed the treetops at the end of the clearing, and I am sure that the pilot never knew in what danger he was. We flew on to Bembe and alerted the garrison, and a patrol set out immediately. We heard later they arrived too late and the farmer, his two sons, his wife and four farmworkers had all been hacked to death.

There were things which I saw in Angola which I would rather forget. I am not squeamish, and the things that I saw in the war and in the forced labour camp and other con-centration camps during the Second World War had, I thought, hardened me against anything, but in Africa primitive barbarism and savagery, heightened by fanaticism and drugs, produced sights which are too revolting to describe.

One day, I flew in to Negage with General Rezende, who later became a close friend. It was quite an important air base, and there were a number of old fighter-bombers parked there. We were standing on the runway, having landed only about half and hour before, when one of these single-seated aircraft took off on a regular patrol. I don't really know what happened, but I think that the brakes on one wheel must have locked in some way, because as the plane was gathering speed down the strip it suddenly started to slew to the left. The pilot cut the engine, but it was too late. The plane smashed into two others parked on the edge of, and halfway down, the runway. We all ran to it as fast as we could to try to get the pilot out before it exploded. He, poor chap, had his throat cut with broken glass from the windshield. We got him free from his harness, and he was still alive as he was pumping blood all over us. I fear that he died shortly afterwards. I found that my camouflage jacket was literally soaked with blood. I was not a very pretty sight. We had to take refugees out that day, and it was like a sort of telephone box game packing them into our aircraft. It was a Dakota, and I would never have believed that so many people could get into it, let alone that we would be able to take off; but we did and got safely back to Luanda. By this time it was pretty late, so before going in to see Honor at dinner, I went to the washroom to try to clean up a bit.

It was there that I first met Kiko Costa Lobo, who was after to become a great friend. He looked at me in horror and asked where I had come from. I told him and he went quite pale. He then said that the following day he was to be posted there.

The accident at Negage had happened at about 3.00 p.m., and it seems that Honor exactly at that time had seen me quite clearly covered from head to foot in blood. She had naturally assumed that it was mine. The vision faded, but she had been desperately worried the whole afternoon, and when the aircraft came in more than three hours late she had begun to fear the worst.

While I was playing soldiers in the north, Honor was going round the hospitals. She knew quite a bit about this, having worked in hospitals during the war. She found them generally in a pretty poor state: they lacked equipment of every sort and were of course never set up to deal with the military and civilian casualties which were now pouring into them. She made lists of the medicines and equipment most urgently needed and talked with the overworked doctors and nurses. It was a depressing job, and she was almost glad to get out of the town to the leper colonies. Although malaria had been wiped out in Angola, leprosy was still a scourge. The leper colonies were better managed and had better facilities than the hospitals, as the war had little effect on them and the numbers of lepers had not increased. On the whole they were satisfactory and were doing a good job. What was most certainly not satisfactory were the private hospitals on the very large estates, like Tentativa, where they had refused to take military casualties, although they had ample facilities and infinitely better equipment and medicines than in the hospitals in Luanda. These estates were still being run as private fiefdoms, and one of the recommendations which Honor made was that they should be commandeered by the Commander-in-Chief for use by both military and civilian casualties of the war as well as estate workers. This recommendation was later implemented and did not make Honor very popular with the immensely wealthy owners of these huge estates, who rarely ventured outside Lisbon and Estoril.

It was a disgraceful fact that, with some very honourable exceptions, too many Portuguese had enriched themselves beyond the dreams of avarice and who, having established model plantations with excellent facilities for their workers, when the war came were reluctant to open these facilities to the military. Their attitude towards the army was one of indifference or even a parsimonious hostility.

Salazar was to take draconian measures to stop this on our return.

Honor also started to make a map of the ethnic areas in Angola based on tribal traditional boundaries and the ethnic languages and tribal beliefs of each area, irrespective of the Catholic overlay which had been introduced during the many hundreds of years during which the Portuguese had been there. This was something which had never been done before and which was to prove useful in the future.

We both continued in our various roles until the time came to leave. There was one incident only two or three days before we left when a friend of ours took us to a restaurant on the outskirts of Luanda. It was, in fact, outside Luanda to the north and considered to be slightly risky, as terrorist groups had penetrated almost into the outskirts of the town. We were assured that it was a wonderful *churasco* (sort of barbecue) restaurant, and we arrived there without incident to find we were alone. The dinner was up to expectations and a welcome change from the food in the Inter-Continental Hotel, with the miasma of drains lurking in the air. It was an open-air restaurant and uncomfortably far out from the town. We had nearly finished our dinner when the bottle of wine which I was pouring was shattered by a shot fired from the edge of the bush about forty yards away. Immediately afterwards two terrorists broke cover and rushed towards us. One had an old sporting rifle and the other a machete. Our host, a Portuguese colonel, was unarmed, as at this time they had a strange mania that to appear armed within the vicinity of Luanda would cause the local population to believe that they were not in control of the situation (which was deteriorating rapidly due to the lack of troops, weapons, vehicles, radios and all the other equipment necessary to deal with a major rebellion and terrorist activity covering the whole of the north of the country). Honor had her .32 Special in her handbag, and I was weighed down with a .45 Colt automatic in a shoulder holster. We got both out in time, and while Honor took one of our uninvited guests, I took the other. We did not stay for another course.

Before we left Luanda, I had several other meetings with the Commander-in-Chief, General Andrade e Silva, and with the director of intelligence, Major (later Brigadier) Renato Marques Pinto, who was later to become a friend.

I think that it was Renato who arranged for me to see and speak to some captured terrorists. I went to the prison to see them. It transpired that the three to whom I spoke could not speak Portuguese. They had come over from the

Congo, recruited by Holden Roberto. (I wondered why nearly all the terrorist leaders had been to schools run by missionaries. This is true of the whole of Africa, which justified my stand against the Reverend Odinga so many years ago at my preparatory school.)

The three in question (one should always be suspicious of anybody paraded to speak to a foreigner under such circumstances) had had training in the former Belgian Congo and had then been brought over the Congo river into northern Angola. I spoke to them in French, which they understood fairly well, and with some difficulty I could understand them. They were curiously simple people: 'Why did you come?' I asked them. 'To make money,' they said. 'How much were you paid?' I asked. They answered willingly, and it was a really very modest sum. They were quietly confident that they would be able to take over Angola without too much difficulty. 'Where did the money come from with which to pay you?' I asked. They did not know, but I later discovered that some had come from American black organisations, some from Sweden and some from European and East European communist sources. The weapons had come from Czechoslovakia for the most part, but some were obtained from United Nations troops in the Congo, who had sold their weapons. I asked them what sort of a life they expected to lead when they had taken Angola, and about this they were all quite certain. 'We will go to the banks,' they said. 'There we sign cheques and draw whatever money we want.' I said, 'But supposing that you have not any money in the bank, what then?' They laughed at me and said, 'When we have taken over all the white men's houses, farms and women, we will have plenty of money.'

I asked then what would happen when they had spent all the money, and again they laughed at me and said that they would just continue to sign cheques and that the banks would give them whatever they wanted. I tried to explain that if there was no money in the banks, the banks would not give them money for their cheques. This they refused to believe, saying that this was just a white man's law and that when they had taken over Angola, the banks would give them anything they wanted.

In a way I felt curiously sorry for them. These were simple people who had been duped with lies and propaganda, sent into a foreign country to kill and be killed on the basis of spurious promises. They were totally convinced that what they thought was right, and I could not convince them in any way that they had been tricked.

We left Luanda and headed south on a wonderful air safari in a four-seater plane. We travelled – the pilot, myself and Honor – right down through Africa to Sa da Bandeira in the south of Angola. We saw herds of elephants, giraffes, zebras, lions – and in fact the whole of the wildlife of Africa. It was quite a long flight, and one which we were never to forget. It was like having a vast zoo paraded in front of one in its natural surroundings. It went on for hundreds of miles. The abundance of wild game in those days was staggering, but now, due to war and man's incredible stupidity and greed, it has gone for ever. Thank God, importunate governments and the cretinism of politicians cannot destroy our memories.

Coming in to land at Sa da Bandeira (I suppose that they call it something else now), we were faced by a huge and sheer mountain wall some three thousand feet high. The pilot flew straight at it and at the last moment pulled up over the top. We landed at what was then a charming and very pretty little Portuguese town in Africa. It has, I believe, been totally destroyed by the conflict between the Marxist troops of the government and the rebels under Jonas Savimbi.

Here we were met by Colonel Borges and his wife. Almost on landing, the colonel asked me to give him my .45 Colt automatic, which I did with some reluctance. This was following the Portuguese theory that to go about armed would cause the population in the south of Angola to believe that the Portuguese were not carrying on business as usual. We were taken out to a tourist hotel on the outskirts of the town to the south and west. A nice hotel, but totally isolated. We were invited that night to have dinner with the colonel and his wife at the casino. The casino part had been closed for some months, but the restaurant was still working, and our host gave us an excellent dinner. We were driven back to our hotel that night.

After some years leading the sort of life which we led, one develops a sense of danger. That night, Honor and I had this sense of acute and imminent danger. Colonel Borges had relieved me of my pistol, but I suppose that it had not occurred to him that Honor might have one too. We piled the furniture against the door of our bedroom – the only time in our lives that we did this. I took Honor's .32 Special and another six bullets in my left hand, and we both lay awake all night. The sense of danger became almost intolerable, but the dawn came and nothing had happened.

The next day we went out to Tundavala, a great cleft in the sheer face of the escarpment which falls away over 2,500 feet sheer into the forest below. It was a place of wonder, with a spectacular view right to the sea and also of giant lizards on the rocks. I had talks with the colonel, and there were various things that I had to do there. Again the garrison was quite unprepared and under-equipped to deal with any real emergency. That evening we left again, and only three days later did I hear that a terrorist raid on the town had been arranged for the night that we were there. It would have come in from the south-west, and our hotel would have been the first target in its path. As we were the only people staying there, it is unlikely that we would have survived.

We flew on to Mocamedes and bathed in the warm sea there. It is better not to swim out very far as there are sharks, but we enjoyed this immensely. We then returned to the interior and to the 'Mountains of the Moon'. These are not the Mountains of the Moon of Rwanda Irundi but are nevertheless very beautiful; the forests are wonderful, and we stayed in a small cottage there. We were asked on arrival if we minded having a python living in the roof above us. I enquired anxiously whether there was a secure ceiling and whether the snake could possibly get into our room. I was assured that it could not, and they said, 'If you don't mind, we do not really want to shoot it because it keeps the rats down.'

We said that we did not mind, but I was uncomfortably aware of a heavy body moving about in the rafters over our heads and occasionally of being observed through small cracks in the ceiling. It was a fascinating place; there are mountains of blue marble there, and we had one wonderful picnic in the forest, but this was rather spoilt by the appearance of an uninvited leopard.

We were soon to return to Luanda and to have further meetings with General Andrade e Silva and with Renato Marques Pinto. The general invited me to accompany him on a tour of the extreme south, but I had to get back to Lisbon. This was just as well, as Andrade e Silva as well as Colonel Borges and several other friends were killed there a fortnight later in an accident with their aircraft. We too would certainly have been killed had we not been booked to return to Lisbon.

It took me three weeks to write up our report for Salazar. It was by no means popular in some quarters, as it showed up terrible deficiencies in training, equipment, weapons, vehicles, medical stores and also in preparedness, as well as in the attitude of certain civilian vested interests. However, Salazar accepted it and acted upon it, although not all of his directives were carried out – a good many becoming lost in the bureaucratic mess and parsimony of the fiscal authorities.

We had flown back from Angola in an aircraft filled with wounded troops. Honor was able to help a good deal, as there were only two nurses on the plane, and she was kept busy the whole time. We landed in Portuguese Guinea for some hours and saw a little bit of that country. A great deal of the area near the coast is mangrove swamp and almost impossible country in which to find and fight guerrillas, but at that time there had not been any fighting there. We flew on. It seemed to be an interminable journey, taking some twenty-four hours or rather more.

We flew over Bathurst and then out over the sea, coming in again over the Spanish Sahara and the Province of Aiun. It looks a very desolate place, and Spanish officers who had served there, and with whom I became very friendly later on, told me that it was even worse on the ground than it looked from the air. We flew rather low and were able to see a good deal of the desert and the desolate coast. Then we had to fly out again over the sea to avoid Morocco and then in over Portugal. Two of the soldiers died on the trip, and as there did not appear to be any air-conditioning or pressurisation in the aircraft, (a DC4, I think) it became terribly hot. With the groans and cries from the wounded men (we did not have enough morphine on the aircraft), it was not a very pleasant journey.

I had considerable admiration for Salazar, a reluctant dictator who got fed up with the whole thing twice and went back to teach at his university in Coimbra, having to be brought back almost by force. I cannot say that he was a warm personality, nor a person who would greatly add to the jollity of a dinner table. He was reserved and spoke so softly that it was sometimes difficult to hear him. There is no doubt that he brought stability to Portugal and did a tremendous amount for his country during the very many years that he was in power.

He lived an ascetic and frugal life, to the point where one could dread having a meal with him – there would be almost nothing to eat and drink. He drove – or was driven – in an ancient and battered Citroen; when urged to change it he asked, 'Why? It still goes, doesn't it?' He acted immediately and drastically against any suspicion of corruption in his government, and any minister, secretary of state or under-secretary whom he suspected of inefficiency (or even worse corruption), would find a little note on his table one morning thanking him for his services and telling him that he was relieved of his post. Salazar himself never took a penny from the state for himself other than an extremely modest salary. Alas, he distrusted the military and even disliked them. He was penny-pinching to a degree, and this was one reason why the Portuguese armed forces in 1961 were so unprepared and even unable to deal with the uprising in Africa. It was only with the very greatest reluctance that he authorised spending on the armed forces. It was a pity that he was never able to delegate authority to really competent men who could have succeeded him. He had very few friends and lived the life of an austere professor.

A great deal of nonsense has been written about the fact that he was kept in power by the 'dreaded PIDE', a sort of international and political police combined with a special branch police force, similar to that in Britain, acting as Security for the state. In actual fact, the PIDE were not particularly efficient. I knew a good many of them, and some were good and able officers who were sent out to

Africa to act as an intelligence service, as the army itself did not have any intelligence corps or military intelligence branch. The PIDE, who were certainly not trained to do this sort of work in Africa, on the whole did a very good job, providing good intelligence about enemy and terrorist movements and intentions. Some of the officers left in Portugal were incompetent, some stupid, and virtually all the best ones were sent overseas to Africa. This was to prove to be one of the main factors which enabled the revolutionaries in Portugal to take power on 25th April, 1974.

In the autumn of 1961, Honor and I went to England for the children's holidays. Marcus, our son, had left Stowe and was at university in Canada, as he wished to train as a geologist. Our daughter, Juanita, had I think just left Chatelard in Switzerland, where she had learnt good French and obtained her Swiss silver medal for skiing. We were all invited up to Scotland for a fortnight's grouse shooting which we all very much enjoyed, and Marcus got some salmon fishing on the Eden.

Then we went back to Portugal and to the CEDI meeting at the Escorial. During this time I wrote a book about the war in Angola; in fact I wrote two. I also met Garcia Arias and was invited to give a lecture at the Spanish War College at Zaragossa. This was a rather terrifying experience as it took place in a very large theatre.

I was instructed to meet at some enormous building, where I was introduced to a plethora of senior officers and escorted down endless echoing stone corridors to an entrance into the theatre, where with a tremendous stamping of feet and slapping of rifles, sentries threw open the doors, and I was ushered into the huge theatre. God knows how many officers there were there – probably some two thousand. I was introduced and advanced to the podium – but the microphone did not work.

For the next two hours I had to shout as loudly as I could in Spanish in order to be heard at the back of the auditorium. With my last sentence my voice died completely, and I was virtually unable to speak for the next twenty-four hours.

At that time I incurred the wrath of the British embassy. I had been much opposed to the British government's official line with regard to the handing over of all the Portuguese overseas territories to a 'one man, one vote' type of democratic government. Having just come back from Angola and Guinea and having seen atrocities which had turned even my stomach, I did not think that giving a vote to drug-crazed Marxist guerrillas was a very good idea – or for that matter to people whose education and resources were so very primitive as those whom I had seen in various parts of the country. The sudden handover of power to a majority or to the native peoples has had a terrible history in Africa.

Many millions have died either by civil war or starvation and before handing over, I believed then and still believe, it is necessary to have a trained local administration made up entirely by the black majority, or with a trained colonial administration prepared to stay on and hand over slowly while training up local people to take their jobs. Democracy does not sit very well on the shoulders of African dictators, and there have been many of them – such as Idi Amin. On the whole the French have handled colonial withdrawal better than either the British or the Belgians. It is to be hoped that the Republic of South Africa will prove an exception, and that with a wise and moderate leader in Mandela sharing power with some of the white South Africans and their trained administration of coloured people of mixed race and Indians, the future for them will be brighter than it was for the people of Uganda, the Southern Sudan, Nigeria, Rwanda and so many other

African states to which instant independence brought death and misery. Even in India, the partition was too hasty and resulted in terrible massacres.

Back in Portugal

The embassy thought that I was interfering in affairs which were none of my business, but in this they were wrong to some extent. I saw in the army the resentment which was engendered by pressurisation and sometimes by folly such as when it was proposed to give a dance in the embassy with the proceeds to go to 'both sides'. To the Portuguese this meant that their oldest ally intended to give money derived from this dance to terrorists who had hanged pregnant Portuguese women by their own guts from trees and had committed unspeakable barbarities, some of which I myself had witnessed. I was able to get this stopped, and thereby I believe I prevented the embassy from being burnt down by infuriated crowds.

A series of terrible disasters began to overtake the embassy and consulate. The consul general, who took a particular dislike to me, fell down dead, and various other disasters overtook the embassy and its staff. I was blamed for these events, and it was actually believed that I had used black magic to bring them about. There was at that time a film showing in Lisbon about somebody who had a pet cat. He used to lie in bed and put the cat on his chest and say, 'Now then, Puss, you have got to arrange for so-and-so to fall ill or to have an accident.' The cat (which was a sort of familiar) used to cause these disasters. The story was spread that this was exactly what I was doing. My dear old Tripitaka was a sort of witch cat, and I was said to shake him and say, 'Come on now, Tripi, do your stuff and bring disaster down on the British embassy and its staff'. This story was largely spread about by an old retired brigadier with huge yellow teeth like a horse and terrible halitosis.

It got to such a stage that they actually had an exorcism service held in the British church to exorcise my malign influence and black magical powers. I know that this seems incredible in this day and age, but it is a fact. Naturally I did not attend the service myself, but its occurrence was reliably reported to me.

There must be comparatively few people who have actually been exorcised, and I did not feel a thing!

Like my dear old friends Nicholas Elliott and John Scott (as well as Charles, Duke of Saint Albans), I have never had an exaggerated respect for civil servants. Many do not feel themselves to be servants of the public and quite a few are not even civil.

There are so many other people whom I should mention when writing memoirs: people like Colin Beer, a staunch and very loyal friend for more than thirty years. Likewise Peter and Minnie Paiva Raposo, Mary Black and Rudy Paumier. We used to send out some three hundred and fifty Christmas cards every year to friends all over the world, and if they are not mentioned in these memoirs I ask their pardon and assure them that it is not because they are out of my thoughts and gratitude for their friendship over the years. The Husums, who lived at Malveira da Serra when we were in Portugal, are a particular case in point, as we had so many happy days with them in Portugal and latterly in London that I can never repay the fun and enjoyment we had in their company and also with Sibille and Kiko Costa Lobo.

I certainly was not popular with everybody, especially amongst some of the more dreary members of the British community in Lisbon. Somebody threw a brick through the window of the British embassy or consulate in Lisbon, and the story was spread that I had done it. In fact I had not, as I do not make a habit of throwing bricks through people's windows. Attached to this brick however was a label which read, 'Here is another one for you to drop.'

In fact the Diplomatic Corps do drop bricks with fair frequency. Sir Noel Charles, whom we liked very much as well as his wife Gipsy, was ambassador in Rome shortly after the war. We were invited to an investiture at the embassy – not that we were to receive a decoration, but several people were, including Monsignor O'Flaherty, a priest in the Vatican who had done the most remarkable work for British citizens and prisoners during the war. There was a long flight of steps down from the embassy into the garden, and those to be decorated were lined up facing this, with Monsignor O'Flaherty on the right of the line to receive a CBE. The ambassador's enormous dog, thinking perhaps that this was a food queue, sat down on Monsignor's right. The doors opened and the ambassador appeared, followed by a secretary carrying the decorations. The sun was in Sir Noel's eyes, and it seemed that he had had a particularly good luncheon. He negotiated the stairs with some difficulty and then, taking the decoration from the secretary, very nearly hung it round the neck of the huge dog. He lurched back just in time to sway forward again and hang it round O'Flaherty's.

On another occasion, another British ambassador had sitting on his right the Princess Torlonia. She asked him, as he was shortly to retire, which of the many countries where he had been 'en poste' he had most enjoyed. He replied that he had enjoyed them all with the exception of Spain and Italy, as he much disliked the people of both countries. The Princess Torlonia said, 'What a pity, Your Excellency, as I was born Spanish and am married to an Italian.' On another occasion another ambassador said that he considered a member of the British community living there to be 'as mad as a hatter' (for which there was some small justification). However this was reported to the man in question, who immediately set about getting to know certain people. His arrangements completed he invited the ambassador to luncheon, and when he came he introduced the other guests saying, 'Your Excellency, may I introduce my friends, Doctor Lupe (pronounced loopy), Mr Batty, Mr Dotti and Professor Madnesse.' The ambassador was not amused and turned on his heels and marched out.

On an even more disastrous occasion we went to a reception in Africa given by a first secretary who was a very good friend of ours and who had a charming, pretty wife. These were in the days before the Pill, and she had recently received a consignment of Volpar gels. These were small, round whitish affairs about the same size as white peppermints. The party began well in the grounds of the embassy. Our hostess had asked her butler and cook to prepare canapés. Alas, in Africa it was necessary to keep Volpar gel contraceptives in the fridge, as otherwise they tended to melt. Honor and I were quite surprised to see a silver tray being handed round with neatly cut little squares of bread in the centre of which were unmistakable Volpar gels. Fortunately our hostess spotted it at about the same time as we did, but it was too late to prevent some of the guests having eaten a few. I gather that they were quite ill afterwards.

Spain and Portugal Again

That winter we had some wonderful shooting at our little syndicate shoot at Cabreiras. I have mentioned that in order to cross the river one either had to use the stepping stones – the river was quite wide – or cross in a mule cart. One evening Honor and I, Léon Paumier and I think two other friends decided that we would return to the cars after shooting in the mule cart. It was already getting dark, and the man leading the mule took it through the wood. Eventually one wheel passed over a great tree root, and as the mule cart was very high off the ground, it tipped over. Honor and I fell out backwards, and with a great cry of 'Merde!' Léon Paumier was catapulted out of the cart. He landed on my stomach. Ione Tanton was thrown into a ravine on the far side, and we were quite extraordinarily lucky not to have had a number of fatal or very serious injuries. As it was we all escaped with only a few bruises. We did not use the mule cart again.

My mother came to stay, and we made expeditions to Spain. I was asked to help an English construction firm to obtain the contract to develop the iron ore mines in the south of Angola and to build a railway from Mocamedes to the mines. This, together with lecturing at the Instituto, kept me busy for the next months and throughout 1962, when we went to the Eo again fishing and stayed with my mother at the villa at Anticoli in Italy. Here I discovered that the local commune had stolen quite a lot of our land with no intention of paying for it. I started a legal action which is still continuing thirty-five years later.

There followed years of an almost idyllic existence. We had our lovely house filled with beautiful things in the Avenida Sanfre at Monte Estoril. They were perhaps the happiest years of our lives. We had our friends to stay with us, and there were splendid parties. We drove down to our little shoot at Cabreiras in the Alentejo, and although it was a pocket handkerchief of a shoot, we probably had more fun there than any other property which we took later. Subsequently we had Marmello, which was much bigger, and there again we had a great deal of fun. We also had Monte Branco, and in the winters, the woods there were alive with pigeons.

Bob Lee and Hunting World

We first met Bob Lee at Lisbon Airport in 1961. We had gone there with our daughter to catch her aeroplane to fly back to school. There had been the usual confusion at the airport, and Honor announced that she was going to the bar to have a drink before we drove back home to Estoril. I found her there some minutes later talking to two men. One was a Belgian whose name was, apparently, Spy (perhaps he spelt it differently, but I suspected that he was well named). We got to know him as Peanuts because whatever sum of money was ever mentioned he always said, 'That's just peanuts.' I don't know what became of him. The other man was Bob Lee, an American who was running a safari business in Angola, where he had a huge hunting concession in the eastern part of the country. Alas, he was not to have it for very long, as guerrilla war was eventually to spread even into this remote area. Bob was later to write a book about this time there, and although we had no idea of it at the time, he was to remain a very great friend for the rest of our lives. He was very interesting about Africa and Angola, and we invited him to dinner a couple of days later at our home. He invited us back to his hotel, the Edward VII in Lisbon, and there we met Diane, a very pretty girl of about eighteen and who was helping him in the business. She too was to become a lifelong friend – virtually an adopted daughter.

Bob was a excellent and very keen shot and had hunted big game in many parts of Africa. He had a remarkable collection of trophies and later was to collect for the American Natural History Museum and explore the deserts of Mongolia and the high mountains of Chinese Pamirs, where no European had been for a very long time.

The following year I invited Bob to shoot with us at Cabreiras, the little shoot we had in the Alentejo. Although an expert rifle shot, Bob had had no previous experience of shotgun shooting. While partridges steamed over his head and a growing pile of empty cartridge cases grew around him, the partridges went on their way unharmed. At the end of one drive a hare suddenly appeared in front of Bob, who hit it. The hare was not to give in so easily and disappeared into the cistus bushes and the cork trees, with Bob in hot pursuit and firing from the hip. Gradually the sound of this epic battle – shots and curses – faded away into the far distance. At last it would appear the hare had become exhausted and surrendered, and Bob reappeared out of the woods grinning like a Cheshire Cat and holding up the 'bunny'. In the years to come, Bob was to become a first-rate shotgun shot – amongst the best that I ever met – and was to go to wonderful shoots in Scotland, England, Spain, Hungary, and elsewhere. However, I rather doubt if any of them gave him the pleasure that he obtained from his 'bunny'.

Bob also came to Marmello on many occasions. This was a much larger shoot which we had some fifty miles away. When he had to give up his safari business in Angola, Bob had started a sports outfitting company in New York. Eventually this was to expand to have outlets all over America, Europe and Japan, and to produce equipment for field sports varying from specially-made guns to clothing of every sort, specially designed tents, camp equipment, glass engraved with hunting motifs, waterproof clothing, riding equipment, specially designed luggage (which not even airlines can break), and a huge variety of things all designed by Bob himself. Hunting World is now a huge business, and Bob has a genius for design. I think that the secret of his success is his meticulous attention to detail: no detail, no matter how small, escapes his attention. On his hunting trips in America and abroad he has tested all his equipment personally, and on one occasion he brought a 'Kalahari

Grill' to Marmello. The trick with this was to use rolled up newspaper as a fuel. One day, when he shot quite a lot of partridges, Bob said the he wanted to cook some on the Kalahari Grill. First we had to get some salt pork, which did not prove to be easy and took some time to find. By then the weather had changed, and it began to rain. Bob and I crouched outside on the top steps leading to the cottage where we stayed, and with some difficulty we got the grill going. That we did at all was a miracle given the rain – apparently in the Kalahari desert it does not rain! We then set about grilling the partridges. It was not a very great success. The sodden newspaper did not throw out much heat, and the howling wind which had got up while we were trying to cook did not help. In fact, I managed to get a rather good partridge (which perhaps had had a rather sheltered position), but most of the others were decidedly underdone.

We had a enormous amount of fun at both Marmello and Cabreiras and some really good shooting. At Marmello we also had two flocks of giant bustards. These are enormous birds, much larger than a turkey but extremely difficult to shoot. They settle on the tops of bare hills and set out sentries. Anybody who approaches within half a mile of them is seen, the sentries sound the alert and the birds take to the air.

One year Bob and I had been trying for several days. I had a 6.5 mm Mannlicher rifle with a telescope sight and a double-set hair trigger. We tried stalking the birds with no success; we tried stalking them with a horse and cart of which they were supposed to take no notice. But our giant bustards knew all about horses and carts. We tried stalking them with a mule, creeping behind it. The bustards were interested; they had never seen a mule with eight legs before. Suddenly the mule kicked, and we had to jump out of the way. This happened several times, with Bob and I jumping about trying not to get kicked and also steering the mule toward the birds. Perhaps the bustards thought that we were putting on an act for their amusement, but eventually they got bored watching us and flew away again. Honor, who was watching us through field glasses almost had a fit laughing.

We tried every sort of trick that we could think of, and none of them worked. On the last day, we were driving back over the property when, topping a rise, we saw two giant bustards barely fifty metres away. They were feeding and seemed oblivious of us. Honor, who was in the back of the Bentley, passed the Mannlicher to Bob, who wound down the window silently. Very carefully he slid a cartridge into the breech and closed the bolt. He got the rifle out of the window, and I was looking forward to roasted bustard for dinner. Alas, Bob was used to big game rifles with a straight trigger pull and not a hair trigger. As soon as he touched the trigger the rifle went off, and the bullet went into the ground five yards away. The bustard looked rather astonished and unhurriedly flew away.

In retrospect I am very glad that we did not ever succeed in shooting one of these huge birds. They are rather rare, although we had well over two hundred on Marmello. Since the revolution they have, I believe, become extinct.

On one occasion, Bob was to bring a girlfriend with him, a New York 'top model'. I must say that she looked rather out of place in her exquisite clothes in the dried up riverbeds and cistus bushes of the Alentejo, but I must give her full marks for her aplomb.

The hotel where we stayed when shooting at Marmello and Cabreiras was not famous for its food. It was really a wayside inn and a pretty primitive one at that. For breakfast the first morning I noticed that Bob's girlfriend's plate contained two slices of fried bacon, a fried egg and three fried cockroaches. She never turned a hair! The next morning there were only two fried cockroaches.

Out final attempt to shoot a giant bustard also came to grief. Bob brought me from New York a 6 mm high-powered Remington with an eight-power telescope. We thought that with that we could probably get a shot from three hundred metres or even further. It was not to be. That year the revolution started in Portugal, and there was no more shooting.

Bob used to come most years, and afterwards, when we had left Portugal, he invited us to stay with him in Montana, where he has a splendid ranch. We had some good fishing in the very fast-flowing Montana river and in the lake at Ennis. Bob is a very good fisherman and was always able to get a few trout. They all had to be put back. I was told that the water of the lake and also river is now so polluted with chemical fertiliser which has been washed in that it is very unwise to eat more than one trout per week – if that. I think that many trout which are landed and then put back probably die and am not at all sure that this is a good conservation policy.

Bob is, like many hunters, a dedicated conservationist. He has set up a foundation, and I believe he is chairperson for conservation of wildlife at the University of Montana.

Crossing the lake at Ennis once, Honor, Bob, Anne and I had with us Bob's ranch manager. The water was a bit choppy, and the boat, which was made of light fibreglass, was bobbing about a bit, occasionally shipping a little water. Bob's ranch manager was a very unhappy man. He turned first white and then a sickly shade of green. I asked him if he felt unwell, as we had been used to the wild seas off the west coast of Ireland and had not noticed anything in particular. The man replied in a tone of infinite gloom, 'I'm a cowboy, not a darned sailor,' and then was violently sick.

We spent many happy days staying with Bob and Anne in Montana – a lovely state, wild and very beautiful.

He is a remarkable man: he has an excellent collection of classic cars and also one of specially made and engraved guns. These will one day be star pieces in a museum. He has built up a very considerable fortune by producing sporting goods of the very finest quality and unique design. He is an author and wrote a second book, *China Safari*, which is enthralling. It recounts his adventures in the most remote regions of western China and in the mountains where that country, India and what was the Soviet Union meet.

Honor and I always remembered our trip with Bob and Anne to the Yellowstone Park. It was before the fire, and I am so glad the we saw it then with buffalo, deer, bears and a whole zoo in beautiful, natural surroundings.

Bob also invited me to go with him as his guest to two or three wonderful pheasant shoots in Scotland. I remember one in particular, as there was an Italian industrialist there who rejoiced in the name of Casanova. I was told that he produced 'bathroom fixtures'. He also had a pair of extremely expensive Italian guns, but alas (perhaps he was having a bad day), like the constipated owl he shot but could not hit. He became more and more furious. He was the next gun to me in the line, and toward the end of one drive, and having missed twenty pheasants in succession, he smashed one of his beautiful guns on a fence post. An Hungarian friend of ours who was with us only made matters worse by shouting down the line so that everybody heard him, 'Casanova, shoot another bidet's length in front!'

All this, however, happened many years in the future, long after we had had to leave Portugal and become nomads. These were golden years. We used to drive down to Seville for the weekend. I can still remember the scent of the orange blossom in Seville and the excitement of the Spanish dancing in the Patio Andaluz. One such weekend, we took the 4.25 razor-edge Bentley and stayed at the Alfonso XIII. The second night that we were there, we went over to the Reina Christina Hotel to watch the Spanish dancing on the roof terrace. We had just finished dinner when the lights on the dance floor grew stronger, the band finished playing and the dancers returned to their tables. There was a sharp rattle of castanets from behind the trellis screen at the back of the stage, and from the wings, a man and a woman stepped out into the brilliant light. The man was dressed in the traditional Andalusian costume of tight black trousers fastened at the waist with a long strip of silk wound very tightly round the body, a white shirt with ruffled lace front and cuffs, a short black jacket or bolero cut short to end at the bottom ribs, high-heeled boots and a flat, wide-brimmed, hard, black hat. The girl wore the Sevilliana costume: long, gaily coloured, flounced cotton, tight at the waist and spreading out over half a dozen or more petticoats, the bodice cut rather high both back and front and with big, flounced sleeves cut off short at the shoulder, leaving arms bare. She was very dark, almost Moorish in appearance, with black hair drawn back into a tight bun and the traditional scarlet carnation above one ear. The guitars throbbed, and the couple began to dance. It was a bolero, and the rhythm swept over the garden and out into the night. The couple turned and twisted, one performing the steps while the other kept time with the castanets. When it came to an end, the two dancers retired and their places were taken by two couples who danced a Sevilliana and a Mollares – quick, light dances, full of grace and movement, swirling colour and the fire of the castanets.

When those dancers had finished, the stage was plunged into darkness, except for a single spotlight which focused on a girl who stood in the middle of the floor. There was complete silence. She stood there alone in the glare of the spotlight, tall, slender and aloof. Her very white skin contrasted with the unrelieved black of her dress. She wore no ornaments of any kind, only a single white carnation pinned in her hair. Slowly, she raised her arms and the castanets spoke. Click-clickity click-click silence. Then again, slowly, deliberately, as if they were asking a question. She stood unmoving and without expression. The castanets spoke more urgently this time. They seemed to have a life of their own, and it was hard to imagine that they had any connection with the figure on the stage. Back and forth, question and answer, growing slowly to a crescendo until suddenly the dam broke and the immobile figure burst into life. Both Honor and I had seen some first-class Spanish dancing from time to time, but this was exceptional. The woman danced with a feverish intensity and with a controlled force which was almost terrifying. Her face changed and became twisted with the agony of physical torture almost beyond bearing. The dance itself was indescribable, sensuous with the heat of uncontrolled passion, demoniac in its wildness and its cruelty, spiritual in that it seemed to move out of space and time, sinuously graceful, beautiful and utterly barbaric. The dance came to an end, the figure once again froze and the light went out. When the light came on again, the stage was empty. Talking about it later, both Honor and I had experienced a similar feeling that this dancing was something inherent to both of us, something that we both felt we knew. We returned to watch it on many occasions.

There are two main types of Spanish dancing: castanet dancing and jondo dancing. In one the dancer enjoys and amuses himself, and in the other he allows himself to be taken possession of by some force outside himself and suffers both torment and ecstasy. The two are diametrically opposed. Castanet dancing follows set steps like any other dance. Jondo is different, as the jondo dancer does not know what he is doing and what he will do next. It is a dance of inspiration, and while once can say that any castanet dance can become jondo if the dancer suddenly becomes possessed or inspired, it is very rare and especially so on a stage.

Whilst castanet dancing is the country dancing of Spain, jondo originated in the area of Cadiz, Jerez and Seville. It has been suggested that jondo came from the Moors, not much earlier than the fifteenth century; but others have suggested it is of immense antiquity. Certainly there is nothing like it anywhere else in the world. There is a legend that somewhere between Seville and Cadiz, the great Phoenician and Etruscan city of Tartesus once stood. Nobody has as yet found the exact site of the city, which was one of the biggest and richest in the ancient world. However, it is known that in the worship of Baal, which at one time must have been one of the main religions of Tartesus, the priestesses danced before the altars and in the smoke of the sacrifices. It is also a fact that the dancing girls of Cadiz were world famous long after Tartesus had ceased to exist.

Those times were glorious: the beautiful drives through Portugal and Spain, which were then still unspoilt and our trips to Granada and Cordoba and through the Sierra Morena.

We took the car on the Italian 'C' line from Lisbon to Genoa and then drove down to Rome. On one occasion when returning in the autumn we ran into a tremendous storm near Genoa. The rain was torrential and continuous, and we found all the roads leading into Genoa blocked by floods. We waited for some hours and decided that we would chance it as the car was heavily loaded and we had a big, powerful engine with a limited slip differential. We came in from the west and only just succeeded. There were some nasty moments as we had empty cars sweep towards us on the floods, dogs, cats and even one human body – or so it appeared in the driving rain and the dark. The following day, we were one of only three cars on the car ferry to Barcelona. At one moment both Honor and I thought that we had taken one risk too many. We gave parties at our lovely home and went to splendid parties given by our friends in Estoril, at Monchique, by Julio Bastos at his beautiful estate near Estremoz and by Oscar and Lillian Husum at Malveira da Serra. My cousin Sir Danvers Osborn visited us and managed to sleep through a really bad earthquake. The ceilings in our bedroom and on the upstairs landing fell down, the walls of our bedroom split and cracks appeared in all the walls. The following morning we saw the sun rise through a huge split in the wall of our bedroom. The landing was full of plaster which had fallen from the ceiling. The noise and the virtual destruction of our home during the night had not apparently disturbed my cousin, who appeared the following morning in his dressing gown and was totally astonished by the fact that much of the house had fallen down during the night!

Trip Through Angola

I began to plan our next expedition to Angola. This time we decided to visit the south, the desert of Mocamedes, and then try to get through the wall of the mountains and the escarpment into what the Portuguese called the 'Lands at the End of the Earth'. This involved a good deal of planning. There had been unconfirmed reports that arms had been landed from Soviet ships in the mouth of the Cunene river, which marks the boundary between Angola and the desert of the Namib.

Honor and I flew to Angola and from Luanda to Mocamedes. There we picked up two Jeeps and a wireless car.

There were a number of local preparations to be made, and I arranged with the Portuguese air force to give us three air drops of petrol and water. Finally all was ready, and we set off through the desert of Mocamedes. This is not a big desert, but it is quite a bad one. The dunes, particularly near the coast, are very high and steep, and we were only able to make very slow progress. Before dawn a mist would come in from the sea and to some extent bind the sand on the dunes, and then we could make some progress. But as soon as the sun came up and the dunes dried off, the sand became shifting and the vehicles started to stick. We carried de-sticking mats with us, but after an hour or two these were more or less useless and we had to lie up for the rest of the day. During the day it was pretty hot, and strangely enough, in the desert there are still flies. At night it became quite cold, and we huddled in our sleeping bags.

There are quite a few sand vipers. These are similar to the asp, and are most unwelcome bedfellows. There are also scorpions which can be equally deadly. However, the nights were marvellous. There is nowhere except the deserts where there is absolute silence. In Europe or America there is always an aeroplane in the distance, or the sound of traffic; only in Africa have I ever encountered absolute silence. Overhead there was a canopy of stars. Again, in the Western world, I suppose due to pollution or damp atmosphere, there are only a certain number of stars which are visible at night even on the clearest nights. In the desert, the whole heavens are blazing with thousands of millions of stars, breathtaking in their beauty. I have written that there is absolute silence in the desert, but this is sometimes broken by a sort of swishing sound. This is the sand moving. One knows that if a person were to remain completely still for several days he would be buried by the sand because the dunes are always on the move.

Finally we got through the sand desert, on to stone desert, and for the first time we began to see animals and in the far distance the blue outline of the mountains.

The first animals we saw were desert oryx, beautiful animals capable of travelling long distances without water; then a desert fox. By now we were driving along fairly fast over a hard desert covered with small stones.

Our first destination was Iona, an outpost at the foot of the mountains where there was a permanent camp with huts, water, food and a considerable degree of civilisation, including an airstrip which supplied it. It was a pretty place, well run and comfortable. The next day we took a trip into the mountains. From time to time there are tremendous explosions from the tops of these mountains: the local people believe that it is the gods who are speaking to them. It is more likely that they are gas explosions, occasionally accompanied by flames but virtually no smoke.

We had been travelling all day in the foothills and that evening came up a long rise. We left the vehicles on the lip of a huge crater ringed with the walls of mountains which must at some time in the remote past have been a great volcano. The crater was about three miles across – or perhaps a bit more – and some six miles long. Down below us were the animals of Africa – there were elephants, two or three prides of lions, hundreds of antelopes of different species, giraffes and several herds of zebras. It was a scene from the Garden of Eden when the world began.

As the sun began to set in a blood-red sky, the grazing animals began to become nervous. The lions emerged from the shade trees and stretched themselves; the night was coming and with it danger from predators. Honor and I stood there in wonder. It was something which we never forgot, and for which I lack the words to describe adequately. There was total silence whilst we were looking down into the valley floor, where already long purple shadows were beginning to creep out from the foothills of the surrounding mountains and spread over the floor of the crater. The zebras herded closer together, the antelopes were nervously moving about, and what had previously been a marvellously peaceful scene became tinged with fear. The whole western sky was now deep red; the sun had gone and a little, chill wind came stirring through the grass.

It was time to be gone. We had a fair way to go to get back to camp, and there were no roads or tracks here. Back at the camp we heard lions coughing somewhere out in the darkness, but the campfire was an oasis of light and warmth.

The following days we explored the region further and made our way south to the Cunene river. The great sand sea of the Namibian desert stretches up nearly to the Cunene itself. It is a bad desert with high dunes but spectacular scenery. We worked our way back towards Iona. We were looking for tracks. Tracks in shifting sand do not last very long, but tracks on a sand and stone desert will last for years. We did not find any, but right on the south-western side of the mountains which then formed the escarpment, we found a tribe of bushmen. They were frightened of our vehicles. It transpired later that they were the first they had ever seen, and the bushmen thought that they were some sort of strange animal. They were living in shelters made from sticks and a little brush wood. These shelters – they could hardly be called huts – were each surrounded by ashes as a deterrent to snakes.

As we approached they vanished into the rocks. We called to them but they would not come out. Honor went forward by herself. She was wearing trousers, snake boots, a khaki blouse and her gun belt; but also she wore a gold bracelet on her wrist and a gold necklace. It was this jewellery which brought out the women of the tribe. First one and then another cautiously approached. They spoke to her, but she could not understand them, and they could not understand her Portuguese. They came closer and closer, and then the bravest lent out and touched her bracelet. Honor showed it to them and also her necklace, and they chattered amongst themselves and then rushed to their huts and came back with their jewellery, mainly consisting of shells strung together, a few beads and animal teeth. Honor admired these jewels. Seeing that no harm had come to their womenfolk, one or two of the bravest of the men appeared from behind the rocks.

They were a little, copper-coloured people, nomads living under the most primitive conditions imaginable, but they seemed to be happy, Honor found herself in the middle of a laughing and giggling group of women and girls. The men were timid and only approached when convinced that we meant them no harm and that the vehicles would not attack them!

Only the headman of the group, which contained perhaps some forty or fifty people in all, spoke some Portuguese. This was necessary for him to communicate with other tribes with which they came in contact on their wanderings.

Some ninety miles further away we came upon the foundations for what must have once been a fairly considerable city, for the most part built of dry stone. The foundations and the building still projecting two or three feet above the ground were not dissimilar to those of Zimbabwe, but nothing was known about this place. The Portuguese knew nothing, and another small group of bushmen whom we met not far away knew nothing.

The following day an aircraft came in low and landed at the Iona airstrip. In this Honor and I flew out towards the sea. We flew very low, hopping over the dunes with a view to being undetected by radar. We skimmed over the top of the last dune and there, anchored off the mouth of the

Cunene, was a Russian 'fishing vessel' festooned with electronic equipment and well inside territorial waters. We circled the ship and I took a number of photographs. Our appearance caused what seemed to be a panic on the Russian ship. People were running about and we then saw them hauling up something which looked suspiciously like a heavy anti-aircraft machine gun. It was time to leave, and we did so instantly.

We flew inland for some way, but there were no signs of tracks on the Portuguese side of the Cunene. However, there did appear to be tracks on the Namibian side, and it is quite possible that SWAPO may have received arms and ammunition as well as other supplies from this Russian source.

Not long after this, we left Iona and started north. We tried to get through the mountains, but that was quite impossible with our vehicles. It would have been very difficult under any circumstances as there was no water and no local people who could act as bearers. Later we often hoped that the gentle bushmen escaped the horrors of the dreadful civil war which was to plunge Angola into misery and starvation and cause the loss of literally millions of lives.

We set off up north, running on sun compass as there were neither tracks nor inhabited places. The Portuguese authorities had given us, before we left Lisbon, a set of maps which turned out to be totally useless. The cartographer, thinking perhaps that large, blank spaces looked rather bad, had marked in tracks and even settlements which not only did not exist, but certainly never had existed.

A day or so out from Iona we came on a desert oryx which had a broken leg. The wretched animal could not move and faced the certainty of being torn to pieces during the coming night by hyenas or lions. I shot it to put it out of its misery and enable it to escape a terribly cruel death. We took the carcass along with us and cut it up that evening. It was extremely tough and not very good to eat. We had built a large campfire as there was plenty of scrub wood about.

We were sitting round the fire after dinner when we saw pairs of eyes reflected in the light of the fire. One can always expect one or two hyenas round a camp, and these animals can be extremely dangerous. They have jaws with which they can sever a man's arm at a single bite, but they are cowardly and will not usually attack unless in a group. It was not long afterwards that we saw a great many more eyes, and they were appreciably closer. In fact they were all round the campfire; I have never seen so many before or since. There must have been one hundred or more of these horrible animals. Attracted by the smell of the roasting meat, they had come from under the escarpment in their scores. They were uncomfortably close, and I fired a shot into the air. They vanished only to reappear a quarter of an hour later. I fired another shot, but this time they were back and closer in a matter of five minutes. The third shot had little effect upon them at all, and our situation was becoming very dangerous.

There were four of us with rifles and we opened fire directly at the eyes, which by now were very close indeed. This was followed by the most ghastly noise, as the living hyenas fell on their dead and wounded brethren and tore them to pieces. I hope I never hear another noise like that, as some of the wounded animals were actually eaten alive by the others. Thank goodness, their hunger satisfied, the hyenas left. We heard no more of them that night.

Moving on, the desert scrub gave way to bushes, acacia thorn and small trees. It became increasingly difficult to maintain direction with the sun compass. We were also extremely hot and very, very dirty. All water was required for the vehicle radiators, and there was a limit to what we could carry. The escarpment lay over on our east, at times visible. Finally we came to a river. It was a glorious sight. First we got the vehicles through. The river was fairly shallow in most places and the water running fairly fast. There was no great problem in crossing over.

Once over the river, we made camp, and Honor started to get our luncheon prepared. Our party consisted of Honor and myself, an Irish friend who had never been out of his home country in his life and two Portuguese friends, one a geologist and the other who had a job working with the military and civilian authorities in Mocamedes. In addition we had an Angolan cook and three driver/mechanics for the vehicles. I have a photograph of our Irish friend taken in the middle of the desert; he has his hands spread out and is saying – only too clearly – 'How in God's name did I ever get to this place?'

We were all extremely dirty, and while Honor was left to supervise an al fresco luncheon with the cook and the three drivers, the four of us went downriver for a couple of hundred yards until we found a perfect bathing place. There was a good flow of water, which meant that there was no bilharzia, and there were a number of shallow rock pools in which we could see that there were no snakes, crocodiles or other undesirables. Here we stripped off, and each choosing his own rock pool, we had the enormous luxury of bathing in the lovely warm water, cleaning and soaking our bodies.

It was delightful, and when I first saw a native with a bow and arrow watching me from the bank, I thought nothing of it. Then I saw another – and another. Looking around I saw that there were perhaps fifteen or twenty of them, and they were not taking much trouble to hide themselves. With reluctance, I climbed out of my pool and went over to the others to tell them that we were being observed. One feels extremely naked when one is totally naked, and I was glad to reach the bank and our clothes and to buckle my pistol round my waist again. We walked back quickly to the vehicles and found a tableau. Honor was leaning up against the side of one of the Jeeps; she was holding her .32 Special and it was pointed at the four Angolans; who seemed to be making determined efforts to touch the sky with their hands.

It seems that not long after we had gone, she started to hear bird calls. She thought nothing of it until she noticed that our Angolan staff were becoming acutely uncomfortable. She asked them the reason and they replied evasively something about the presence of 'bad men'. Not long after this, Honor noticed that the bird calls were very much nearer and seemed to be coming from all directions. It was then that our gallant Angolans got into a huddle and started whispering together. A moment or two later they made a determined rush for the vehicles and that is when Honor drew her gun and invited them to line up with their hands raised as high as possible. They had all seen her shoot at Iona where she broke six lemonade bottles with six shots in as many seconds at twenty metres. They had no doubt that all four of them would be dead as mutton before they could reach the vehicles and make off with them, leaving us to be killed by the 'bad men'.

The natives in this remote part of Angola were known to use poisoned arrows and they had from time to time attacked geologists, cartographers and hunters. We called to them to come out and speak to us, but our repeated invitations were met by silence. Not long afterwards the bird noises were repeated, but closer. A shot from a .375 Magnum brought about instant silence, and I invited Honor to come down to the river and have a bathe there under armed supervision. However she declined, saying that she preferred to remain dirty for a bit longer, and especially so if I would bring her a jerrycan of water from the river which she could use later. We also decided to have our al fresco luncheon fairly quickly and then press on. On the way, and about four hundred yards from where we were camped by the river, we came across a band of some twenty Angolans with their bows and arrows. They did not seem to be very pleased to see us, or our rifles, and did not respond to our greetings.

Continuing on, the bush gradually thinned out and we came across a track which led to a road and then back towards the escarpment. It was clear that we would have to go back to Sa de Bandeira in order to get over it, and this we did. We spent another night in this charming little town, and one day went out to visit Fenkovi, an Hungarian who had a splendid estate there, with the best strawberries I have ever eaten. Honor was also able to take her long delayed bath.

We did not stay long in Sa de Bandeira but set off again south towards the Terras do Fim do Mondo (the Lands at the End of the Earth). This is a strange place, or was in those days. We travelled again on sun compass for five days without seeing anything – no people, animals, water or tracks. We called in an airdrop on the wireless and the Portuguese air force dropped in petrol and oil for the vehicles, one or two spare parts – which we were beginning to need – and also water and some food. We continued on south and east. It is largely waterless land except for some water-holes here and there; in the vicinity of these we saw a good many animals. There were 'wait-a-bit' thorn trees, scrubby acacias and baobabs, but not much else.

However, down towards the Cunene again there is some forest and also one or two settlements. The people here are Cunhamas, while further north and round Sa de Bandeira they are Huambos, who wear the most extraordinary and elaborate hairstyles. Their women pile their hair up into fantastic shapes, plastered with cow dung and decorated with multicoloured beads. There is a fascination about this part of the world; the silence, the desolation and the strange beauty. I fear that much if not all of it has gone now, as there has been very fierce fighting throughout all this region in the civil war. The desert and grasslands are more than likely strewn with broken armoured vehicles and mines, and the people, as well as nearly all the animals, have probably been killed.

Thank God we saw it when we did. It was much as it had been since the beginning of time and something that neither Honor nor I were ever to forget.

We moved east towards Macuso and then north. Macuso used to be a hunting reserve and was filled with game of every sort. In fact the world's largest elephant – actually shot by Fenkovi, the Hungarian – was shot down in the south-eastern part of Angola and is now to be seen in the Natural History Museum in New York.

By now, we had travelled a long way and had been out from Mocamedes for some four to five weeks. It was time for us to strike north and make for Jamba, where there are iron ore mines, an airstrip, a large permanent settlement and even a small town with a good hospital and modern facilities. We spent our last night in the jungle surrounded by the noises of the forest. We heard a leopard cough and further away there were lions. Well before dawn the following day we were on the road, and we drove into Jamba in the morning. We were shown round the camp and the iron mines. These are driven deep into a mountain of haematite. Later, Jamba was to be taken over by Savimbi in the civil war and there was to be heavy fighting in that area. Jamba indicates that it was a major migration route for the elephants. We did not see any as it was the wrong time of year but were told that there were always a certain number around. Probably they have now all been killed, as has most of the wild game of Africa, in civil wars and the massacres, and in political upheavals following the with-drawal of the colonial powers and their replacement by Marxist dictatorships.

We were driving out to the airstrip when an enormous snake reared up in the middle of the track and struck at the jeep in which we were travelling. In fact it came right across the bonnet of the jeep, and had not the windscreen been up it would have come right in amongst us. As it was, it slithered off the bonnet and back down on to the road. We flew to Luanda and that same night got on a plane to Lisbon. The following night we slept in our bed at Estoril. Only forty-eight hours previously we had been in the African bush, sleeping round a fire in the jungle.

Canada

A few weeks later and after I had finished my report for the Instituto, Honor and I flew to Canada to see our son receive his master's degree at his university. He had first gone to McGill, but found that the university was too large. There were several hundred in the Physics classes, and formulae would be flashed on the screen. There was no tuition system and nobody to whom he could go if he wanted further explanation of some point which he did not understand. After his first year, he asked to go to a much smaller university in Nova Scotia. I had never heard of it, but later discovered that Acadia had turned out more Rhodes scholars than almost any other university in the world. In a way this was not surprising, in that there was absolutely nothing to do there other than work. Many of the girls looked like polar bears, and being a Baptist area, it was 'dry'. Honor was disgusted when on our first day there Marcus invited us to a small restaurant at Wolfville. She asked for some wine and might as well have asked for prussic acid. She was stiffly informed that they did not serve wine. 'Well, a glass of beer then,' she said. She was then told that it was either water or milk!

The autumn colours were very beautiful indeed, and we made a number of trips in Marcus's car in the locality. We both appreciated the beauty but found it a strangely depressing place with an enormous number of neat and beautifully maintained cemeteries. In fact every village appeared to have a very much greater number of dead citizens than ones who were still alive. Also the woods were extremely dense, almost impenetrable and very dark. There did not seem to be any wildlife, although I was told that there were deer and many wildfowl on the hundreds of little lakes.

The ceremony of graduation and the conferring of the degrees went off well, and afterwards we were invited to a luncheon. It was not very warm, and Honor was delighted when she saw what she took to be a glass of whisky and soda by her plate. It turned out to be cold tea. We flew on to New Brunswick and from there to Boston, where we met Joan O'Shea, who had been our cook at Bantry in Ireland. She had married an Irish-American and was living in Boston. We had a very happy reunion with her before going on to New York and then back to Lisbon. In New York we stayed at the Pierre Hotel, which we both liked very much, and met old friends who entertained us royally.

Portugal and Travelling

We returned to Portugal, and at about this time the Portuguese gave me a medal as Knight Grand Officer of the Order of Military Merit. This was at that time a fairly good honour and amongst the Portuguese orders ranked second only to the Tower and Sword. It has since become much debased and now more or less comes up with the rations after a certain number of years. They should really have given Honor something as she did more than I. The Spaniards made me a Knight Commander of the Order of Isobel la Cattolica, and this confers certain privileges, such as being able to wear a plume in my hat and to travel about with an escort of cavalry. This second privilege intrigued Honor very much, as it also included that I should be accompanied by my personal priest and that I could wear the robes of the order at all times.

She suggested that we should go to Gibraltar, load up a caravan of mules and donkeys with various things which were cheap in Gibraltar and expensive in Spain, and then wearing my robes, accompanied by a priest and wearing the plume in my hat, we should cross the line into Spain and make a considerable profit from the goods carried by the 'escort of cavalry'. There was also the privilege of building, at my own expense, a Chapel to the Order, but this I did not take up. It was useful, though, as when I wore the button of the Order in my lapel, we were waved through customs and frontier posts in Spain and received priority in hotels, restaurants and so on.

There were certain disadvantages, as I was to discover shortly. One Saturday evening I received a telephone call in Estoril asking me to fly to London the next day.

I went upstairs to my study, packed a bag and collected my passport and traveller's cheques. We had been staying with old friends of ours who own the wonderful old house of Mateus in the north of Portugal. As always when travelling in Portugal, I had a .32 Browning automatic and a box of cartridges for it in my briefcase. I removed the pistol, and early the next morning I went to the airport in Lisbon, eventually arriving in Paris as I could not get on any direct flights to London. I was in a hurry to get to Orly, having come in at Le Bourget, for my onward connection to London. But first I knew that I had to change a traveller's cheque as I had no French money. I waited in the queue to do this and when my turn came produced my passport and the traveller's cheque – only to find that they were Honor's and not mine. I tried to telephone the embassy but there was nobody there on a Sunday afternoon. I searched my pockets and found a little Portuguese money and two pounds in English money. I then asked a taxi how much it cost to get to Orly. I had just enough with one Franc over.

I dashed down and got my bag from the reclaim, and then made a fatal mistake. There was a queue waiting to go through customs. There were two customs officers on duty: one was a man with a queue in front of him, the other was a woman with no queue. So I went to the woman. French women customs officers are a special breed, and she went through everything that I had and found the pistol cartridges which I had forgotten to take out. She called the chief customs officer, a rat-faced man who eyed the button of Isobel la Cattolica in my lapel with distaste. 'I suppose that it was Franco who gave you that,' he said. As there was nobody else who could have done so, I said that was so. He sneered at me with obvious loathing. 'Now, where is the pistol?' he asked. I explained what had happened. 'Do you always carry a pistol when you go to visit your friends?' he asked. I replied that I usually carried a pistol when travelling long distances by car at night in Portugal, and that I had removed the pistol but forgotten the cartridges. He disbelieved every word that I said, and for the next two hours we played 'Hunt the Pistol', looking in litter bins, going through my bags time and again and ripping out the lining, looking in the water cisterns in the lavatories and virtually searching the whole airport. He could not have been more unpleasant, but eventually he said, 'Well, on this occasion you can go, but we will sequester the pistol cartridges and you will have to pay a large fine.' I explained to him that I had no money and only traveller's cheques which were my wife's. He had now become convinced that I was a lunatic, and with a dismissive gesture he said 'Oh, get the hell out of here!'

I got a taxi to Orly and gave the driver all that I had, leaving myself just one franc. I wanted this for a cup of coffee as I had had no food all day. I was then told that coffee cost one franc fifty centimes. It was not my day.

At last I was seated on an aircraft to London and began wondering how on earth I was going to get into London from the airport. It was Sunday evening, my club was closed and the few friends we had in London I knew were away for the weekend. It was not a very good outlook. At that moment a Japanese man appeared with a tremendously long parcel which he had difficulty getting into the luggage rack. He then sat down, introduced himself and produced a visiting card written in Japanese. I was not really very much interested but the man was determined to enter into conversation. He told me that he was going to England to give a demonstration of Japanese archery. I could not have cared less. He then said, 'I have problem with Japanese bow. Japanese bow very long and will not go in bus.' I became interested immediately. 'You will have to take a taxi,' I said. 'I will help you and will persuade the driver to take Japanese bow in taxi into London, and I will even come with you.' He was effusive in his thanks and insisted on buying me a drink. We got the bow into the cab with a bit of it sticking out through the window, and the Japanese archer obligingly dropped me at Boodles, where I had booked rooms for a couple of nights. The next day I was able to go next door to my club at Whites and get some money.

At about this time Alex Hutchens appeared. He was a Texan oil man, and almost a caricature of the genus. He wanted oil concessions in Mozambique and had arranged a consortium of various American oil companies to carry out exploration and drilling there. He asked me to help, and after long negotiations I was able to get a concession for them of the whole of Mozambique. Under this agreement I was to get half of one per cent overriding royalty at well-head on all oil produced. This would have made me a millionaire many times over, and Honor and I spent many happy hours discussing how we would spend our millions. Alas, there were to be many delays, and the consortium drilled three dry holes and then started to quarrel amongst themselves and eventually split up, so our dreams came to nothing. However, there was a huge gas explosion at Pandé in Mozambique, and I have no doubt that there is oil there as well. The Pandé fire lasted for more than a year before it could be extinguished, and Honor and I were to fly near it the following year when it was still burning. It was an awe-inspiring sight, with flames shooting over one thousand feet into the air.

Our Silver Wedding and then to Mozambique

1966 was a special year for us as we had our silver wedding anniversary on the 10th February and gave a big party for all our friends in Portugal, and others who came from Italy, England, Spain and elsewhere. We also planned our next trip to Africa. We flew to Luanda first and there we met up with an old friend, Sir John Biggs-Davison MP. He had been in Luanda for some days, and we had arranged to go on together to Lourenco Marques in Mozambique, which is now called Maputo. There too we met Cedric Salter, who was working in public relations for Toby O'Brien.

We stayed at the Polana hotel, at that time one of the best hotels in the whole of Africa. Lourenco Marques was a pretty town, and from there we made a number of trips south to the Limpopo, where, on the frontier area with South Africa, the Portuguese had a huge agricultural scheme going on which was interesting. We also went north to the port of Beira, which had been used by the Rhodesians as their main port for imports and exports from Rhodesia; but with sanctions declared against the Smith Government and a virtual blockade of the port, the town was suffering a very serious economic depression. From there we flew into Gorongosa, a game park, not far from the Rhodesian border.

There was a permanent tourist camp there which was very well built, with every modern convenience and comfort. From it, we went out in hunting vehicles to look at the animals. These tourist safaris were very well run, and there was an enormous amount of wild game to be seen. The original camp which had been established there some years before, consisting of about twelve to fifteen brick-built houses, had been abandoned when the new and much more luxurious camp was built, and lions had taken over the empty buildings. There must have been fifty or sixty of them there, sunning themselves on the flat roofs and peering out of holes in the walls where windows had been. Some came and rubbed themselves against the vehicles in which we were. I got some photographs of lions only three or four feet away. There were also a number of elephants, Thompson gazelles, antelopes of all sort, zebras, giraffes and virtually all the wild game of Africa.

We spent three or four days there and then flew back to Beira. From there Honor, John Biggs-Davison and our son, Marcus, who had joined us from Rhodesia, flew north. At this time Marcus was at Magdalene College, Cambridge, doing his PhD, but he had just been carrying out some research work in Rhodesia. This time we flew in military aircraft and went to Nampula, where the headquarters of the army were located.

Thousands of terrorists had crossed into the north of Mozambique from Tanzania and over the Rovuma river. They were well equipped with Soviet weapons – Kalashnikovs, machine guns, rocket-propelled grenades and mortars – and they also carried in thousands of mines. Quite a considerable area of the north of Mozambique, stretching from Lake Niassa in the west to well to the south of Nacala on the sea to the east, was largely overrun by terrorists groups. John Biggs-Davison and I flew in a four-seater Dornier to Vila Cabral, an army outpost commanded by one of my former pupils from the Instituto.

He entertained us very well, and the next day we flew on to Lake Niassa. Our pilot, a Portuguese from Goa, was apparently as mad as a hatter. He thought it a tremendous joke to fly as low as possible and straight for a mountain ridge. At the last possible moment, when we were certain to drive straight into the forest, he would pull up, skimming the tops of the trees and screaming with laughter. To add to this hazard, we were flying over enemy territory, and soon our aeroplane looked like a colander, with bullet-holes in the wings and fuselage. I was really very thankful – and so was John Biggs-Davison – when our pilot circled the naval base on the lake and came in to land.

Here the Portuguese had a permanent base on an isthmus jutting out into the lake and five or six motor torpedo boats fitted with 40 mm cannons and machine guns. The base was comfortable and offered excellent conditions, although the cavalry regiment of Portuguese troops that was stationed there for its protection were housed in wretched conditions in a makeshift camp made out of empty four-gallon tins.

Our daughter, Juanita, was by now twenty. She was an exceptionally pretty girl who had a throng of admirers, not all of whom I considered to be in any way suitable. Some of these I had sent to serve their president and country in Angola, Mozambique and Guinea.

When we landed in our bullet-riddled aeroplane, a very smart young officer came forward in immaculate white uniform, saluted and asked, 'Don't you remember me, sir?' He had grown a beard, and I had not recognised him. He was one of those to whom I referred as 'Juanita's creeps'. I had despatched him to this Godforsaken place surrounded by terrorists, hundreds of miles from anywhere. I felt a pang of conscience, but he seemed to bear me no ill will and was apparently quite enjoying himself. He was in the navy and had excellent accommodation. I cannot imagine that any of the army personnel there could have enjoyed it much.

John Biggs-Davison, who had been a Royal Marine Officer, was especially interested in the operations, and we went out several times with troops on the motor torpedo boats, landing troops further up the lake to make contact with the enemy. On occasions we were fired upon from the shore and returned fire from the semi-automatic 40 mm cannons and machine guns, but in fact I never actually saw any of the enemy, as they were well hidden in the forest on the lake shore.

It was time to move on, and with some reluctance we climbed into the remnants of the Dornier. We flew south along the shore of the lake. On one occasion I saw what I thought was probably a group of terrorists, but although the madman pilot (who later killed himself) continued his hedge-hopping, we were not shot at. The terrorists seemed to be to the north and east of the naval station on the lake.

We made one or two more stops, one at an air force base where some very necessary repairs were carried out on our plane, and then flew back to Nampula. There we found that Honor and Marcus had made several rather short expeditions into the surrounding country under escort, but it had been too dangerous for them to go far from the town.

From Nampula the four of us flew down to the coast at Nacala. This is probably the best deep-water harbour in the whole of East Africa, and after the Portuguese withdrawal from Mozambique following the revolution in Lisbon in 1974, the Russians were not slow to turn it into a major navy and aero-naval base of considerable size.

From there we took a motor launch belonging to the governor out to the island. This was Mozambique island, and was the site of the first Portuguese settlement in south-east Africa. They settled there in the fifteenth century and built a huge fort with stone brought as ballast by ships from Portugal. Mozambique island was the base from which the Portuguese carried on their further explorations to the east: to Ceylon, the Islands of the Moluccas, Indonesia and Timor; and to China, Macau and eventually Japan.

The great fortress on the island of Mozambique is still there, and there was a garrison with some enormous seventeenth and eighteenth century cannons. We were met by the governor, who was almost entirely round and like a huge snowball in his white uniform. We were greeted effusively and taken by rickshaw to the hotel, which was really very comfortable. That evening we had a dinner given by the governor in the hotel. It consisted of the most enormous lobster that I have ever seen or even dreamed could exist. It must have been well over four feet long. Alas, I cannot eat lobster, as I have an allergy to most sorts of shellfish. Anyway, I thought that this marine monster would be inedible anyway. I was wrong. Honor told me that it was the most wonderful lobster she had ever eaten, and the others in our party agreed.

The next day she and I bathed, but did not venture out very far as there are sharks about. The water was clear and wonderfully warm. We then went on a tour of the island. It was what I always imagined that a 'Spice Island' would be; in fact the whole island smelt of spices and was covered with tall palm trees. Many of the inhabitants, in fact the majority, were of Indian or Arab extraction, and most were Moslems.

It was an enchanting place and we would all have liked to have spent much more time there, but once again we had to move on. We took the launch back to the mainland but started late. Nor was there any aircraft available to take us to Nampula. A car and driver was produced, but the man was so nervous that we wondered whether it would not be better to wait until the following morning. However, John Biggs-Davison and I had an appointment to see the commanding general the following morning, and to keep this we would have to leave that evening. The driver explained that the road was quite frequently the scene of attacks and ambushes. I had an M1 semi-automatic carbine with me, and both Honor and I had our pistols. We gave the carbine to Marcus because John Biggs-Davison, as a very respectable British Member of Parliament, could not be seen to be carrying arms.

We set off at dusk, and the driver drove like the wind. Finally we were able to slow him down a bit saying that we would rather take our chance in a shoot-out with terrorists than face the certainty of death by being driven by this Jehu. In fact we reached Nampula that night without incident, although the next day a car travelling along that road was shot at and the occupants killed.

The time had come to move on again, and anyway we had exhausted supplies at the local hotel. The food was so revolting that we had lived for some time on bread and piripiri (a sort of very hot red pepper), but to compensate we had discovered that the hotel had some excellent Portuguese wine. By now we had finished the last bottles of that and flew south. During this trip I had found many of my pupils and friends from the Instituto, and I was sorry to say goodbye to them.

We spent some more days in Mozambique, in the centre of the country, and then flew from Beira to Salisbury as it then was (it is now Harare). At the hotel there, we were met by the Duke of Montrose – or rather Lord Angus Graham, as he preferred to be called. He was the defence minister in Ian Smith's government. We found him a most charming man, and he invited us all to dine with him at his house that evening.

Rhodesia

The following day, John Biggs-Davison was taken off to see the parliament and meet various politicians, and Honor, Marcus and I spent the day sightseeing in Salisbury, which was a pretty town. We met Peter van der Byl, who was the foreign minister in the Smith government.

The purpose of my visit was to have talks with the defence minister, Lord Graham, and with the Rhodesian intelligence services. I was introduced to the head of the special branch of the police, and I understood that he was also in charge of intelligence generally – a man called Ken Flower, who had been a policeman in England. I did not like him, and I believe that the feeling was mutual.

While we were out, somebody had been through the things in our hotel room. I had expected this and arranged a few things which would have to be moved if there was to be any search. When we got back to the hotel, they had been moved. I thought – in fact I was quite sure – that Mr Flower had ordered this search. At this time, 1966, the terrorism had not really started in Rhodesia, so it was completely safe to travel anywhere in the country. However, I wanted to arrange some sort of liaison or exchange of intelligence and information between the Portuguese in Angola and Mozambique and the Rhodesian forces. I found this extremely difficult, as the attitude of the Rhodesian security services was suspicious if not hostile. It was certainly lacking in any spirit of co-operation.

They were also convinced that they knew everything and that there was absolutely nothing that I could tell them about anti-terrorist operations, based on my experience in Angola and Mozambique, which they did not already know.

Lord Angus Graham invited Honor and me to spend a long weekend with him and his wife at their lovely farm, some forty miles outside Salisbury. They were both extremely kind and hospitable. On the first day we were shown round the farm, which must have been a model for any other in Rhodesia.

That evening I suggested that we might have some talks together, but Graham said that there would be plenty of time for that the next day. We spent a delightful evening with them and the next day were taken on a further sightseeing tour of the estate and the country round about. I suggested that evening we might begin our talk.

Angus Graham asked me if I knew any Celtic songs, and I replied that although I could not sing at all I did in fact know some Irish songs. We spent a splendid evening with Angus Graham at the piano and all of us singing. The next day was a repetition of the previous one, and that evening I again suggested that the time had come for our talk, which was the reason for my presence in Rhodesia. This time Angus asked me if I knew anything about the British Israelite movement and incautiously I said that I did not. So he told me all about it for the next three hours, until it was late and time to go to bed. In fact, I never did have the opportunity to discuss terrorism and intelligence with him, as the following day we had to go back to Salisbury. I think that the main reason was that he knew nothing about the subject whatever.

He had been a naval officer during the war and anti-guerrilla operations in the bush were a completely closed book to him. However he did arrange for me to address a conference at the army staff college, and to this most of the senior officers came as well as police and the ubiquitous Mr Flower. I spoke to them for about an hour and answered questions, but I might just as well have been speaking to the wall. They knew it all – or a least they thought that they did.

It was pretty well an abortive mission from my point of view, but we attended a session of the parliament and met Ian Smith and various of his ministers and politicians, as well as seeing something of the country, which was lovely.

I fear that I made myself rather unpopular by suggesting to Peter van der Byl that one thing which was required urgently was education for the children. He agreed enthusiastically, but misunderstood me. 'I mean the white children and for that matter also their parents,' I said. 'It is quite clear that very many of the people living here have come from England and from a society in which they certainly never had any servants. Now in Rhodesia they have, and I have noticed that they treat them with arrogance and gratuitous rudeness. You see whites pushing blacks off the pavement, and the children are being brought up to think of the blacks as inferior people. I am not suggesting that there should be an integrated society as both races have their own and quite different cultures, and they seldom mix, but courtesy to all irrespective of race or colour would go a very long way towards better relations and very greatly reduce the risk of a revolt of some sort.'

I had noticed that in the hotel, black staff were treated with rudeness and a total lack of courtesy, as were black men and women in the streets and in a few people's houses. However, Lord Graham seemed to be on excellent terms with his employees. He had respect for them, as they had for him. Unfortunately this was the exception, especially amongst people who had come from a background in England where they had never been used to having servants, let alone being courteous and considerate towards them.

We enjoyed Rhodesia. It was a most beautiful country, but unfortunately we never went back again. We flew on to Luanda on our return journey. Here the situation was very different. The terrorism had been held in the north, confined to a relatively small area in the environs of Ambriz, Ambriset, the Serra de Uige and Nambongongo. There were some pockets of trouble out in the north-east of the country which became more serious until my good friend General Jose de Bettencourt Rodrigues brought the situation under control.

John Biggs-Davison and I flew into Santa Eulalia, a major Portuguese base and a brigade headquarters, on the eastern edge of the Nambongongo forests and somewhat to the north. There was some fighting going on round about, so we went out on a couple of patrols with the troops. Things, however, had improved enormously in the five years since it had all begun, and if one avoided the comparatively small areas in which terrorists were still coming in from the Congo, one could travel in complete safety throughout the rest of the country. To say that it is impossible to win a war against terrorists and guerrillas is nonsense, and by 1974 the war had been completely won in Angola, and was a good way to being won in Mozambique. Only in Guinea was there really serious fighting. This was largely due to the nature of the country itself and the huge areas of mangrove swamp near the coast, with continual infiltration from Guinea (Conakray) and also from the north. I was able to complete a detailed report on the situation. Meanwhile, Honor completed her ethnic maps of the different tribes, their languages and their beliefs, and revisited the hospitals.

Portugal Again

My mother came to stay with us in Portugal that winter for three months. Alas, that was to be the last time I saw her, as she died in the following March.

We had some wonderful shooting for snipe in the rice fields, where we used to go with Leon Paumier. There was also partridge shooting at Cabreiras, Marmello and Monte Branco. We spent a very happy Christmas all together. In 1967 we had to spend some time at Anticoli at the villa there, and several friends came to visit us: Carlos Abecasis and his wife Flavia, and Brigadier Paul Roos and his wife Jill. We attended the CEDI and I carried on with my lectures at the Instituto. We went fishing on the Eo for salmon and attended another meeting of the CEDI in London. During this time I wrote a couple of novels. I also wrote two more books on counter-terrorism and the war in Angola.

Our daughter and her friends came out to stay. She had been involved in a nasty motor accident, so I was worried when she used to come back very late. However, she was grown up by now, and perhaps we worried too much. One night I heard her come in at about midnight and the front door shut. There was silence for quite some time, and then I heard a strange noise coming from the drawing room. I thought perhaps that a burglar had got into the house. Slipping out of bed (it was in the summer and I was sleeping in the nude), I picked up a sub-machine gun which I kept beside my bed and crept downstairs. There was a light on in the drawing room and I tiptoed in silently. There was nobody there. Then I heard a noise from the high-backed Charles II love-seat, and suddenly two figures exploded from it. One was Juanita and the other an unknown young man. For a moment or two he stood quite still, taking in the sight of a naked man pointing a sub-machine gun at him. Then, as in the cartoon films, he leapt into the air and his legs were working like pistons when he hit the ground. One moment he was there and the next he had vanished – and was never seen again. Our daughter was not pleased with me.

In the years that followed, Juanita was to travel the world. She got a job organising public relations for industrial fairs. This was interesting work and involved organising stands (to some extent supervising their construction), handling press releases, organising receptions and arranging protocol. Her work took her to America, Brazil, Argentina, Chile, France, Switzerland, Portugal, Angola, South Africa, Mozambique, Tehran, Kuwait and goodness knows where else. She also did it very well; and it was well paid. She was – and is – an adventurous girl who thoroughly enjoyed the travel, and her languages were a great asset. She also worked for the Angolan Diamond Company and organised major exhibitions and public relations for them.

Our son meanwhile was still at Cambridge, working on a monumental thesis for his doctorate but he also took consultancy work, which sent him to many countries.

At about this time, Keith Collins appeared. He was a friend of ours and of Peter Paiva Raposos and his wife Minnie. Keith was an oil man who wanted a concession, and they had asked me to help him. It took quite a long time, but eventually we obtained a concession for the Islands of Sao Tome and Principe. There are oil seeps there and I am quite certain that there is oil – possibly a stringer coming south and west from Nigeria, but quite likely a good deal more. Unfortunately, it took so long to negotiate that the revolution in Portugal came before much work could be done, and the concession issued by the Portuguese government became null and void.

My old friend Carlos Abecasis became president of the Angolan Diamond Company, and he invited me to become a director of one of their subsidiary property companies, which I accepted.

I continued to lecture at the Instituto. I wrote. We went fishing and shooting in Portugal and Spain and stayed with our friends; and there were wonderful parties given by Sibille and Kiko Costa Lobo, Julio Bastos, Oscar and Lillian Husum and many others. Life was busy and very good indeed. We spent part of our summers in Italy up at the villa, where Lisa and Antonietta Cuccato helped us to entertain our friends, and part of the early autumn in Portugal.

We drove up to Spain for the CEDI meetings, and it was when we were returning from one of these with our friends, Ewald and Gundulla von Kleist, that we saw a most remarkable thing. I have read about 'a convocation of eagles', but like most people, we had never seen one. One day, after the end of the CEDI meeting in Madrid, we were driving back to Portugal when we saw a number of eagles circling high up over the mountain of Miravette. They circled lower and landed, and then more came in from every point of the compass.

We stopped halfway up the mountain and, looking across a valley, we saw very many of the eagles had already arrived. We were there for about two hours and counted about one hundred and thirty imperial eagles. Some must have come from North Africa, some from the Pyrenees. In fact, when I told the authorities in Spain about this, they said that they did not think that there were more than about eighty or ninety in the whole of Spain.

The eagles landed in a field about three hundred yards from where we were. Some perched on stone walls, some in trees and some – quite a lot of them – were walking about like chickens in the fields. It was a most extraordinary sight. Alas, none of us had a camera, but I have never seen anything like it and never will again.

Ewald and Gundulla had a house in the Algarve, and every year they invited us to stay with them. In those days the Algarve had not been 'developed' and totally ruined. There were long stretches of deserted beaches. We used to picnic and swim there, and Albufeira was still just a small fishing village. There were no high-rise blocks of hideous apartments and very few hotels. The interior of the country was unspoilt, with acres and acres of almond trees, little white cottages and not a golf course in sight. There were few if any tourists; and in many ways it was still a paradise.

Nothing lasts for ever, and in 1968 Salazar was to have the accident which was to lead to his death two years later. Things began to change.

There were legitimate grounds for dissatisfaction in the armed forces. Troops would be sent to Angola or Mozambique, or even worse to Guinea, and were supposed to do a two-year tour there; but when the time came for them return to Portugal there was not the shipping to take them, and bureaucratic inefficiency frequently meant that soldiers would have to wait for a year or eighteen months, sometimes longer, before returning home. Many of the troops on active service lived in very poor conditions without any recreational facilities at all; the pay was miserably bad and the food not much better.

In very many cases, the years of separation from their families brought about a collapse of family life. Wives would go off with other men, and there was virtually no system for home leave during the entire period of service abroad. Some of the officers brought their wives out and this caused jealousy. Junior officers could not live on their pay, and I know of very many officers of the rank of captain with ten or twelve years service who came to the Instituto and whose homes were miles away from Lisbon. They could not afford to take apartments near or in Lisbon and their pay did not cover even the barest necessities of life.

In order to make more money and to make ends meet, some officers volunteered for two tours of duty abroad (sometimes even three), as they were paid more when overseas. However, this meant six or nine years separation from their families. It was a thoroughly bad system, and I criticised it in writing to senior officers and chiefs of the general staff, many of whom I knew very well. This did not make me very popular in some political quarters, although my friends in the army much appreciated it.

Marcello Caetano had taken over as prime minister, although Salazar continued to hang on to life for another two years until 1970. The trouble really only started after his death, when there was open grumbling and dissatisfaction. The Americans, the British and the United Nations also started to increase pressure on Portugal to hand over its overseas provinces of Angola, Mozambique, Guinea, and the Cape Verde Islands, as well as Timor and Macau in the south of China, and others in the Indonesian archipelago. The Indian Army had already seized the almost undefended Portuguese enclaves in India, although soldiers put up what resistance they could. However, this was a bitter psychological blow to Portugal.

The revolution was to come in 1974, still in the future, but from 1970 onwards there was serious trouble brewing. The Communist Party was outlawed in Portugal, but it remained under cover and fairly active, run by Cunhal from Czechoslovakia. It was, however, very small. If there was to be a revolution in Portugal, it had to come from within the armed forces – and that is what eventually happened. However, this was still not for some years.

For ourselves, we continued our lives travelling between Italy and Portugal, driving up to Madrid and to Seville and Granada, fishing on the Eo, shooting in the Alentejo south of the Tagus and attending the Wehrkunde meetings in Munich. These were organised by Ewald von Kleist, and here I met the foreign ministers and defence ministers from all the NATO countries – although I was the only representative from Portugal.

I also met people like Senator John Tower from America – politicians, secretaries of state – and the meetings were always extremely interesting. There were the CEDI meetings too, dinners and parties with our friends, weekend house parties with Julio Bastos at his lovely estate near Estremoz and trips to Badajoz (which was only just over two hours away in the Bentley) and the Algarve, to stay with our friends there.

I continued with my lecturing at the Instituto and also had director's meetings of the Torres do Tejo, the property company in which the Angolan Diamond Company was a major shareholder. Keith Collins and Alex Hutchens were still about, and I was helping them with their oil concessions. I was also very much interested in what was developing on the political scene in Portugal and the situation in Angola and Mozambique.

Two or three years before, Honor, Ewald von Kleist and I had gone to Madeira with the Archduke Otto Von Habsburg and we explored the island, which in parts is very beautiful. Honor made a collection of orchids there. She was a very knowledgeable botanist and many of the volumes which constituted her considerable library of some four thousand books were botanical in content. She grew a beautiful garden with the orchids which she brought back from Madeira, as well as plants and flowers from Angola and Mozambique. In fact, when we came to leave Portugal, it was a considerable wrench to leave all of this behind.

Marcus received his doctorate from Cambridge and came to live in Cascais in a small flat there, earning a good income as a consultant geologist. At the same time he worked at the Geological Institute in Lisbon, as well as making trips to Brazil and Africa on consultancy work.

A communist administration had been elected at Anticoli, which set about making my life a hell there with seizures of land, taxes and continual irritations. When in 1972 dear old Liza died, who had been our cook for more than thirty-five years, I decided that we would have to sell the villa in Italy. We either had to live there ourselves or sell it, otherwise it would be robbed, and the communist administration would make things even more difficult for me with nobody living in the house or taking care of it. Our last summer there was in 1972, and I sold the place with very great sorrow in 1973.

1972 and 1973 were the last really good years in Portugal and we had a wonderful time, with visits to Madrid to the CEDI, to which we took Juanita. For her birthday, Juanita gave her mother and me tickets to the concert given by Maria Dolores Padeira in the Retiro Gardens, something that we always remembered. We went fishing again in Spain, travelled to Italy and entertained our friends at the villa in 1972. I went to the Wehrkunde meeting and the CEDI. We had a meeting in Estoril, where we invited eighty-five of the members to a sit-down dinner and reception at our house. We had our syndicate shoots at Marmello, Marcellonas and Monte Branco, for partridges and snipe shooting in the rice fields. Marcus became engaged to be married, and we gave a big party. His fiancée was Lucia de Faro, a member of a cadet branch of the Braganza family, long resident in Brazil. I had a good deal of work to do at the Instituto and also as a director of the Torres do Tejo, but already the storm clouds were brewing.

Our Son's Wedding

There was considerable difficulty in arranging for Marcus's marriage. It would have taken him months to get the necessary papers in Brazil, and it would have taken Lucia equally long to arrange the necessary papers in Portugal. I finally hit on the idea of getting them married in Gibraltar. The governor-general and commander-in-chief at Gibraltar could give permission for anybody to be married virtually without any formalities. Marshal of the Royal Air Force Sir John Grandy had joined Whites club in the same year that I had, and he had become a friend of my father-in-law, Air Marshal Langford-Sainsbury. I got in touch with him and all was arranged. My father-in-law had died some three years previously, but he remembered him well.

In 1973 I had the trauma of selling the villa at Anticoli in the late autumn, and now with the arrangements for Marcus's wedding, I was too preoccupied with my own affairs to become really aware of what was happening in Portugal.

The day eventually came when Marcus, Juanita, Honor and I set off for Tangier. The land frontier with Gibraltar was still closed, and we drove first to Seville where we spent a last night together watching the Spanish dancing at the Patio Andaluz, which we all loved. The next day we drove to Algeciras, left the cars there and took the boat across to Tangier. We arrived there in the evening, and having finally got through immigration and customs, we waited for our luggage. It did not come.

I sent Marcus to look for it and he came back to report that it was still on the quay while the Arab porters were fighting each other as to who was to carry it. So we went there, picked it up ourselves and got it loaded on to a taxi. Suddenly, about twenty Arabs besieged the taxi demanding money for having not carried the luggage. The taxi driver managed to shake them off and we got to our hotel.

The next morning we flew to Gibraltar and put up at the Rock Hotel. The Brazilian party was supposed to arrive that afternoon, and the wedding was to be the next day. We called on the marshal of the Royal Air Force to thank him and went to the register office to make sure that all was in order for the wedding. I then got in touch with the hotel manager and asked him to arrange for flowers to be put in the Brazilian party's rooms and a bouquet for the bride. The manager then explained that all flowers had to be imported from Spain, but this was no longer possible. However, he suggested that I leave the matter to him.

The next morning there were lovely flowers in the rooms and a beautiful bridal bouquet. He explained to me that he had an arrangement with some local boys, and that during the night they had 'arranged' the flowers from the gardens of local people on the Rock. I felt sorry that we had to accept stolen flowers, but they had already been stolen and beautifully arranged, and one could hardly put them back!

That afternoon, we went to the airport and met the aircraft from Madrid. Lucia, her sister, her brother-in-law and a maid of honour descended from the plane as a tremendous thunderstorm broke with torrential rain. The party were all wearing thin clothes having come from Brazil, with the girls in little silk dresses. They had about one hundred and fifty yards to walk to the airport building, and when they arrived they might just have well have been in the sea for an hour or two. Marcus could at least see very clearly what he was marrying.

They were all extremely wet and very cold, and we took them to the Rock Hotel as quickly as we could. Suddenly there was an outburst of gunfire. For the first time in years a major squadron of the Navy came into the Grand Harbour, led by three cruisers and with a destroyer escort. As they came in they fired their guns in salute, and the batteries on the rock replied. In those days we still had a lot of guns. It was quite a barrage. Suddenly, the door of our room burst open and our future daughter-in-law appeared in dishabille with her eyes popping out of her head. '*Revolucao!*' she cried. 'They are all shooting at us.' With some difficulty my son was able to quieten her and the other members of the Brazilian party. I even explained that, far from it being a revolution, the salute was in their honour! I think that they even believed me!

The wedding went off without a hitch, and then Honor and I were invited to have dinner with the commander-in-chief and governor-general, whilst Marcus and his bride went off on the first part of their honeymoon. Honor, Juanita and I left the next day and flew to Tangier, and then took the ghastly boat again to Algeciras. We had frightful difficulty in getting on, and I had to get hold of the chief of police and speak very loudly and clearly to him in order to get the three of us personally escorted on to the ship. I hoped very much never to see Tangier again and in fact never did.

We returned to Monte Estoril for ten days of celebrations and had our friends come from Italy, Spain, England, France, Greece, Austria and in fact from all over the world. The dinner we gave was a seated dinner for ninety people, and two of Marcus's friends arrived in 'uniform' – one dressed as an American general and the other as a Russian general. Robin Behar and Zaf Zafiropulo made the party. We had put on the invitation 'evening dress or uniform', as some of our friends in the Portuguese Army did not have evening dress. Robin and Zaf decided to take this literally and hired their uniforms from Moss Bros. We gave a luncheon at the Seteais Hotel in a private dining room for some thirty or forty people, and at the end of it all we were exhausted. While Marcus and his wife went off on the second part of their honeymoon in Spain, we went down to stay with our old friends, the von Kleists, at their villa some miles from Albufeira.

We spent a very happy ten days there, only marred by the fact that I lost my signet ring when bathing. I was very superstitious about this, as if by any chance I left it off, some disaster happened. I had been sunbathing and was covered with oil and had not intended to bathe. However, I walked with Ewald along the edge of the sea. Suddenly a big wave came, and I found myself swimming. Once in the water, I decided to swim out with him and then found that my ring had slipped from my oily finger. In spite of several days searching with a mask, I never found it. I told Honor at the time that a terrible disaster would follow. I did not have to wait long.

On 25th April, 1974, Honor and I drove up to the Portuguese/Spanish frontier. We took side roads and noticed nothing abnormal; even going through the Portuguese frontier everything was as usual. Once in Spain, I wanted to change some money into pesetas and went to the bank in the customs post. I found that it was closed. Asking why, I was told that they only changed escudos but that they were not even changing them. Again I asked why, and was told that 'They have had some sort of revolution over there'. We drove into Badajoz and waited for Marcus and his wife to join us, but they came very late. When we tried to get back into Portugal, the frontier had been closed.

Chapter Six

Revolution in Portugal

The following morning I went to the boundary again: out through the Spanish frontier into a sort of no-man's land in between the countries, and then to the Portuguese post. Here I found everything in confusion. I demanded to speak to the general staff of the army and eventually got through to a friend of mine who was the duty officer. He told me that there had been a revolution and that nobody at all was to be allowed in or out of the frontiers.

I then tried to find the PIDE officer, but he was at home, and when I went there I found him and his wife packing frantically. There was nothing for it, and we had to go back into Badajoz. The first problem was to try and get Marcus and his wife back to Brazil. They had booked on a Spanish ship which was coming via Cadiz to Lisbon and then on to Vigo before crossing the Atlantic to Rio de Janeiro.

I got in touch on the telephone with the managing director of the line in Seville, who said that while my son's passage and that of his wife were booked, they did not know if they would be going into Lisbon or not, due to the revolution in Portugal. I then got hold of my old friend General Carlos Vallespin, who was the captain general of the north-west of Spain. He had been military attaché in Lisbon some years before, and we had become great friends with him and his wife. He said that he would do all that he could for us but that first we had to come into his area of command.

I then got in touch on the telephone with our daughter, Juanita, who had remained in Lisbon. I asked her go to Marcus's flat, pack up all his things and get a truck; then take the whole lot down to the quays in Lisbon in two days time in order to get herself and all Marcus's things on to the ship. I told her to meet us in Vigo in the event that the Spanish ship did actually come into Lisbon.

Honor and I, Marcus and his wife then set off along the Spanish side of the frontier from Badajoz to Vigo – a considerable distance over very bad roads with enormous potholes in them – and spent the night in Salamanca. We were tired and hungry and looked for a restaurant in which to eat. We had a grading system: each establishment would be either a one-priest restaurant, a two-priest restaurant, a three-priest restaurant or a four-priest restaurant. One-priest restaurants were the worst, and four-priest restaurants the best.

Priests know their food, and wherever there are the most priests eating that is the best restaurant in town. We found a pretty good one – a three-priest restaurant, if I remember correctly – and had dinner there. The next day we drove on to Vigo, and immediately when we arrived I telephoned the commanding general. Carlos Vallespin had been as good as his word, and the general sent his ADC immediately to our hotel and took us on a tour of the town. He then invited us all to dinner with him and his wife. He also told me that the captain of the port of Vigo had been informed that the Spanish ship had in fact called into Lisbon and was expected in Vigo harbour the following morning.

Early the next day, we were escorted down to the docks. The commanding general, his ADC and a dozen senior officers were there with the captain of the port. As the ship docked we saw our daughter and we all went on board. The general offered us all drinks. Finally, Juanita came ashore with us, and our son and his wife set sail on the ship for Brazil.

Juanita's journey had been filled with drama. She had been to her brother's flat, packed up everything, been able to get hold of a truck (and a driver) and had loaded everything on to it, including our son's collection of rocks. (Being a geologist, he had assembled a dozen or more very large and heavy boxes filled with rocks, taken from various places in Portugal, Spain and elsewhere, around which he had written his PhD thesis at Cambridge.) There was also an empty gun case – he had already taken the gun to Brazil about a year previously – and there were trunks of clothes, scientific instruments and so on – a considerable amount of stuff.

On her arrival at the docks with the truck, Juanita had at first been denied entry, but had managed to talk her way in. There were a good many revolutionary soldiers about, generally looking for trouble. The driver unloaded his truck, dumped everything on the dock and then leapt into his vehicle and fled.

The customs authorities at first refused to even look at the collection of boxes and trunks, and Juanita tried every trick in the book: charm, tears, cajolery, threats – everything. Finally, with very bad grace the customs agreed to look at the stuff to be shipped. The first thing was the empty gun case. Where, they asked, was the gun? Juanita explained. Then they opened one of the large wooden cases. It was filled with stones. They opened another, and that was filled with stones, too. The third, fourth and fifth – all filled with stones. 'Is your brother a lunatic?' the customs man asked. Juanita explained that was the opinion which some people had of geologists. 'There are twelve boxes of rocks,' Juanita said. The ship's captain then intervened and said that his ship must sail and they must either allow the passenger and the luggage to be brought on board or else leave without them. By this time the customs men were certain that not only was Juanita's brother mad, but that she was as well. Furthermore, they wanted to go off and howl and caper in the street with the revolutionaries. So they told her to go to hell and take herself and her mad brother's rocks with her.

So she went on board. The rocks and other stuff were carried up and put on deck, and the following morning she appeared through the morning mist at Vigo to be met by us. In fact, she had been very brave and successful.

When the ship had sailed, we were invited by the captain of the port for luncheon, but said that we had better be starting back as we had a long way to go. The general had his intelligence people working, and he warned us not try to get through the frontiers on the north as they were still closed. Even more serious, there was no petrol for the car to be bought from pumps in Portugal. We drove back to Salamanca, and that evening we were joined there by one very old friend, David Ramsay, who had helped me considerably in the past on many occasions. (We had also been at school together more than thirty-five years previously.) We always saw David in Madrid, where he had lived for many years, and he used to come down to stay with us in Lisbon, where his father, a retired ambassador, had lived. He came with us the next day and we had a picnic luncheon on the road, finally leaving him at Badajoz. Honor, Juanita and I remained in Badajoz for a day or two until the frontier was re-opened, and then with a full tank of petrol which would take us back to Monte Estoril we started back, stopping for a few minutes at Julio Bastos's house to see if he was all right; he was not there. On the way we passed several truckloads of scruffy sailors, armed to the teeth and clearly looking for trouble; but the car had foreign number plates, and we passed them at speed. We reached our home in safety and then tried to find out what had happened.

At first everything was in a state of complete confusion. A committee of National Salvation had been set up, and I went there to see who was doing what. I saw a number of officers whom I knew, and was able to get a certain amount of information. As I had suspected, some of my former pupils at the Instituto had played a considerable part in the revolution, but the hard-core consisted of a handful of communist officers, many of them from the navy, and virtually none from the air force. There were also officers whom I had never met and who had never been to the staff college. One of my pupils, Major Victor Alves, was a prime mover, together with Colonel Braz and many others. Some were socialists, some Christian democrats, and at first they were a very mixed bag with no very clear political orientation. The communist element were the only ones who knew what they wanted and had a very clear plan of how to achieve it.

It was also extremely tiresome that the banks and safe deposits had all been closed, and for some time it was impossible to get any money.

A sort of political/military militia had been formed under a Captain Otello, who was promoted to brigadier and who was in command of the filthiest soldiers I have ever seen in my life. These dirty, scruffy, unshaven ruffians scoured the country in trucks picking up suspected 'fascists' who were then taken off and confined in the barracks of the Second Light Artillery Regiment on the outskirts of Lisbon. There many were subjected to hideous tortures. General Spinola, who had written a book advocating autonomy for the Portuguese provinces of Angola, Mozambique, Guinea and so on, was called in to be the new president. Admiral Tomas, the former president, and Marcello Caetano, the former prime minister, were bundled off into exile in Brazil.

It is not part of my purpose to write a short history of the Portuguese revolution, but as it radically altered our lives, I must mention some of the effects which it had upon us. During the summer of 1974 things began to get worse and worse. COPCON, the gang of ruffians commanded by Otello, went about arresting people, and a considerable number were confined in prisons and in concentration camps, including a good many of my friends and senior officers in the army.

We began to hear stories of raids made on people's homes by armed gangs who terrorised their victims and stole whatever took their fancy. We also started to get our friends coming to our house at night, asking to be hidden. I hung a large flag from our bedroom window which overlooked the garden and the road, and put a notice on the door to the effect that the premises and the persons therein were under the protection of the embassy. This was not in fact true, but I think it dissuaded the more gung-ho of the COPCON scoundrels from bothering us.

An attempt was made to steal one of the Bentleys one night, but Honor fired a few shots over the heads of those responsible and they ran away. However, it had become decidedly unpleasant, so we made up our minds to leave Portugal. (I was also advised to do this by my friends in London.) The problem was how to get anything out, as the new communist-dominated government and the left-wing local administration told me that everything in our house – including my wife's jewellery – was wanted for 'a people's museum'. Already the employees at my bank had seized the keys of the strong room from the bank's directors, who had been literally kicked into the street. They could not tell me if the bearer bonds which I had there were still there or not, as from the day of the revolution they themselves had not been allowed into the strong room of the bank.

We began to make enquires as to whether there would be a frontier with Spain where the wheels of progress could be oiled for trucks bearing our possessions to be allowed through. Eventually we found one and also discovered the type of 'oil' required and the amount necessary. The next thing was to arrange the requisite export documents.

While General Spinola was still president of the republic and before he had been overthrown by the far left-wing, Honor had persuaded him to give her an order to our bank in Estoril where we had a strong box and where she kept her jewels, to allow her access to the box. We went there and the manager refused absolutely to allow us to go down to the strong room. Then Honor produced her authorisation from the president of the republic, and the manager went quite white. He telephoned his superiors at the head office of the bank, who could hardly disregard a direct order from the president. So we were allowed to go down and in a few minutes had transferred all Honor's jewellery into plastic shopping bags. We relocked the box, now containing only empty jewel boxes, and left the bank, never to return.

The next thing was to get the cars out of the country. I sold the 4.5 litre Bentley, and the other we managed to get safely to England (as I have recounted previously). I sold the Allard to a museum for old cars. One of our Barraducas was already in Spain, and eventually we took the other to England on the same ferry as we had taken the Bentley. Meanwhile, David Ramsay in Madrid was working on suitable export documents, and I was also able to get some genuine documents from the local authorities.

There was no shooting that winter, as the private estates and shooting reserves had all been sequestered or abolished and the mass massacre of all the wild game in Portugal was in full swing. All the planning work on the Torres do Tejo, of which I was a director had been stopped, and the Instituto had been closed (or rather taken over by a villainous crew of young and scruffy soldiers). There was a good deal of planning to be done before we left, and we lingered on in the hope that things might change.

In fact, in the spring of 1975 there was an attempted coup made by Spinola and a number of other officers; but it was badly planned and failed abysmally. I was actually in Beirut when this happened and was acutely unhappy there. It was perfectly obvious that the country would be plunged into civil war in a matter of days (if not hours), and I could not get out fast enough.

However, I had word from Honor that the authorities intended to arrest two of the people who were with me in Beirut as soon as we got back to Portugal. So we flew to Rome first, and there one of my friends was met by his son. He then went on to Paris. Another of my very good friends managed to escape from Lisbon and arrived up on the Spanish frontier in the north, where he had to be towed on a large log across the Minho river by his brother, as he himself could not swim.

I arrived back in Portugal without incident, but it was clearly time for us to leave. The failed coup had brought the communists in the revolutionary council and in the government a good deal closer to seizing complete power. In the autumn of 1975, had it not been for the socialists and the farmers in the north of Portugal, they would almost certainly have succeeded.

It was with very great sadness that we packed up and left our lovely home in Portugal, with all the friends we had made over the years and all the wonderful times we had: the beauty of the Alentejo in the dawn mist, the cork forests, the deserted and unspoilt coast of the Algarve, and the very many years of happiness we had spent there.

It was a chapter of our lives which was closing, and a completely new life lay before us. I have written of the wonderful parties which we had there, and were never to have again, and two stand out in my memory.

The first was the one which we gave in our house for our son's wedding, seated for ninety guests, with our beautiful Georgian silver, our eighteenth century Venetian glass, the Derby, Rockingham and Dresden china, the whole housed filled with flowers and everything, as always, all prepared in the house by our old cook Marguerita, who always became royally drunk whenever we gave a party but cooked the most wonderful food. Since then Marguerita has alas died, but we keep in touch with Josefa (who was the house parlour maid) and her family and hear from them regularly.

It makes rather a sad gloss on those splendid days that the Portuguese had a depressing habit of taking small pieces of silver and bibelots away as 'mementoes', and we had to keep an eye out for this. Nevertheless, we did lose several pieces of early eighteenth-century silver, a seventeenth-century pepperpot and several other things.

The other party which I particularly remember was given by Sibille Costa Lobo in the summer before the revolution. It was a 'Mexican' party, most beautifully done in the garden. Kiko Costa Lobo's father appeared as a Mexican peasant riding a donkey. Honor went as Mercedes, the wife of the local inn keeper. I went as the Bandit 'El Gordo'. For the occasion I did not shave for several days, borrowed Honor's black hairpiece – which hung down from my Sombrero in greasy looking curls – and wore cross-cartridge bandolieros and a gun belt with an ancient Frontier Colt.

The whole effect was completed with a large, drooping, black moustache and my face suitably darkened with brown boot polish. Juanita went as the local tart and our son as an officer in the Federales. When we arrived at the party that evening, nobody recognised us. There was a great deal of tequila, a band and dancing, and a wonderful Mexican meal which Sibille had prepared especially.

Again, it is sad to remember that so many of the guests ate until they could eat no more and then got up and left. For ourselves, we stayed on until the dawn, when I found myself in the children's paddling pool together with my host solemnly dancing a passadoble.

We Leave Portugal

In April 1975, the day finally came for us to leave. Five days previously the three huge twenty-metre long trucks had arrived: one by sea on the Lisbon to Southampton ferry and two overland. Each had a driver and his mate, and we also had four expert packers sent out from England by air. We put them all up in the house and the trucks were hidden amongst some trees at the top of the road. For four days and nights they packed the house and everything in it. At dawn, or rather before on D1, we loaded everything into the trucks. I gave the driver foreman the 'oil' (which consisted of gold sovereigns and whisky) which would, I hoped, facilitate the frontier crossing. I also handed over the excellent export documents.

We estimated that it would take several hours for them to reach the frontier and that they should cross it at about 2 p.m. The aircraft for London left at 1.30 p.m. and a good two hours before then Honor and I presented ourselves at the airport together with some eighteen suitcases. These were loaded on to a wagon, and the porter, who knew us well, whispered to me that we should not attempt to speak Portuguese or understand it.

I had taken the precaution of changing our passports so that they showed that we were tourists and not residents, and we had dressed for the part. Many foreign officials expect (or perhaps I should say 'expected') English to look like English, and in fact American tourists are fairly easily identifiable even today. I had put on my bowler hat although it was April and fairly warm, and I carried an umbrella. As I wore an eyeglass in those days, I had this screwed firmly into my eye. Honor had also dressed for the part.

We found a howling mass of people at the airport. There was a long queue with a turnstile. Behind a table there was an unpleasant individual sporting a huge brass hammer and sickle in his buttonhole. For many months previously all the old customs officers had been changed regularly, and we had been reasonably certain that we would not be recognised although we had been through the airport so many times in the past years that most of the former customs and immigration officers knew us. Now they were all new men and good party members.

This particular specimen was taking an immense delight in being really bloody to everybody. He snarled at the people coming before him and ordered them to open all their cases. He then tipped everything out on to the table in front of him, frequently ripping the linings out of the empty cases. People were crying and protesting, and he was shouting and throwing his weight about. As we got nearer to the turnstile, Honor and I started to talk to each other very loudly in English.

'Incredible. I've never seen anything like this before! We come here on holiday and find that we are in the middle of a pack of Nazis and madmen. We damn well won't come here again!' 'Can't think what the fellow is doing. We've never been treated like this before anywhere.' 'How can they expect to have tourists if they treat them like this?' And so on. Finally, we came up to the table, and before the man could say anything I barked at him, 'Speekee English?' He replied in passably good English that he did, but I repeated my question. 'What! Speekee English?' Again he said that he did. I turned to Honor and said. 'Good God, darling. He says that he does speak English. Wonder where he learnt that. Well,' I continued, glaring at the man through my eyeglass, 'what do you want? What! You want us to open our cases? Yes, of course, they are all our cases, whose do you think they are? We came here for a holiday, tourists, you know. We won't come here again, though! Anyway, where are your white gloves? International regulations – all customs officers must wear white gloves when examining travellers' luggage!' Honor then came in with her bit and said, 'Ugh! Just look at his filthy fingernails!'

By this time the man was bright red in the face, the people round about were beginning to titter and he was losing his authority. It was a calculated risk, but there were really only three things that he could do. He could insist on opening our luggage, and I would then have insisted that he obtained and wore white gloves, thereby exposing him to further ridicule. He could arrest us – but for what? In any event, I expected that the embassy would demand our release immediately. Finally, he could get rid of us as quickly as possible and continue to bully other people. I expected him to take the third option, and that is what he did. He waved us through as quickly as possible.

A few yards further on a sort of Irma Grease (The Belle of Belsen) appeared from behind a pillar and suggested to Honor that she wished to make a body search. Honor just looked at her without saying anything. The large, blowsy woman hurriedly gave a sign against the evil eye and retreated instantly behind the pillar. We passed through that and were met on the far side by the station head of British Airways, or BEA as it then was, whom we knew well. We were installed in first-class seats with third-class tickets and called for champagne.

And so we left Portugal. For some weeks previously and before my visit to Beirut, I had heard that there was some sort of a warrant out for my arrest. I did not pay much attention to that. I then heard that I was on a list of people to be assassinated. I paid even less attention to that, until I heard some time later that two people whom I knew only very slightly but were also supposed to be on this list had disappeared. As far as I know, they have never been seen again. This caused us to think that the time had really come to make a move. In any event, things were becoming more unpleasant every day, and the communists were within an ace of seizing power.

In the end, they got the bearer bonds which we had in the bank in Lisbon, as these were in a different bank and a different strong room to where we kept Honor's jewels. Before we could get another letter from Spinola he had been overthrown, and I was told that anything that I had in the strong room of the Lisbon bank could not be removed and was under the control of the Workers' Committee. I tried for years to get these bonds, as they were valuable. Finally I was told that the envelope containing them could not be found, and although I got a letter from the former director of the bank to the effect that to his knowledge the envelope was in the strong room of the bank, this was ignored.

I had the matter taken up by the embassy and by various ministers; the foreign minister said that I should be paid for them. I had a list of what had been there and their values. The finance minister also added a note that I should be paid, but the Workers' Committee in the bank vetoed any payment. Thus we lost many thousands of pounds worth of bearer bonds, and I think that we were lucky to have got anything else out. Even the bank directors said that I should be paid, but the Workers' Committee was all-powerful and could and did ignore their own directors and government ministers – including even the deputy prime minister, who also said that we should be paid. The value of the bearer bonds today after twenty years would be well in excess of £250,000.

A New Life and We Become Nomads

Our new life was very different to our old one. Alas, I had sold the villa at Anticoli only in the autumn of 1973. Had I still had it when the revolution came in Portugal in April 1974, we would have gone back there.

When we left Portugal, we spent some time looking for another home. We thought of Spain and went to see various places there, but the country was changing and the old Spain which we knew and loved was being transformed into the Spain of the package tour and the fish and chip shop, with beaches covered with bright red bodies, packed like sardines and covered with oil and sweat. The damnable disco had come and the nights were made hideous by a ghetto-blaster cacophony where before you could hear the gentle strumming of guitars under the moon.

Madrid had become filled with millions of people and so polluted with traffic fumes that even the trees were dying. Even in remote country areas, broken-down farmhouses had suddenly become immensely valuable. Austria was too expensive, and Switzerland too dear and too dull. We even thought of Alderney. John Scott took us there in his little aeroplane which he flew himself; this was made exciting by the fact that he is very short-sighted. We spent a fascinating few days on Alderney, but this is a haunted island and Honor had the most horrible dreams of prisoners buried alive in subterranean tunnels; moreover, we found a certain brooding melancholy hanging over the place. We went to see a lovely house in the Lot and others in the region of Cahors.

France might well have been a solution as we both spoke the language fluently and it was Honor's mother tongue, but events really changed all this. Honor's uncle died and left a house in Jersey and various things which he said he wanted to come to Honor on the death of his widow. He made a will in which he stipulated this. Alas, when the really dreadful and partly mad old woman died it was discovered that she had ignored her husband's wishes and had left everything to a local Anglican priest – who, with avaricious fanaticism, defended his inheritance. In spite of a Jersey law which precludes the church from inheriting real estate, we were forced to abandon the claim for the restitution of Honor's family money and possessions.

As it was, we became nomads. Every summer we spent three or four months in Italy, where my cousins have a large house with a garden of several acres and in which they built a cottage for us out of the stables. We travelled to stay at our daughter's flat in London; we travelled to see our son in Brazil and spent some weeks or months with him there; we went to see our friends in Austria, sometimes in the autumn for the shooting; we travelled to France and Spain, and latterly (from about 1978) we spent a month or two in America travelling and lecturing. Twice we went back for very short trips to Portugal, and I also went to the Wehrkunde meetings in Munich and to other meetings in Germany. We went to Greece and briefly to Argentina.

I started lecturing and gave testimony in the Committee Rooms of the House of Commons and the Lords. I lectured two or three times at the Royal College for Defence Studies, and every year for about ten years or more we travelled all over America lecturing. I spoke at the Defence University in Washington, the US Army War College at Carlisle, the US Air Force War College at Montgomery, Alabama and the US Air Force Academy at Colorado Springs. I also lectured at the military colleges at

Lexington and the Citadel in Charleston, South Carolina, and in fact all over America. Honor always came with me, and we got to know the United States fairly well.

However, when we first left Portugal we went to our daughter's flat in Knightsbridge, and it was there that we sent our cats. These had remained in Portugal as sort of rearguard with Juanita, our daughter. My dear old Tripitaka had died. He was nineteen and had become rather old, but was still able just before his death to kill a bandit cat who had attacked his dear companion Tao, who had been abandoned by his owners when they left Portugal, and who had come to live with us. Tao was a cat who enjoyed his food and a peaceful life, and was asleep in the sun in the garden when a robber cat pounced on him. Tao was no fighter, and his howl for help brought Tripitaka to his rescue. In a matter of minutes of blood and flying fur, the robber cat was no more.

Tao, Joe and Rose now came to our daughter's flat in London. Rose we had found as a kitten, starving on a farm in the Alentejo. She was nearly dead when we rescued her, but we were able to save her and several of the other cats. She was one of the most affectionate cats we ever had. She too lived to a ripe old age of nineteen, and Tao lived to be twenty-three and then died largely because he ate nearly all of his personal turkey which our son had sent him for Christmas. Joe was another Siamese, and after we left Portugal he was sitting in the sun in the garden when a gang of yobbos (of which there were many about after the 'glorious revolution' of 25th April), came down the street. Shouting that he was a 'fascist cat' they hurled a rock at him which broke his leg. It was badly set in Portugal, but when the cats all arrived in London we got him completely well again. The cats played a great part in our lives and gave us infinite pleasure.

I began to look for another job. My very good friend Sir Arthur Hockaday, who was then second permanent under-secretary at the defence ministry told me I was already far too old. In the event he was proven to have been quite right, as I was unable to find any employment. I had written some three hundred or more articles which had been published in fourteen or fifteen countries, and I thought that by lecturing and writing I might be able to make some money. I did a good deal of both but made very little.

We also started urgently to look for another home. Unfortunately, the loss of our bearer bonds in Portugal and the enormous cost of saving our possessions and getting them transported to England had depleted our capital very greatly, and the cost of the storage alone was a huge burden. We spent several weeks with our daughter Juanita in the Lot and Dordogne in France but could not find anything that we liked or could afford. Although we all liked the area, it had already become too popular with expatriates from Britain.

The beauty of nature has given me infinite pleasure all my life. There are millions of people who go though their lives without even seeing it, let alone obtaining very great pleasure from it.

Both Honor and I derived wonderful satisfaction from nature. There was the ethereal beauty of the mountains of the west of Ireland: the drifting cloud and mist, the sunlight on the heather and the gorse, the deep red glow of the fuchsia hedges, the purple of the rhododendrons; amongst the rocks and crags, the green and red of the rowans, and, in the boggy patches, the brown of the whin grass, and flecks of white cotton grass. There were the lonely loughs hidden amongst the mountains, brown with turf water and edged with green reeds, silent and sometimes strangely sinister, as if they held dark secrets in their depths. I felt a part of it, as if I belonged there. There was a danger there, as there is always in beauty. There were sinkholes even on the mountain tops, where a false step could plunge the unwary into a bog, where the more he struggled the quicker he would be sucked down. The mountains are lonely, but they are not silent: there is the cry of passing curlew, the sudden flurry of a snipe or a woodcock, the wind in the whin grass and sometimes the bleating of unseen sheep.

In the desert it is lonely and the nights are silent. There is an almost palpable stillness. The heavens are ablaze with stars, countless millions of them, and with the dry clear air one sees them in the desert as it is impossible to see them in the land outside. The silence of the desert is fascinating: there is no distant dog barking, no singing telephone wires, no passing aeroplanes, no distant sound of traffic and not even the wind. The dawns and sunsets are a miracle of light and colour.

In Portugal, when we were shooting in the Alentejo, the crisp frosts of October brought with them an opalescent mist as the sun rose in the early morning, turning the cork forest into a magical world of diffused light and shape. The silence of the woods in winter, in the dawn or dusk, waiting for the wood-pigeons to take flight, and where one could hear the trees speaking to each other with the quiet rustle of leaves. Then there were the hot days of September, with the sun blazing down on the deep shadows of the cork and live-oak trees, the cistus bushes with their pink, yellow and white flowers, and the heady scent from them which, as they give laudanum, induces sleep. Then there is the beauty of Italy, the alpine meadows in the spring, the cliffs and azure sea coast and the bare mountains of Umbria painted with cloud-shadows.

There is so much that nature gives us, even in the winter's storm with the sea crashing against the cliffs and the spray flung high into the lowering clouds. There is the beauty of the sun on the hoarfrost of the winter's morning, glinting on a million tiny spiders' webs and turning them into nets of diamonds.

Honor and I were lucky enough to see this miracle of nature and to have had such infinite pleasure from it. Cities are alien places for me, but Honor enjoyed them as I think most women do. The cities of Italy are beautiful also for me, but I do not enjoy the modern towns of today.

Brazil

We went back to Rome, and then in 1976 we went to visit our son Marcus in Brazil. He and his wife had a lovely flat overlooking the beach at Ipanema, just to the south of Rio, and also a house about an hour's drive away up in the mountains at Petropolis. They took us round Brazil – or more accurately a small part of it, as it is an immense country. Although we travelled for many thousands of kilometres, we actually only saw a fraction. We went to stay with friends of theirs on their farm in the country.

The Brazilians for some reason like to sleep on very hard beds, but we always remembered the beds at this place as they were surely made of concrete. Marcus took us shooting in the jungle, but as I have a pathological horror of snakes, I made so much noise hoping to frighten any snakes away that we never saw anything to shoot. There were flights of parrots in the forest, and it is a strange and mysterious place. Under the canopy of the trees there is a rather dull green light, and little sun gets through. There are lianas and creepers everywhere. In places there are billions of banana flies, which have a painful bite and get into one's hair and everywhere.

I had been armed with a dreadful old gun, rusty and quite likely to explode if fired. We were told that there were jaguars in the woods and I had no wish to meet one. There were also armadillos, which apparently the Brazilians eat; a bird which from its description must be something like a wild turkey; peccaries, a small type of South American wild boar, dangerous in a pack; and Capi Barras, another sort of South American wild pig. There are also thousands of snakes and billions of mosquitoes.

It was a very interesting experience, but we had no wish ever to return to the Brazilian jungle, although it is very beautiful in places. The flowering trees are wonderful: the golden ipes grow to a great height and are covered with bright golden-yellow flowers, the red ipes are covered with deep red and sometimes almost mauve flowers, the jacarandas have electric blue flowers, and there is a silver ipe which has silver leaves. These beautiful trees in Brazil left one of the most lasting impressions on us. There are many varieties, both in the forests and also in the streets and private gardens of the towns. They are a marvellous sight, and on the edge of the jungle they stand out against the background of green as huge, towering masses of red, gold, white and silver.

Rio itself is a beautiful city. The setting is spectacular to a degree, and no matter what has been built, there is no disguising the wonderful, natural beauty. It is also a strange place in that there are super luxury hotels and only a matter of two hundred yards away wood and tin shanties on the Montes – great, high and steep outcrops of rock. Here a swarming population of extremely poor people live in usually unsanitary conditions. It is a dangerous town, too, and gangs of criminals (some as young as seven or eight) will attack and kill without a second thought, if they believe that they can rob you of a few valuables. There have been many outcries in the British and American press against the Brazilian 'death squads', and there is no doubt that they do kill children who are gangsters, but the press does not say that these children are in most cases much better armed than the police and have now Kalashnikov assault rifles, Uzi machine pistols and even RPGS (rocket-propelled grenades). They do not hesitate to kill the local inhabitants, tourists and the police.

Our son and his wife gave several receptions for us as did their friends, and we also enjoyed trips into the interior of the country to the old 'gold towns' of Oro Preto and others, which have over the centuries provided an enormous quantity of gold and jewels. It was a new and fantastic world, quite unlike anything that we had seen before anywhere. In places it is extremely beautiful, but there is danger in beauty, and in Brazil both Honor and I were keenly aware of danger lurking in the forests, in the dark streets at night and in the insalubrious suburbs and shanty towns through which the roads pass now and again.

We went to many places – to Bom Jardin where our son had a small coffee plantation and to San Salvador de Bahia, a really rather lovely old town where we stayed in a converted convent with a great swimming pool in the central courtyard. One evening we went out to a Macumba ceremony. This took place some thirty or forty miles away off the roads in a huge marquee. Macumba and Canton Blé are the unofficial religions of Brazil. They were brought from Africa by the slaves. The priests were unable to stamp it out and so they partly Christianised it. Imanja, the Goddess of the Sea, is portrayed as being white and frequently standing on the crescent moon. She is equated with the Virgin Mary. The African War God is now portrayed as Saint George; there is the God of the Forest, the God of Thunder and so on, with strange Macumba incantations. At crossroads, even in the Centre of Rio, there are frequently to be found lighted candles, packets of cigarettes and bottles of the local fire-water put out as offerings to the gods.

On the beach at Ipanema and Copacabana and in front of the luxurious hotels at the New Year, candles are lit all along the beaches, and offerings are set out for the goddess

Imanja to take with her as the tide comes in. An enormous number of people – politicians, the social elite, business-men, lawyers and doctors as well as the swarming hordes of people who make up this nation of some one hundred and forty million people – secretly consult priests of the Macumba, take part in the ceremonies and ask for commu-nication with the dead or predictions for the future. The power of Macumba and Canton Blé is very considerable, although nearly all Brazilians would deny this.

I was interested in the ceremony, as these are not easy for an outsider to penetrate. When we got to the marquee, there was a long table at the far end, in the centre at which there sat an elderly black woman – the *Mae dos Santos* (Mother of the Saints). On either side of her sat her assistants and Macumba dignitaries. Immediately in front of this table, which was on a raised dais, there was a very large, circular dancefloor. On one side there were seated the drummers. Then on chairs facing the dancefloor and the dais there were several hundred people. There was a wide variety of people: expensively dressed girls (the daughters and wives of the local elite), white girls with expensive jewels, and also people – black, khaki and white – from every social level and profession. There must have been well over one thousand people there when the ceremony began.

It started with rhythmic drumming which gradually increased in tempo, until one of the people at the 'top table' – so to speak – got up and began slowly to circle the room, dancing and waving a small axe. This, I was told, was St George. Soon he was joined by more people from the audience and also others from the 'top table'. The drum-ming increased to a hypnotic rhythm and worked up to a crescendo. The audience began to sway and the dancers circling the floor to chant. Suddenly, one of the dancers – a middle-aged woman – gave a great cry and collapsed, and had to be half-dragged and half-carried out of the tent to recover. She was clearly in some sort of hypnotic trance. The *Mae dos Santos* then addressed the congregation. I understood very little of what she was saying. She then sat down: she had a stately and dignified presence.

The drumming and the dancing started again, and more and more of the audience and the dancers became overcome and fainted or collapsed in a form of trance. It was interesting, but I could not ask Honor what she thought of it all as at the entrance to the marquee all the women were seated on the left and the men on the right, with a central aisle running down the middle. People were shouting, chanting and dancing, and the drummers had worked themselves up to a frenzy, when I felt something crawling on my back. It got up to nearly as far as my neck when a man sitting in the chair immediately behind me brushed it off and said, '*Aranha*', (spider). I looked down and there it was scuttling away: a tarantula!

My interest in the future proceedings began to wane by the minute, and I was quite prepared if necessary to go into a trance myself if it meant being carried out of the tent. In fact, I am not very much frightened by spiders (unlike snakes), but I did not relish the thought of any more crawling all over me. I whispered to Marcus that I thought that it might be time to leave and asked whether this would be possible. In fact we had been there for some time, perhaps three hours, and I had noticed that some of the congregation had got up and left. So that was what we did. Alas, I am largely tone deaf and the rhythmic drumming had no physical effect on me at all, but it certainly had on Marcus's wife and to a lesser extent on Marcus himself. Honor told me that she had a much accelerated heartbeat. It was an interesting experience, and I believe that Macumba and Canton Blé is still widely practised.

In another way, I was very much interested in the activities of the 'Church of Liberation', a form of Catholic teaching which varied hardly at all from communism. A certain Father Boff was one of the founder members of this movement, and Honor and I arranged to go to the church where this form of Catholicism was being practised, attached to which was a seminary where the priests of the Church of Liberation were being trained. We duly went to Mass there, and at the door we were each handed a pamphlet to read while the service was in progress. It was very interesting indeed. It invited revolution and could well have been produced in Moscow or by the Socialist Workers Party in Britain, but in some ways it was even more extreme. The sermon was also interesting and again invited revolt.

It must be said that there appeared to be a great deal of social injustice in Brazil at the time. There was a vast gulf fixed between the incredibly rich and incredibly poor. The poor were really incredibly poor, and in many cases living far worse than any animals. The Amazon jungle was being burnt down to provide grazing land for rich farmers, and in many cases the workers on the big estates were treated almost as slaves. There was a good deal about which the church could protest quite legitimately. However, what was going on was quite a different matter: it was using the church for organised subversion. When we left, we had to hand back the pamphlets which we had been given. Unfortunately, I had 'lost' mine, and as I did not understand any Brazilian and was an incredibly stupid foreigner anyway, I was able eventually to get it back to Rome. Father Boff was suspended for some years and was summoned to Rome to answer for his actions. We enjoyed Brazil and our time there.

We returned for a few weeks to our daughter's flat in London before being invited to go to Austria for a wild boar

shoot on the lovely estate of Count and Countess Draskovich. This is right up against the Hungarian frontier in the
Burgenland and had in fact been a part of Hungary until
after the First World War.

Austria

Here we met again our old friends from the Moosburg.
Cara Nostitz had married Seppel Stubenberg and Karl
Draskovich had married Monika. Prince and Princess
Franzi Ausperg were there too, as were Pacetta Countess
Kuefstein from Bernstein and Mathias Thun-Salm, who
married Lori Hoyos.

The castle had been occupied by the Russians during the
war and was in the Russian zone after the war until they
finally withdrew. They had used the drawers of the furniture as lavatories, and the floors in most of the rooms were
ankle-deep in excreta. All the floors had to be taken up and
the furniture (or what remained of it, as much had been
used for firewood) had to be burnt. This had taken some
years and a great deal of money. Only a few of the rooms of
the castle were being used again, but there our friends gave
a great party for us, dressed formally for dinner with
beautiful silver and china on the great dining table. It was a
splendid occasion, reminiscent of the Vienna Congress of
more than a century ago.

The next day there was a boar shoot. We assembled
shortly after dawn on a clear, bright, sunny but very cold
morning. There were fourteen people shooting, including a
Prince Battyany, a cousin of Karl Draskovich and a distant
relative of mine. We were driven from a clearing in the
forest to our stands. The forest covers a huge area of beech
and oak woods with some conifers and extends in all to
some four thousand hectares. There were rides cut through
the woods, and in front of the stand where I was there was

a wide-open space of fairly tall grass, bracken and bushes. To my left there was a lake, about one hundred and fifty yards away and perhaps one hundred yards wide, with a beech forest on the far side. It was very beautiful in the clear sunlight but also very cold. Cara Nostitz came with me to keep me company, as did one of Karl's keepers.

There were some fifty beaters in two packs. Each man was armed with a boar spear, as wild boar can be very dangerous indeed and can rip a man open like an envelope.

I had the foresight to bring with me a flask of whisky, for which we were all most grateful.

In the far distance there was a shot; then a horn sounded and the beat began. It lasted until the early afternoon.

Now and again there was the sound of shots, some very far away and faint and the others nearer, but no boar came my way at all. The morning was advancing when a boar appeared on the far side of the lake, trotted round the bank and disappeared. I waited and waited and then he started to cross my front about two hundred yards away, only visible from time to time between the grass and the low bushes. At last I was able to get a shot and followed it up with a second one. The boar disappeared.

Not long after this there was a most remarkable sound. It was like a great wind, rustling the leaves of the forest floor. Then, through the sunlit beech forest on the far side of the lake there came perhaps seven or eight hundred wild boar. It was a sight never to be forgotten. They were milling around and moving all the time and it was a long shot, two hundred and fifty to three hundred yards away, but at last I got another shot and I saw the boar fall.

Not very long after this the horn was sounded again to indicate that the shoot was over and that it was safe to leave one's post. I went over and found the first boar quite dead. The first shot had been a little far back from the heart but the second had killed it instantly. The second boar on the far side of the lake was also quite dead.

We all assembled back at the clearing in the forest where there was a large thatched cottage. Here there were glasses of schnapps, as by now the sun was setting and we were all very cold. There was some very welcome hot food too: Hungarian goulash!

While we were in the cottage, great bonfires had been lit in the clearing outside and the dead boar laid out in a long row. There were some forty of them placed on pine branches as a bed. Behind each stood a keeper or a beater, holding his boar spear in one hand and a flaming pine torch in the other. By now it was quite dark, and the only illumination came from the great bonfires and from the torches. It was a scene from the Middle Ages. The head keeper then reported to Karl Draskovich while we all stood in a line behind him. Then a bugler sounded the family Hunting Call and there was a moment or two of absolute silence. The bugler then sounded the *Mort* (a sort of last post), and as the last notes of this died away all the beaters and keepers doused their flaming torches in the earth. There was total silence for three or four minutes while the smoke slowly drifted away back into the forest. It was later explained to me that this was symbolic of the spirits of the dead boar returning to their lairs in the woods. It was very moving and rather eerie.

The following day was bitterly cold, and all the guests other than ourselves left in the course of the morning. After luncheon, Karl Draskovich suggested that I should accompany him back to the forest. It appeared that there were three wounded boar, and he wanted them shot. The technique, so he told me, was for us to walk some three hundred yards apart through that part of the woods where the wounded animals were supposed to be. He lent me a double barrelled rifle with hammers, and we took a light truck back to the forest clearing and then along tracks to the area where he wanted to search. We divided, and I walked some one hundred and fifty to two hundred yards to the right; and he did the same to the left. Then he told me the general direction to go and that about three miles away I would come to a very broad ride in the forest. There would be others ten yards wide, but the big ride was at least twenty yards across. There I was to turn to my left and walk towards him; he would be waiting on the big ride a maximum of a quarter of a mile away. It was rather dark and great, heavy, black clouds were gathering.

The forest was fairly open, but scattered about there were large clumps of bushes. Karl had told me that the wounded boar would probably be found in one of them. I started my search, but soon realised that my hands were so cold that I would not be able or have the time to cock both hammers of the rifle. I did not like carrying the weapon cocked as there were brambles about everywhere and it would have been very easy to trip over them. I compromised by cocking one barrel.

It then started to snow and the forest became gloomier and darker. The snow fell silently and continuously, and I began to realise that I would probably not see a boar until I practically stumbled over it, and that in any event the snow had obscured the sights on the rifle. The dark, gloomy silence continued and I saw no living thing. I began to hope most fervently that I would not come across any of the wounded boar, as my chances of survival seemed slim. I came to a ride but it was not wide enough. My hands and feet were like ice, the snow continued to fall and it was getting very dark. Then I came to another ride and there, about fifteen yards away, was one of the boar facing towards me and about to charge. I threw up the rifle like a shotgun and fired. Thank God, the animal fell dead. I found that in spite of the cold, I was sweating profusely.

This is not a sport which I can recommend, and I think that I was lucky and Honor was glad to see me back.

Italy and America

The next year we spent most of the summer in Rome, preparing lectures for the autumn. In the spring we had been to Sienna with Dickie and Evelyn Metcalfe; we had spent a very happy fortnight with them in Tuscany. Sienna itself is a lovely city, and the countryside round about is beautiful, with little medieval towns perched on the tops of hills with good and in those days inexpensive restaurants where we ate and drank well. We also went to Paris for my birthday, invited by our daughter and son-in-law. We had dinner at Fouquet's and afterwards watched a show at the Lido.

I was also asked to fly from Rome to Washington to see the American under-secretary for defence, the deputy director of the CIA and Breshinsky (whom I had already met a number of times at the Wehrkunde meetings in Germany). It was rather an odd journey. On arrival at my hotel in Washington, I telephoned the CIA contact, who was very mysterious about it all. He gave me a map reference for the meeting. There was absolutely no reason for such secrecy as far as I knew.

The following day I hired a taxi and asked the driver to take me to a spot some miles down the road leading to Arlington. We got there; but there was no sign of the contact. We tried another place, moving from Maryland to Virginia as I thought that perhaps the map reference was in some way wrong. Still there was nobody there. There was nothing for it, and I telephoned Langley. I was given an entirely different reference, this time on the freeway from Washington to Dulles International Airport. We went there and sure enough there was a petrol station and a black sedan car with two hard-faced characters sitting in it. I left the taxi and went over with some misgivings.

Finally we reached a very high fence with a sort of cage entrance with armed guards. I handed over my passport to a black guard who then got on his walkie-talkie. I heard him say, 'There's a guy called Dook.' On occasions I have had letters addressed to 'The Duck'. I suggested that we might try again, and this time they let me and my escort through and into some considerable parkland to the main building, which was very large. The entrance hall was enormous, but there were barriers where passes were checked, and also a physical check. I got through all this and into a waiting room, where a secretary gave me a plastic cup of some indescribable liquid which I suspect must have been a mixture of orange juice and coffee.

I was about to rush to the lavatory to get rid of this foul mixture when two very senior officials of the CIA entered. We had two hours together; either they did not have any sense of humour at all, or if they had they had been well trained not to show it. For the first hour the going was decidedly sticky. I tried a few jolly jokes but they fell like lead balloons. Finally, I found a subject which interested them, entirely due to a chance remark about the Normans in Sicily. After that relations began to improve, and towards the end we were on good and even cordial terms. So much so that before I left they offered to show me round the building, and we passed two offices labelled 'Spook 1' and 'Spook 2' – the offices of the director and his deputy!

I was eventually escorted back to Washington, and my next visit was to the Pentagon. It is a vast building so big that they use small electric cars to move about the miles of corridors. I got in all right and had all my papers checked. I was then directed to the second floor and to the office of the under-secretary. I was shown to the lift and provided with a map – just in case I should get lost and be wandering for ever, like the Flying Dutchman, in the corridors of the Pentagon. I got into a lift and pressed the button for the second floor. The lift, in which I was the only passenger, promptly descended into the bowels of the Earth, the doors came open and I found myself faced with a door marked 'No Entry'. I pressed the button for the second floor and nothing happened. I looked for some alternative exit but there was none. I spent some time doing this, and then in desperation I went into the room marked 'No Entry' and found myself in a sort of atomic bunker operation room.

This was very interesting indeed, and I wandered about a bit until an armed security guard appeared. I said that I knew that I was in the wrong place and explained what had happened. The security guard shrugged his shoulders and said, 'Those God damned lifts! It happens all the time.' He took me through to where there were some stairs. I climbed back out of the underworld and finally to the second floor, where I found the under-secretary who was quite charming and very helpful.

I had one more session at the National Security Building and then flew back to Rome. I had great difficulty getting my expenses paid as the hotel had booked me in as Mr Ronald Henry; in fact, during the years to come and over the course of the very many visits I made to America with Honor, it was always a struggle in any hotel to get our names properly registered. I find this strange: many Americans have strange names like Cyrus Gotterdammerung, but *this* does not seem to bother American hotel clerks.

We would often get up at 5.30 a.m. in order to have our baths, dress, pack and then go down to breakfast at about 7.30 a.m., with a view to leaving at about 8.00 a.m. We would then be driven to the airport, perhaps an hour or so away. There we would catch a plane (say at 9.30 a.m.) and fly for an hour or an hour and a half, arriving at 11 a.m. We would be picked up by a car from the next place where we were to lecture and then driven there, arriving at, say, 12 p.m. We would be shown to our quarters for the night and then be taken for luncheon.

Although some of my very best friends are American, I have encountered some rather odd attitudes there. During the years that we were lecturing in the United States, we discovered strange ideas about 'Demon Drink'. All my life I have drunk wine with my meals, and when asked if I would like a 'Coke' or some revolting soft drink, I would ask if it would be possible to have a half-bottle of wine, or even a bottle, with Honor. This request was inevitably met with astonishment and the reluctant admission that there *might* be a bottle or half a bottle of wine – which, after a delay, would be produced. The instructors or professors would then watch me with gloomy apprehension. I could almost hear them thinking, He's going to be drunk. He's a win-o. We'll have to cancel his lectures, as they watched the bottle being emptied slowly. They were invariably astonished when it appeared to have no effect and I was able to lecture to different classes for the next three or four hours without keeling over or becoming unintelligible.

Another strange custom was to produce for every meal a salad made from tasteless iceberg lettuce and accompanied by a revolting little pool of either pink dressing ('Italian dressing') or a sickly, yellow dressing ('French dressing').

Another habit which I found deplorable was the inevitable large white bread bun in the centre of which there was a piece of overcooked meat.

Occasionally I was billed as the Duck of Valderano, sometimes as Mr Henry (one of my Christian names), and they seldom got it right. In fact, we would answer to 'Hi' or any other loud cry.

Radio phone-ins with questions also produced some extraordinary methods of address.

However, in the streets of the very many towns we visited we were always met with great courtesy, people actually going some distance out of their way to point us in the right direction when lost, which was not infrequently. Honor got totally lost in Washington once, and somebody came up to her in the street and said, 'Lady, do you know that you're in the red light district?' He insisted on accompanying her back to a more respectable part of the town.

We came to London and I gave a lecture in the Committee Rooms in the Commons. I had invited Jack Harrison to come to this; he was the Irishman who had been our companion on the wonderful journey through the Desert of Mocamedes and the Terras do Fim do Mundo. Unfortunately, he had a heart attack in the middle of my lecture. He was carried out and I never saw him again.

I gave another lecture at the Royal Defence College, and then we were invited to lecture in America and flew to Washington. There Tony Harrigan and his delightful wife Elizabeth had organised a splendid tour for us. First we went to a semi-secret place on the edge of the Blue Ridge Mountains in Virginia. On arrival there we found a Cotswold manor house and I was told that it had been imported stone by stone from England. It was a most lovely house, in a glorious setting overlooking the foothills of the mountains.

That night after dinner I went out for a short walk before going to bed. It was a cold night, with the sky filled with stars and the woods with moonlight. I was discouraged from any further exploration by the sudden glare of security lights and the not-very-distant noise of dogs and their handlers. Thereafter, Honor and I admired the scenery from our bedroom window.

Our next stop was Wilmington where there are some wonderful gardens, comparable to Kew Gardens in London. I was due to give a lecture at Delaware University, but this turned out to be an after-dinner talk to a group of the professors.

Then we went back to Washington, but not without some difficulty as it appeared that there were only two taxis in Wilmington. One was engaged and the other broken down. We had had the same trouble on arrival two days previously: there had been absolutely no transport from the station to the hotel, which was some way away. I eventually telephoned the police, and we were taken to our destination in a police car.

Our next scheduled trip was to Roanoak in Virginia. There we were met by a car which drove us a good many miles to Lexington, where we were established in a rather charming old house. Probably the oldest in Lexington but it had a really very strange atmosphere. However, it was comfortable, and we could walk from there to the Military Academy. We were taken out to luncheon, and Honor was let loose on a sightseeing trip. She was particularly enchanted with General Lee's stuffed horse.

I gave a couple of lectures in Lexington. One was to the assembled military cadets of which there were, I estimated, over one thousand. It was all very military, with a very large central ground for marching and counter-marching. We returned again to Washington and saw Tony and Elizabeth Harrigan and their children before going down to Charleston in South Carolina to visit our cousins, who have been established there since about 1680. They took us to several places round about and to a wonderful plantation belonging to Gertie Legendre.

Chapter Seven

Research Foundation for the Study of Terrorism

When in the mid-1960s the supreme Soviet decided to support terrorist groups around the world, even when they could not themselves directly control them, it really opened the doors for terrorist expansion. Cuba received money to fund training camps, and at one time there were at least a dozen of them on the island. Libya also received funding; East Germany and Czechoslovakia provided specialist instructors. It is probable that the provisional IRA received some funds, either directly or indirectly, from the Soviets. Training camps were set up in the Soviet Union itself, especially for Africans. There were two advanced training schools in Czechoslovakia, and one or two in East Germany. Weapons were provided mainly from Czechoslovakia, as well as explosives and detonators at which the Czechs excelled – Semtex is a Czech invention initially, although later produced in other countries. East German inks, paper and engravers went to Syria and later Iran to produce forged currency – especially US one hundred dollar bills. Libya set up more than a dozen training camps attended by recruits from all over the Islamic world. There they met terrorists from the Basque movement ETA and Red Brigades from Italy, as well as other Italian terrorist groups, a few specialists from the IRA, and even some Americans who had gone as tourists to Paris and were then taken by the underground organisation to Libya. Libya set up an organisation on Malta, and the Basque ETA movement facilitated movement from Europe to both North Africa and to Cuba through ports such as San Sebastian, Santander and Vigo.

In the very early stages, Feltrinelli had financed terrorism in Italy. Through his Swiss bank account in the name of 'Robinson Crusoe', he assisted Italians and Spanish terrorists to go for training in Cuba and Czechoslovakia, obtained arms and set up safe houses. He introduced Baader to Meinhoff to form the Red Army Faction in Germany, produced false documents and printed terrorist manuals. However, the real financing and assistance to terrorists was to come from the Soviets, until the collapse of communism there as well as the financial collapse of the Soviet Union. However, before this happened, quite independently funded and organised, terrorist training had been set up in the Bekkar Valley of the Lebanon, in Syria, in Iran and also in the Sudan. These terrorist training facilities were financed mainly by Iran and Syria, and had a totally Islamic orientation, while North Korea provided training for south-east Asian terrorists.

The purpose of the Soviet backing for terrorism was that they believed that it could be an important factor in destabilising the capitalist world. The driving force behind Islamic terrorism was the destruction of Israel and an attack on all those countries or individuals that supported Israel. In both instances, the United States of America and its civilians were a prime target. It was mainly this warning that I attempted to convey in my lectures in America, and to point out that the service personnel posted abroad, diplomats, UN, American personnel, businessmen and tourists were all considered to be legitimate targets. While I gave lectures to the men, Honor, in informal meetings with officers' wives, gave them the message that they and their children would also be considered prime targets.

There is, of course, a difference between terrorism and organised crime, but that difference has become blurred in the last years and the two are now virtually indistinguishable. This is in part due to the disappearance of funding from the Soviet Union. Terrorist organisations have had to find an alternative source and that source is usually drugs. In the days before the Second World War, the Sicilian Mafia would not touch drugs: it was not considered 'honourable'. Today the Mafia is everywhere – in Italy, America and worldwide – and some of its members deal in drugs. Money laundering and counterfeiting are also major sources of income, while kidnapping, extortion, corruption of politicians in order to obtain lucrative public work contracts, prostitution, blackmailing of corrupt officials and so on all play their part in obtaining funds for terrorism. At the same time, terror tactics such as threats, assassinations and bombings all are used today by organised crime groups in order to obtain money. Thus, a third prime target can be added to the two previously mentioned – terrorism to obtain money.

With the break-up of the Soviet Union, many former senior KGB officers, as well as some military officers, have gone into organised crime. We have what is called the 'Russian Mafia'. However, this sort of Mafia exists all over Europe today, as well as into the Americas and even Asia. Terrorism is no longer used only to obtain territory, a political ideology, a religious objective or any combination of these; it is also used to obtain money. The boundary between terrorism and organised crime has vanished.

My cousin Tom Waring is the senior partner in the leading firm of lawyers in Charleston, and together we set up a foundation for research into contemporary problems. One of these was the terrorism which had begun to sweep over Europe and was stretching into North Africa, the Middle East and even America. A few months later I set up the Research Foundation for the Study of Terrorism in London.

In short, since nobody wanted to employ me, I had decided to employ myself with these two foundations. They have given me a good deal of work, both in research and also in lecturing in the past fourteen or fifteen years.

From the outset, it was clear that in order to keep up to date and provide material for the lectures, it was necessary to have an European foundation as well. I asked the Archduke Otto von Hapsburg, who was a personal friend, if he would become patron of it. I then recruited an advisory council, consisting of an admiral who had been director of the Royal College for Defence Studies in London, a former permanent under-secretary of state at the Defence Ministry, an assistant secretary general of NATO, a former head of the Anti-Terrorist Squad at Scotland Yard, a former head of Italian Army security, the former minister for the army in Portugal, a former very senior member of the French secret service, the former director for Europe of MI6, (the secret intelligence service), an expert on low intensity warfare, a former minister and two or three members of the British Parliament, three members of the European Parliament, a bishop with direct access to the Italian parliament, a very senior member of the Spanish security service, a German member of the Bundestag with special interest in security and an expert in international law. The council had correspondents at a high level in Scandinavia, Greece, Turkey, Austria, the Netherlands, the Middle East, Pakistan, Africa and South America, and about another four from the United States, including members of the security service, the DIA and so on.

All these people worked on a purely voluntary basis, as we had no funding from any government agency. In fact we did not want it, as I feared that this would tie our hands in some way. We received some money from private contributions to the foundation, but it was little enough, and in spite of appeals and also a major conference which ran at a conference centre near Windsor, we received almost nothing. The degree of cowardice – and I can use no other word – displayed by business and industry generally was, to me, totally staggering. The typical response to our solicitations was, 'If we were to give anything to you, terrorists might get to hear of us and we would become targets for them and they might take reprisal against us.' We had even set up special accounts to which donations could be made with absolutely no connection with terrorism, but it made no difference. We told members of the food industry that they could well be targets for terrorists and attempted extortion by the actual, or threatened, contamination of their products, but they made the same excuses. It was an exhibition of craven cowardice which I find totally inexcusable. Over a period of twenty years and by means of personal letters, seminars, presentations, conferences, targeted mail appeals and every other possible means, we received only a few thousand pounds in all.

Wealthy individuals found a variety of excuses, suggesting that the existing organisations were totally adequate, and that nothing else was necessary. They were motivated by fear of reprisal against themselves and their families. Businesses huffed and puffed and came back with the same excuses or bald statements that they had their own security which was totally adequate. We suggested possible scenarios to the airlines – which were to be proven later to be tragically true – but in which they were not interested. We suggested dangers to supermarkets, which were later to cost them millions of pounds, but which were dismissed. We suggested that we had a network of people in different countries who were in a position to warn of possible dangers, but they were not interested. A balance sheet prepared by accountants was of greater interest, and if something untoward *was* to happen then they could deny responsibility and fight interminable court proceedings by relatives of those killed or injured. Anyway, it might not happen to them.

A huge golden statue to Mammon, the false god of money and greed, should be set up in most of the major financial centres of the world. Irrespective of lip-service to the leaders of the major religions of the world today, Mammon is the one which is mainly worshipped by the people of today.

I may be accused of bitterness, and I would plead guilty to that. I despise cowardice and find insensate greed disgusting. The lives of those destroyed by terrorism and their relatives, the maimed and blinded are for me rather more important than an extra penny in the pound on dividends or a few thousands a year paid to the directors.

I finished up funding the foundations largely by myself and have ruined myself in the process, but at least I did what I knew was right.

Airey Neave, who was a good friend and who eventually was murdered in the underground car park of the House of Commons by the IRA, urged me to go ahead. Norris McWhirter, whose brother was murdered by terrorists has helped me; Michael Ivens, who really understands the threat of terrorism, has helped me more than I can say. John Scott, a solicitor, has provided me and the Foundation with totally invaluable support over the years. All of them have given without any reward and even without expenses, which for all of them have been considerable, I can only offer my total gratitude. To Richard Shannon, who has been a trustee and who has greatly helped in so many ways, I am more than grateful; to Kristy Prenn and so many others, I can only say thank you. I believe that you have all contributed to something which was very much worth doing. To my cousin, Tom Waring, who set up the American Foundation and who gave all his services for free, to Anthony Harrigan and to so many others, I would like to put on record in this book my appreciation and my never-dying thanks.

With virtually non-existent financial resources, I believe that we achieved a good deal. For very obvious reasons I do not wish to go into details; the Foundation is still in existence. We worked with the police in many countries, and I was given an award by the Italian state police fairly recently which I treasure. We have worked with the French police, the Spanish police, the British security forces, police and intelligence as well as with the Americans, South Americans, and even in the Middle East and Asia. I suppose that my lectures and those of others in the Foundation have reached more than a quarter of a million people: civil servants, members of the foreign service, military men, tourists, businessmen, industrialists and those from the security services of many countries. I hope that they may just possibly have saved some lives. There is no place in this book to recount in detail what we have done or the lectures we have given in the American Defence University, the American Army and air force colleges, the US Air Force Academy, the military schools, the security and intelligence services and also in Europe.

At least I believe that given our financial constraints, we did what we could.

Generally speaking, we had a very much greater response and appreciation in America rather than Europe. The European Commission and Parliament were totally negative. They just did not want to hear. I believe that this was largely due to the fact that they perceived the Foundation as a possible 'threat to the boys'. They had their own agenda for 'European security' which would provide immensely well-paid jobs for many thousands of the faceless bureaucrats of Brussels.

The late 1970s and the whole of the 1980s saw terrorism proliferating across Europe, with the rise of the Red Brigades in Italy and some thirty other terrorist organisations (both of the far left and the far right). In France there was Action Directe; in the Low Countries and Belgium the Fighting Communist Cells; in Germany the Red Army Faction; in Spain GRAPO and ETA. In Ireland and England there were the IRA and so-called loyalist terrorist groups. In Greece they had two if not three major terrorist groups, and even in America a former director of the FBI identified twenty-two terrorist organisations.

In virtually every country there are terrorist groups, from India and Pakistan to Sri Lanka, to North Africa; witness the multiplicity of Islamic terrorist groups varying from Hamas to Black September; from Abu Nidal's group to Gadaffi's training camps and support for terrorist groups from all over Europe and Asia Minor. In Cuba there was Castro, again with a multiplicity of terrorist training centres, and the Soviets had finally agreed to support international terrorists, training, arming and equipping them even when they could not control them, on the general theory that terrorism destabilised the West and Western capitalism.

It involved a tremendous amount of work, to keep up to date on who these terrorist groups were, where they were trained and who financed them, and to gather information on their armaments, objectives and ultimate aims (in some cases these were not by any manner of means clear). Also, it was necessary to study why they had become terrorists, if there was any sort of terrorist mentality common to the majority and what were the links between the different terrorist groups in the different countries and even within the same country. We also had to obtain profiles on terrorist leaders and information on the special modus operandi of certain individuals and groups – some specialising in car bombings, others in small arms and grenade attacks, others in kidnapping, others in individual assassinations, and so on.

Nor was this entirely without a certain danger. Over the years we have received about a dozen death threats, mostly anonymous, and on occasion we have been supplied with armed security guards at lectures where it was thought that some lunatic might wish to assassinate the speaker. While I admit that there have been occasions on which I have felt like this myself, to stop some verbose speaker at international meetings from going on with an endless soporific speech, I don't take kindly to this idea if I am the speaker.

In the course of our research over the years we have been careful, but inevitably now and again we have attracted unwelcome attention.

Our research work in Italy involved going to places where our enquiries would not have been welcomed. I had a permit to carry a pistol, but that would not have been much value against a *lupara* – a sawn-off shotgun – which is the favoured assassination weapon in southern Italy and Sicily. We had to invent reasons for our presence: a search for an ancestor – perhaps there was record of such a person living there before the First World War? Alternatively we were writing a book about the area, local dishes, local customs, interesting churches or monuments. It was also important not to give the impression that we were at all well off, as that would have made us targets for a possible kidnapping. This involves paying only after a very careful check on any bill and then reluctantly, small note after small note, with nothing obviously of much value left in the wallet. Credit cards would, of course, invite suspicion and would probably not have been accepted; even traveller's cheques might imply a certain wealth. A really old battered car was also an advantage. In fact my cousin had one, an ancient Opel which had been hit so often both front and back that it greatly resembled a closed concertina or accordion. Old and very well-worn clothes and suitcases held together with string also helped.

On a couple of occasions we found ourselves becoming the object of open hostility, and things had begun to look very ugly. One such time was down in Calabria – very definitely 'bandit country', and the local inhabitants fully fitted the countryside. We were staying the night in a small hotel in a village. It was not very clean, and Honor had sprayed the bed with anti-bug spray, a standard part of our kit. We had just finished a rather nasty meal that evening, and I mentioned that we were looking for family of a distant relative. I cannot at the moment remember the name which I mentioned. It was only an opening gambit in trying to enter into conversation with the hotel owner for local gossip. In any event, it seems that I mentioned the wrong name. It certainly meant something to the local people and they did not like it one little bit. The hotel owner – it was in fact little more than a run-down *trattoria* with a couple of rooms upstairs – reacted violently at its mention. He turned a nasty shade of green, backed away and disappeared. Honor and I finished our bottle of wine and were just about to get up from the table and go up to bed when six men came in. Two were carrying sawn-off shotguns. They stood over us at the table, and one of them asked, or rather demanded, 'Who are you, and what do you want here?'

I replied with my story that we were looking for possible descendants of a distant relative who we thought might have lived in that area long before the First World War. The man bent down, thrusting his face into mine and shouted, 'Liar!' Who are you really? Answer me now or my *lupara* will ask the next question?' It seemed that by some ill-chance I had used the name of some local person who was wanted either by police or by some others it was better not to know about. It was a difficult and dangerous moment: as these people kill first and ask questions later. I said as calmly as I could, 'I really do not know what you mean. I only mentioned the name of somebody who might have been distantly related to me a long time ago. We are passing through the district and I only asked casually.' 'Liar!' the man bawled in my face again. He cocked the hammers of his gun. It was all so unexpected that I really was at a total loss for words. Suddenly, in a very quiet voice, Honor said, 'You had better ask who *I* am, son of a whore!' The man was so taken aback that for a moment he said nothing; then he shouted, 'Well, who the devil *are* you?' Honor replied very quietly, so quietly that it was difficult to hear her. 'Perhaps you may have heard of Marilena La Stega. I am her niece.' The six men immediately jumped back from the table, giving the three fingered sign against the evil eye. Honor got up from the table, and she had a very strange look on her face. She said, 'Go now, all of you; and do not look back, or this night you will die and my aunt will come for your souls.'

No room has ever cleared quicker. One moment they were there and the next we were totally alone. We had not unpacked, so we collected our suitcases and loaded the car and drove away. We never paid for our room or our nasty dinner, as we never saw the *trattoria* owner again. He had disappeared as completely as his unpleasant companions.

After some miles, I asked Honor, 'Who on earth is Marilena la Stega?'

'Well,' Honor replied, 'I was reading about her a couple of nights ago. You remember there were some books for tourists in that hotel at Cosenza. It seems that she is a very well-known local witch who can summon the Devil, and people around here are terrified of her. They are all very superstitious, and it seems that Marilena la Stega is something special.'

'It was very clever of you to remember her name. What made you think of it?' I asked.

'I really don't know,' Honor replied, 'but things seemed to be getting out of hand and her name suddenly came to mind.'

'Are you sure that you are really not her niece?' I asked. 'You had a very strange look on your face when you told those thugs to go, and you were speaking in dialect which you don't know.'

'Oh, I don't think so,' Honor said smiling. 'But, remember, I used to play with the gypsies when I was a little girl; they told me a lot, and told me that they would always look after me.'

On many occasions we would go into the small towns or villages and find that stillness and feeling of fear and quiet menace. On one occasion, also in the south, we found a political meeting of some sort going on. We found a small hotel, parked the car and went to see what was going on. Just as we arrived there was a sudden burst of sub-machine gun fire. The crowd ran in all directions, and as we ran with them I saw two *carabinieri* lying dead on the steps of the Casa Comuale.

In Tuscany there was a different sort of danger. Here the Sardinian shepherds used to come every year, and they had their own organisation which specialised in kidnapping. Amongst our many friends we had one who was a Sard. Years ago he had killed somebody or other in Sardinia, and he had fled to take service in the Foreign Legion. He was a very tough little man. and I once asked him whether he could help if we had any trouble with the shepherds in Tuscany. He looked at me a little quizzically, tapped his nose and said, 'I'll just pass the word to see that you have no trouble.' Italy is an ancient land full of dark secrets.

We usually suffered nothing other than abuse coupled with vague threats, but on occasions the latter were more specific, and then we were obliged to take precautions.

My work for the Foundation over the years has differed in one major respect from that I had done previously for other intelligence operations. I set up the first Foundation in America really with a view to lecturing there, and Tony Harrigan, who was in charge of the educational side of the United States Business and Industrial Council, of which he was the president, was responsible for my starting this. He organised lecture tours for Honor and me which sent us all over America. I owe him a debt of gratitude for his great kindness, which I can never repay. Without him I certainly could not have done it, and he and his beautiful wife Elizabeth and his charming family all became very great personal friends.

Somewhere on our travels, I had picked up a remarkably unpleasant form of amoebic dysentery called giardia. This gave me diarrhoea to the extent that I lost some thirty-five kilos in weight and had to make hurried trips to the nearest lavatory up to fourteen or fifteen times a day. My life began to be governed by plans as to where I could find the nearest lavatory. I eventually qualified to write a book on the lavatories of the Western world; some are almost unbelievably horrid. It also made lecturing difficult, in as much as that one can not interrupt a lecture to perhaps some six hundred people by saying, 'Just wait a moment. I will be back with you shortly.' It also made travelling difficult and everything exhausting, as I seldom got more than an hour and a half's uninterrupted sleep. Had it not been for Honor, who supported me throughout and on occasions, because I became so weak, had to almost carry me to the bathroom at night, I could not possibly have carried on.

My anti-terrorist activities are things of the past. Others who are much younger and more qualified than I can accept the risks, but terrorists or organised crime groups inevitably have fanatics and do not welcome any intrusion into their affairs.

As terrorism has become merged with organised crime we have had to contend with organisations such as the Sicilian Mafia, N'Dranghita, the 4th Mafia, the Camorra, the Sardinian Shepherds, the Anomima, and so on – the list can be extended indefinitely. Now we have the addition of the Russian Mafia and their links – which are probably by far the most dangerous, encompassing the whole country as well as Eastern Europe – are now spreading. In fact, they have already spread all over Western Europe.

However, as the Foundations will carry on and will in fact expand, I do not wish to write at length here as to the exact work which we do, and that which we have done in the past. I think that I can say that due to the lectures in the United States, Canada, Latin America, Britain and throughout Western Europe, we have made many thousands of people aware of the threat of terrorism in its very many forms, as well as that of organised crime, which is spreading at a terrifying rate and which has already become a major threat in almost every country.

With the disappearance of the Berlin Wall and the end of the Cold War, many people thought that the main danger to the world had passed. It has not. In fact, with the break-up of the former Soviet Union the danger may well have increased. Nuclear weapons are becoming more and more readily available to irresponsible states, and even to criminal organisations. In Japan, we have witnessed the use of nerve gas, which can be manufactured relatively easily and can become a weapon of mass destruction in the hands of criminal organisations or even individuals.

The empires of the twentieth century have ended, as Rees-Mogg recently pointed out in a newspaper article. The authority imposed by the empires of Britain, France,

Germany, Italy, Belgium, Japan, Portugal, Austro-Hungary, India (as a part of the British Empire), Ethiopia, Spain, Turkey and Holland, have all come to an end this century. We see incidents such as those in Chechnya, Algeria, almost the whole of Black Africa and very much of Asia, the former Yugoslavia and the Middle East (with the rise of militant fanaticism), and the list can be extended worldwide. We are entering, and in fact have already entered, the day of the terrorist and that of immensely powerful cartels of organised crime.

I believe that we are about to enter the age of the anarchist and the warlords of the Dark Ages, brought up to date. Nor is it only a matter of drugs, violence and terrorism on a major scale: it can also extend into the world of international finance, which can destroy individuals and even communities as effectively as weapons.

It has been a fascinating study, and one in which Honor helped me more than I can ever possibly say. Now that she has gone, I have become old and tired; I am going to give it up and let somebody else take on the job. My friend since our days at Cambridge together, Nicholas Elliott, who was a mainstay to the Foundation, has just died. John Scott, who was not only my oldest friend but also invaluable to us as a trustee and legal adviser, has retired, as he wants to spend the rest of his life sailing in Mull and doing other things which he enjoys. Without Honor, I do not really wish to carry on; I have neither the interest nor the will to do so. I will stay in a purely advisory capacity for as long as I am wanted, but I think that it is now up to others to carry on with the work. However, I like to think that Honor and I together with our friends in the Foundation have made a contribution to combating the evils of terrorism and organised crime.

Austria and Greece

The two Foundations were set up towards the end of the 1970s. For the next fifteen years or so they occasioned Honor and me a very great deal of work and travel, but we also had a lot of fun. For one of Honor's birthdays we were again invited to Austria; this time Marcus came with us. We arrived at Bernstein, a splendid chateau fort in the Burgenland which had belonged to Count Almasy and then to Pacetta Kuefstein-Almasy.

The following day was Honor's birthday, and there had clearly been planned some surprise for her. There were whisperings and the prime mover seemed to be Michael Bull, who was staying in the castle. He was constantly making mysterious disappearances. That evening we were called from our rooms and asked to come up on to the battlements. There was an enormous yellow thing lying on the ground: this proved to be a balloon made from yellow paper, which they were even then inflating with hot air. Gradually it filled and then majestically floated off over the battlements towards the east. The evenings usually brought a breeze from the west, and now this splendid balloon floated into the sky and off over the Hungarian frontier, which was only a few miles away. On its side it bore in black paper letters: 'HAPPY BIRTHDAY, HONOR'. Its appearance over the frontier caused a tremendous stir, and before long we could see tracers from anti-aircraft guns and machine guns pouring into the sky. The poor balloon was not proof against this, and it came down in flames. However, I hope that enough of it remained for the legend, to be read by the Hungarian border guards.

Marcus shot his first roe buck but, was not so happy when he discovered that the owner of the shoot traditionally gives a hearty whack on the backside of the person who has shot his first buck; this Pacetta did while Marcus lay across the carcass. We went on to stay with Karl and Monika at Gussing, and Marcus got his first wild boar. Then we went on to stay with Cara and Seppel Stubenberg at Guttenberg, another magnificent early medieval fortress perched on a bluff.

Here I nearly came to grief. I had gone shooting with Seppel's eldest son, and he introduced me to an immensely tall tree on the edge of the forest and to what appeared to be a stairway to the stars: ladders which disappeared into the top of this tree, where there was a small and flimsy platform. From here I shot the best buck that I have ever shot in my life and also very nearly fell off the platform. I find it difficult to estimate height, but it must have been the best part of eighty feet down. I think that would probably have put paid to me. From there we went on to stay with Franzi and Dorgie Auersperg at Goldegg, an enormous castle near St Polten.

In the evenings we used to assemble in the kitchen, where we had drinks. We would all take part in the cooking and then carried the food solemnly one hundred yards or so to the state dining room. They had no servants; how some of our Austrian friends maintain these vast castles by themselves, with the aid of only a few guests, I will never know.

From Vienna we went to Italy to stay with David Craig, an old friend since we were all together at the end of the war. He now has a lovely house in a forest which runs down through a sandy path to the sea. It is a beautiful, peaceful place – except when the shooting season starts in Italy, when the whole countryside resounds to incessant gunfire. Not that there is anything to shoot, but the Italians love to fire their guns. Any bird, even if it is imaginary and several miles away, attracts a barrage of shots.

We spent ten days there happily bathing and walking amongst the pines; then went back to Rome by train.

A fortnight later we flew to Athens and there we met Julian Guest and Diane Wilson. Julian was the brother of Viscount Wimbourne; we had met him in London in about 1977, introduced to us by Diane Wilson. Diane we had known for many years. We first met her in 1961 in Lisbon when she was working with Bob Lee on a safari business in Angola. They had a huge hunting concession there in the south-east. Both of them have remained close friends of ours for more than thirty years. Diane had married Ed Wilson a few years after we first met her and they had two children. Ed Wilson died and Diane came to London. Ed had been the son of the President of General Motors with a considerable fortune.

Over the years Diane has become a sort of adopted daughter. I can never begin to thank her for her kindness to us during the time that we have known her. She was present with me when Honor died, and nothing that I could ever write or say would be sufficient to express my gratitude to her. She has become part of the family and will forever have my deepest affection.

Honor and I had previously been to stay with Diane and Julian when Diane rented a most beautiful villa in Majorca, and we had spent a very happy two or three weeks together there. On this occasion it was Julian's brother, Wimbourne, who had offered us a-ten day cruise on a wonderful yacht *Korvalan*. She was lying at an island some twenty or thirty miles away from Piraeus, and we joined her there by means of a Soviet-built hydrofoil which covered the distance quickly. *Korvalan* was an old yacht, beautifully built and appointed with a captain and a crew of seven. She was the last word in luxury for the four of us. If one can, this is the way to see the Greek islands!

It was ten days of bliss: of splendid food, beautiful and interesting islands and secluded, sandy little coves where we anchored for the nights, away from the tourists and the discos. Here and there we landed to go bathing or to explore the small villages in the interior of the islands. It was the trip of a lifetime and it had everything; the food and wines on board were superb, as was the cooking. The crew were all charming and so was the captain. All were English and the motor yacht, which was about ninety feet long, was comfortable and totally delightful.

Many people now know the Greek islands; but very few, I think, have had the pleasure of seeing them as we did. The weather was pretty good. We only had one storm and one day of fairly rough seas, but as Honor and I were used to going out in a full gale into the Atlantic and crossing and re-crossing the Irish seas in really dreadful weather, the whole voyage seemed to be as calm as a mill-pond.

Our cruise on *Korvalan* ended at Sounion. We came in from the east and the sun was beginning to set through the ruins of the great temple perched high on a bluff projecting into the sea. We dropped anchor in the little bay and went ashore, and then up to the temple. It is one of the wonders of Greece, and in the evening afterglow with the dark blue of the bay below it was incredibly beautiful.

Many of the Greek islands are beautiful but also very barren; millions of the population have emigrated, and the terraces which were carved into the steep slopes of the mountains and which once grew olives, vines and corn are now abandoned and arid, totally lacking in vegetation. Anything which is green is immediately eaten by the thousands of goats. With billions of dollars poured in by the European Community in Brussels, I believe that these terraces and the irrigation channels are being rebuilt; but today there is a glut of olive oil, corn, wine and oranges. Many thousands of tons are destroyed every year, and in so many European countries farmers are now paid *not* to grow crops on their land.

As a city Athens had little to offer, apart from the ruins of the ancient Greek civilisation. Athens is a modern town and for the most part ugly. At the time of the liberation of Greece from the Turks about one hundred and fifty years ago, the total number of inhabitants of Athens amounted to barely two thousand, and they were concentrated in what was little more than a village. The Athens of today has all been built since then. Probably one of the nastiest of God's creatures on earth is the Athens taxi driver. This creature is usually accompanied by an odoriferous companion sitting in the front seat or a more odoriferous dog, and sometimes both. Occasionally he will stop if a would-be passenger signals to him, but then as likely as not, he will refuse to take the passenger because he does not want to go that way. They he will drive off – preferably over the passenger's feet. Frequently he is exceedingly rude.

Westerners, and in particular British and Americans, are not popular. While thousands of tourists flock to the islands they are regarded as a necessary evil and tolerated with a snarl because they bring money. After four hundred years or more of Turkish domination, the Greek of today bears about as much resemblance to the ancient Greek as does the present-day inhabitant of Britain to the ancient Briton.

Back to London, France and Italy

We spent that Christmas in London at our daughter's flat. London as usual was decorated with lights and Christmas trees, while loud speakers blared out *Jingle Bells* and carols. In one store, which shall remain nameless, I came across a splendid Father Christmas. He was seated on an upturned beer crate and his white beard was askew, as was his hat. Honor and I edged closer to look at this remarkable sight: Father Christmas was royally drunk. Surrounded by a circle of wide-eyed children, he was waving a toy of some sort in one hand and a bottle in the other. 'Come 'ere, you little bastards!' he roared. 'Father bloody Christmas will give you something – just see if 'e don't! 'E 'as got all these fuckin' presents just to give away to you little buggers.' He waved the toys and took a swig from the bottle. Some mothers were scuttling away with their children, and an assistant manager emerged with a couple of beefy doormen. Father Christmas was forcibly removed, struggling and cursing. It had made our Christmas!

Scotland

Before I became struck down with giardia, we went to the extreme north of Scotland, where Ewald Von Kleist (whom I had first met in the bathroom at Merano during the war) and I took a walking moor near Thurso. Honor and Gundula came too, and the children. Honor spent the days fishing the river for trout, while Ewald and I, with a couple of keepers and their dogs, walked the moors. This is an extremely exhausting form of shooting: each day we must have covered more than twenty miles over the peat hags and up the mountains through knee-high heather and bog. It was hard work, but in the evenings we had delicious grouse for dinner. One day when we were not shooting, I managed to get a couple of salmon on the Thurso river.

Alas, the end of the trip was marked with a bad accident. Honor was walking along the river bank watching a trout rising and lengthening line when she fell into a deep hole, tearing all the ligaments off the foot and ankle of one leg. She was alone and somehow managed to get back across the river and up the bank to the road about two hundred and fifty yards away. She was found there and taken to a doctor, who gave her half a bottle of whisky to drink and bound up her leg. However, she could not walk at all. I got her back to London, where she was a prisoner for some eight weeks.

She could only move about the flat on hands and knees. We used to say that she had fallen off the edge of Scotland.

We gave a conference of the Research Foundation for the Study of Terrorism in a large house near Windsor which was used as a conference centre. This was well attended by people from all over Europe and from America, as well as by most of the members of the Advisory Council.

The next year Dickie and Evelyn Metcalfe invited us to go with them to Tuscany again. This we enjoyed very much, and I took them to see the grim fortress built by my ancestors five hundred years ago, where the family lived on and off until my grandfather sold it after the First World War.

The Pyrenees

A few months later they invited us to go with them to St Etienne de Baigorry in the Pyrenees, a most beautiful and tranquil place right on the Spanish frontier (which was just across the mountain). We stayed at the Hotel Arce there, and every year for the next nine years we went back. The drives through the chestnut forests and the mountains round about were a constant delight, as were the small inns and restaurants where we had our luncheons each day. We would return each evening for dinner on the terrace beside the river and then retire to bed in this wonderfully peaceful place with just the sound of the river running past the hotel.

I was very much interested in this area as it is ETA country – the Basque separatist movement which is ideologically Marxist. We found that it was very easy indeed to cross over from France and into Spain down the little-used mountain passes, and that there were no border controls whatsoever at most of them. We already knew that they were used for the movement of personnel and also weapons and explosives from France into Spain and vice-versa, and that wanted terrorists used to move into the Basque area of France, which they used as a rest area or when pursuit by the Spanish police became too close. We explored the area very thoroughly and then the Foundation made specific suggestions to the French and Spanish authorities.

On returning there the following year, we found that these reports and recommendations had been totally ignored, and we submitted them again. The third year we went back again. We found that the Spanish and French authorities, who had ignored the Foundation reports of the two previous years, had finally implemented them and done it very well indeed. Now the French and Spanish had established checkpoints from anything up to twenty kilometres from the actual frontier. They were manned with armed troops and police and moved daily. The checkpoints tended to be located around a sharp bend and the checks that were made were very thorough. In this way the authorities were able to arrest a considerable number of terrorists who were using these routes from Europe to the ports on the north-west coast of Spain and from there to Cuba, or to the Middle East and North Africa.

These trips to Tuscany in March and later to St Etienne de Baigorry in June became a regular feature of our lives, and we enjoyed them immensely. Sometimes they were funny, as when Evelyn's knickers fell down in the main street of Sienna. Sometimes there was drama, as when Evelyn cut her leg getting out of a wheelchair at Bordeaux Airport, and fountains of blood caused a small lake to form in front of some wretched passenger in the waiting hall, who took one look and was sick on top of it. The first-aid brigade of the airport arrived to bind Evelyn up, and then the sanitary squad refused to mop up the blood as they said that it might be contaminated with Aids. I pointed out that

Evelyn was a most respectable lady of over eighty but they still refused. We left them to it.

The previous year, when we were staying with them at a charming small hotel about eight miles from Sienna, she fell down and cut her head open. Again there was much more blood. A doctor was called and wished to remove Evelyn to the local hospital. With some considerable knowledge of Italian hospitals, we knew that she would never come out alive. It took all Honor's powers of persuasion to get the doctor to agree to Evelyn remaining where she was. Once again there was an ocean of blood and the manager called the head waiter, but he was violently sick at the sight of it.

On yet another occasion Evelyn developed an acute appendicitis while we were in France. We got her back to Heathrow and into an ambulance only just in time.

In the Basque country of France and north-western Spain, elderly tourists with an octogenarian lady, barely able to walk, did not excite suspicion. Apparently unable to speak anything other than schoolroom French, people talked freely in the local patios, Spanish and Basque. However, there were hazards.

After my beloved Honor died, Evelyn asked me to take her to the area again. I could not refuse, although it was infinitely painful for me to visit the same places where only a year before I had been with my darling Honor. Memories came flooding back. The mountain passes were the same; the narrow, one track-roads the same; the clouds came down over the mountain tops in the same way, obliterating all visibility; the hairpin bends were the same; the rock walls on one side and the sheer drops on the other were the same.

Evelyn suddenly said, 'Stop! I must pee.'

I replied, 'Evelyn, dear, that is impossible. This is a very narrow one-track road. There are clouds and nobody can see more than twenty yards ahead. If somebody comes around the corner we will be driven like a golf ball down the mountain. Anyway, there are no bushes, and just the precipice.'

She replied, 'I don't care. I must pee. Stop the car!'

She got out and stood on the edge of the road. There was virtually no verge and no guard rail; only a sheer drop down into a misty depth, hundreds of feet below. Evelyn surveyed the scene. Then, with the imperviousness of the English grand dame, she announced, 'You will have to hold me!' She dropped her knickers (which had a sort of life of their own, having previously fallen off in the main square of Sienna some three years before, to the delight of the populace), extended her hands for me to hold, lent outwards and peed into the abyss. Any car coming the other way, if it had not hit us, would have thought that I was pushing her over the precipice.

The French have a saying, 'Les vieilles dames Anglaises – (old English ladies). Yes, I know what they mean – they are a breed unto themselves.

During the summers, I spent some time writing up my lectures for the autumn tours in America. We were in the little cottage in the garden of my cousin's house on the outskirts of Rome. I used to sit in the garden in my bathing suit and type. I also wrote up the reports for the Foundation. Emilio Fina (the nephew of my stepfather General Bacchiani, Count of Savana, whom my mother married after her divorce from my father) is a doctor, as is his wife. They were incredibly kind to us over very many years. We went for trips with them for many hundreds of miles round Italy when they got a break from their hospital duties. These were enormous fun but not without hazard, as my dear cousins have a regal disregard of traffic lights – a fact borne out by the state of their cars, which in some cases were – and still are – barely-moving heaps of scrap metal.

In fact one car looked literally like a closed concertina, totally flattened at both ends and crumpled in the middle.

There is a certain magnificent unworldliness about my cousin, Emilio. Once, when Julian Guest was staying with us in Rome, it was announced that we were going to a *vendemia* (grape harvest) in the country. It was at least one hundred and fifty miles away, and we had some difficulty in finding the place. We arrived and the doors were opened by our astonished host. 'We have come for the *vendemia*,' Emilio announced. 'Alas, that was three weeks ago,' our host replied.

However, it was decided that we would have a luncheon party there instead, and we were all sent off to look at the Etruscan walls in the nearby town while a meal was prepared. We returned to find that they had luncheon ready, and that there was the local priest and a retired general and a couple of other guests as well as the seven of us. It was a good luncheon, and afterwards I repaired to the lavatory. High on the wall above the seat was the cistern with a chain suspended from it. I pulled the chain and the whole thing – cistern, pipes, chain and everything – fell down into the lavatory, demolishing it entirely. It all came down with a frightful crash, and I have never been back there since!

That evening, back in Rome, we took Julian to a tavern, where we had a vast meal and a great bowl of grappa. My stepfather and Emilio burst into song: old Fascist songs which it is forbidden by law to sing, grand opera and somewhat ribald ballads. A couple of seedy individuals approached – possibly plainclothed police. Emilio turned on them and said, 'Who are you – Garibaldi?' They melted away into the darkness.

A few days previously, we had taken Julian to Subiaco up the valley of the Aniene for luncheon and afterwards walked back to the car. On our way we passed the Autoscuola Furia (the Fury Driving School). A mile or so down the road we came on a huge pile of junk cars with a sign over the gate which read: '*Auto Distruzione*'. Honor remarked, 'I suppose that it helps to keep the population down.' These interludes in our work for the Foundations – the research, preparation of reports, travelling, lecturing and constant updating of lectures, television and radio interviews and discussions with police and intelligence people, were tremendous fun, but we also had worked very hard.

America Again

We flew to America in the autumn, where we did a round of the universities in Mississippi, Nashville, Memphis, Jackson, Philadelphia and Indiana, as well as one or two others. We finished up with a talk to CIA and intelligence people in Washington and also a talk on airline security in the Sky Club on top of the Pan Am building. We then flew on to Montana where we were met by Bob Lee.

Some years later we went there again, but this time we met Marcus and his wife, and I gave a series of lectures at the University of Montana. Marcus, who had been working in that area for some months, had bought an enormous second-hand car, and in this we toured the whole area around Missoula: north to Flathead Lake near the Canadian border and south to Bute. Marcus and I were taken shooting round the mountains and lakes just to the south of Flathead Lake, where we saw thousands of geese and ducks as well as pheasants and partridges, buffalo, antelopes – a whole natural zoo. We climbed up a fairly high mountain and from there had a view of hundreds of square miles. It was not possible to see any indication that man had ever been there: there were no houses, cars, fences or roads, no telephone or electricity poles – absolutely nothing in any direction. It was a wild and very beautiful place.

We flew on to Spokane and Seattle and stayed with our friend Professor Bonica and his family there before returning to London.

Both Honor and I were very much impressed with the extraordinarily good manners of the American university students. Over the years our travels took us to Minneapolis, Chicago, Salt Lake City, San Francisco and Denver on a number of occasions; also to Colorado Springs and even to Galveston Island in Texas. From east to west and north to south, everywhere we were met with unfailing courtesy. The students were interested and extremely polite. The only exception in all those years was at some small college down on the Gulf of Mexico at Texas City, where a rather gorgeous 'student' was extremely rude. He was most beautifully dressed and wore a gold bracelet on one wrist and a large gold watch and bracelet on the other. He must have been at least thirty-five and he turned out to be an Iranian who occasionally attended at this miserable little place. Nobody knew anything about him, and I often wondered what he was doing there.

It would be tedious to recount all our travels in America, but certain incidents stick out. On one occasion Honor got locked in the ladies' lavatory at Denver Airport. She could not get out and the lock would not budge. The flight was called and there was still no sign of Honor. I begged them to hold the flight for a moment, and just when they told me that they could hold it no longer, Honor appeared. It seemed that finally her cries for help had been heard by two large ladies who had thrown their combined weight against the door, broken the lock and released my wife.

In the Rockies, when we were at Colorado Springs for the first time, we were taken to Cripple Creek. This had been a gold mining town or settlement and the whole area was pitted with the old workings. The town really only consisted of a single street, but just behind it there was a really good and substantial house, by far the best building in the little town. I was told with great pride that this had been the local brothel and that it was now maintained as a museum – still set up as a brothel – as it 'had brought home comforts to so many of the poor, lonely miners at the turn of the century'. Nor could we ever forget seeing the thousands of geese when we were staying at a splendid hotel at Colorado Springs. The lake at the back of the building was frozen over. However, three or four holes in the ice were kept open, and every evening thousands of geese would fly in for the night. The following morning they got out on the ice and did warming-up exercises before flapping madly and sliding all over the ice until they finally became airborne again.

The most outstanding impression must be, however, the extraordinary kindness and generosity of our cousins in Charleston, Tony and Elizabeth Harrigan and their family, Bob Lee and Anne, and all those other friends whom we made on our travels in the States.

Bob Lee and Diane Wilson we see often; in fact Diane, who lives in London, we see most of all. Bill Graver, Nathan Adams and Tony and Elizabeth Harrigan come over to London from time to time; I see them when they do. Also, of course, our cousins, the Warings from Charleston.

The Roman Cats

It must have been about 1983 when we were staying with our old friend Maria Pifferi in Rome that we first heard about the cats. Both Honor and I were very fond of cats and I still am. It appeared that some dreadful communist female who was in charge of the ancient monuments in Rome had a great hatred for cats. Filled with zeal, and with the excuse that the cats were unsanitary, this appalling female had given an order that all the cats which inhabited the ruins of ancient Rome were to be rounded up and destroyed. Many already had been. Honor got hold of Signora Fanfani, the wife of the president of the senate; I wrote a series of red-hot articles on asbestos paper for publication in the Italian and foreign press. Finally we were able to get this revolting business stopped. Both Honor and I pointed out the fact that, with the demise of many of the cats, Rome was becoming infested with rats and that they bring very many diseases, including bubonic plague.

Subsequently, we were able to get a law through the parliament declaring the cats to be an integral part of the ancient ruins of Rome and inflicting dire penalties on anybody who interfered with them. The infestation of rats stopped almost immediately, although the cats are fed by *gattiere*, mostly elderly women who daily bring food for them. We used to tell each other that when we were ultimately called upon to recount anything good that we had done in our lives, this would be the best thing we had ever done.

People are sickeningly cruel to animals in all countries – including Britain, where the incidence of cruelty to animals increases yearly and where the magistrates impose paltry fines when offenders are brought to court. As supposedly a nation of animal lovers, the British appear to be suffering from self-delusion. However, humanity as a whole is a revolting species: cruel, destructive of every other living thing (other humans included), destructive of the world in which they live and of its beauty. The teaching that 'Man was created in the image of God' must be a mistranslation: the word should be 'travesty' or 'parody' rather than 'image'.

Brazil Again

Some two years later, we made another visit to Brazil to see our son and his wife. This time they took us to Angra dos Reis, one hundred and fifty miles or so to the south of Rio. Here there are a number of islands. We duly sailed out to one of them in a motorised schooner. Friends of our son had lent us their house on this island: it was really a tropical paradise. From the little harbour, a track led steeply up the hill to the villa amongst the trees, surrounded by a wild and beautiful garden. It was a place of enchantment, with large red, blue and green parrots flying across the sea from one island to another, and yellow and green parrots climbing about on the roof of the thatched restaurant where we used to have most of our meals ten minutes walk down the forest track to the end of the harbour. We bathed and swam in a fairly warm sea. The water off the Brazilian coast is not very warm; perhaps for that reason there are rather few sharks, unlike the Indian Ocean which is infested with them.

We spent several marvellous days there, then had to return. We went down to the harbour, but no schooner arrived to take us back to the mainland. After several hours, I began to doubt if any ever would come; but as for most Latin Americans time is relative – a few minutes are not even considered, a few hours are of no consequence – some people there will miss appointments by several days and do not think that to do so even requires an apology. A schooner did eventually arrive; we sailed back to the mainland through a night of stars, over a totally still and unruffled sea. Now and again we passed little islands, illuminated in the darkness by millions of fireflies winking from the forest trees which came down to the edge of the sea.

From Rio we flew to Sao Paolo and from there to the Foz do Iguacu on the Parana river. There is a good hotel there, not far away from which are the famous Falls of Iguacu.

This magnificent spectacle must be one of the wonders of the modern world. There are very many falls and they make Niagara look like water falling from a roof gutter; even the Zambesi Falls are not to be compared. These majestic falls which are, perhaps well over a mile wide were once a place of sacrifice for the Indians who lived in these parts. Young girls, and also latterly missionaries, were sacrificed to the river gods, being tied to logs and sent crashing over the falls. There are very many falls, some quite small and others enormous, with great curtains of water falling down into the river below. Through these curtains of water, birds like swifts dart to their nests in the cliffs behind the falls, totally protected by the curtain of water.

Cascavel (Rattlesnake), on the Brazilian side, was a pretty wild place. Most of the men carried revolvers strapped to their legs, and I was told that at the weekends there would be shoot-outs in the street, as in the old, Wild West films. In fact, much of Brazil is still like this, a huge and, in parts, still unknown country. It was fascinating, but time to return to Europe.

Paraguay and the Argentine

Another day we drove into Paraguay, to Strossner City. Here one may see the world's best collection of ancient and broken-down vehicles. Taking the road across the bridge from Brazil to Paraguay is a lengthy business, as certainly two or three of these ancient cars will have broken down and will be being pushed across by their owners.

At the far end of the bridge were representatives of the Paraguayan Army. They hardly presented a military appearance: shaving every day is clearly not a requirement, their uniforms would have been rejected by a scarecrow and rusty rifles were propped up against the parapet of the bridge while the soldiers were engaged in conversation with local girls and busy sucking soft drinks out of straws inserted into bottles. Passports were, apparently, unnecessary, or the customs were asleep during their siesta.

Strossner City, which nowadays, I am sure, has another name, consists largely of one street crammed with stalls and booths, each filled with junk of one sort or another. Incredibly cheap watches are on sale by the million; by some miracle, the stallkeepers have been able to devise a way in which they can be made to work for about twelve hours before ceasing to work ever again. The only really good things to buy are leather holdalls. We bought one which, after many hundreds of thousands of miles of travelling, is still as good as new.

Strossner City was a really scruffy town. Exhausted, we went to the best hotel there and in a fly-infested hotel lobby we had some remarkably good beer. I then remembered that the dictator of the time, Strossner, was the son of a Bavarian brewer; if he did nothing good in the rest of his life, he brought excellent beer to Paraguay.

The interior of Paraguay is rather flat and uninteresting, or at least that small part of it which we saw. There are great cattle ranches and it is, or rather it then was, remarkably cheap. However, the only things worth buying were the leather bags and steaks which were excellent and, of course, the beer.

From Paraguay we went into the Argentine, which was very different. There were good roads, and military camps were tidy and appeared to be efficient. We were, of course, in a frontier zone. We also approached the Iguacu Falls from the Argentine side down an immensely long wooden walkway built out into the river. In some ways the falls are even more impressive from the Argentine side. They are something that nobody who has seen them could ever forget.

On our return to Europe, we went to stay with David Craig at Castiglione delle Pescaia. This was always one of our favourite places, with the peace and the beauty of the pine woods, the deserted beach and warm sea. In the evenings we would all drive out to the little restaurants in the hills nearby and feast on wild boar and red wine.

A few weeks later – back to America

We flew to America again over the Greenland icecap. It was a crystal-clear day with brilliant sunshine and the desolate beauty of the snowfields sparkled in the sun. We flew fairly low and finally came to a great glacier flowing into the sea to the west. The western coastline was marked with jagged, black mountains jutting upwards and to the west, falling downwards into the frozen sea. It had a terrible beauty of loneliness and cold.

We lectured at Hillsdale again, but first we flew down the Hudson Bay. That too had fascination. It was a place of dark, snow-filled forests, and icebergs floating on an icy sea.

When the seminar at Hillside was over, we flew south from Detroit to Raleigh in North Carolina, where we stayed with Sam Cambata and his wife Gunnilie. Tony Harrigan and Elizabeth drove up from Charleston and we returned with them; a long drive but fascinating as we went through the area where the hurricane had struck and saw the hundreds of square miles of forests flattened by the wind. We stayed with them at Kiawah Island, just off the coast of South Carolina, and with our cousins at Charleston. Tony and Elizabeth drove us back to Raleigh, and from there we flew to Washington and back to London.

Italy

Honor and I made several trips to Sicily and southern Italy in order to obtain first-hand information – and here I should thank my many friends in Italy who, not without a certain risk to themselves, helped us in our research and the collection of information. To quote an old army adage: 'No names – no pack drill'.

For some time I had been interested in the Mafia and its many rivals and offshoots, and in the growth of organised crime. Initially the Mafia was not a political terrorist organisation in Italy. Their killings were amongst themselves, against rival groups such as the Camorra. They were concerned with drugs and to some extent with kidnapping, extortion and protection rackets, the acquisition and control of public works contracts and that sort of thing. This developed into a desire for control of politicians and political parties. The Mafia itself has not had much in the way of a political ideology, but terrorism, which was the proper business of the Foundation, takes many forms which need not of necessity be political.

Islamic terrorism is, in many cases, based on religious fundamentalism; ETA in Spain has a political Marxist ideology but also is Basque nationalist; the IRA has mainly territorial aims coupled with a desire to bring about a sort of Irish Marxist state in the whole of Ireland. The Red Army Faction was almost totally ideological, as were Action Directe in France, the Fighting Communist Cells in Holland and Belgium and the Red Brigades in Italy.

One should be careful. At least one member of the Foundation has been murdered and others have received threats, including ourselves.

The shadows were beginning to lengthen. Our visits to London became rather more frequent; we stayed with Evelyn Metcalfe down at Waltham St Lawrence and saw 'something of our many friends down there. After Dickie Metcalfe died, I took his gun in a small syndicate shoot near there with Basil Sparrow, enjoying this for a couple of years or so. Bob Lee invited me to shoot in Scotland, and my cousin Tom Waring invited us to Constable Burton, the home of the Wyvills and a most lovely place where, I think, I had some of the happiest days shooting with Honor and our friends.

Chapter Eight

Sunset

I had to go to Brussels and to the European Parliament there, but it was a case of beating the wind. I was passed from one office to another and round and round until I finally found a languid individual, an escapee from the Foreign Office, who told me that he supposed that terrorism might have something to do with his department but hastened to add that they had no money. I said that I happened to know that he had several million ecus a year for his department. He replied that this was all used up on administrative expenses. 'But don't you actually do anything at all?' I asked. He replied stiffly that they ran the department. I could see what he meant at the hotel nearby where I was staying. For luncheon and dinner every day the people with whom I had been talking during the day would come trooping in to eat and drink enormously and very well indeed – and then sign the bills. No doubt the administrative expenses leave no money at all actually to achieve those things for which they get enormous salaries and expenses.

My lifelong friend and distant cousin Charles Duke of St Albans died, as did Andrea Count Novellari, Peter Baden Powell and many others.

Honor had not been feeling well for some time and used to get very tired. It was finally discovered that she had cancer; she had a major operation to remove her colon. It was successful, and she recovered so much that we could go to Italy again. We stayed with HRH The Prince Cesare Altavilla Sicilia Napoli at the castle of Roppolo near Turin. We went again with Evelyn that summer to St Etienne de Baigorry in the Pyrenees; this time we even managed to get her back neither as walking wounded nor in an ambulance. But then I developed cancer and had radiation treatment for it. Then, in the spring, Honor began to feel ill again, and we found that the cancer had spread. She died in July of 1993.

We had a good life together. It was filled with friends, with fun and adventures, with travel and excitements, with the wonderful places which we have seen and the perhaps unusual things that we have done. Now the sun has gone down and it is time for others to take on the joys and burdens of life. We enjoyed it all.

Honor had been created Dame Grand Cross of the Order of St George and Dame Grand Cross of the Order of St Ignatius of Antioch some years previously, and I was created Knight Grand Cross of St George and Knight Grand Commander of the Order of St Ignatius at the same time, as well as being given Hereditary Knighthood of the Cingolo Militare. I don't know that we really accomplished very much, other than helping the cats of Rome, but we had a wonderful life together and, who knows, perhaps we may be able to continue it together elsewhere.

For fifty-two and a half years we were married. We lived, loved and laughed together. We were virtually never apart, except for the short time when I was in Italy during the war. Finally, we became virtually a single person: we thought of the same things together and established a sort of telepathic communication between us. Her extraordinary gift with languages and natural ability to make friends at every level of society and wherever she went were enormously useful, as was her remarkably good judgement of character. She would say, 'Don't trust that man [or woman]', I would ask her why, as they seemed pleasant enough, but she was invariably right.

She painted well, receiving a gold medal from the Royal Academy, and also drew. She was a most excellent cook and actually wrote a cookbook. She shot wonderfully well, but never birds or animals as she never wished to kill anything. She was an accomplished dowser who sighted wells for many of our friends. Her tremendous zest for life shone through everything that she did. She helped me in everything that I tried to do and without her help I could have accomplished nothing; fearless and interested in everything, she was the perfect companion. Her beauty and charm live on in the memories of all her hundreds of friends. When she died I received cards of sympathy signed by the matron and some fifty of the nurses who had looked after her, from the girls in the reception, to the girls in the outpatients' department, from the nurses floor to those who had treated her in X-ray and the radiation department, from those who had brought her food to the girls in the accountancy department. It was a most remarkable and perhaps unique tribute to a remarkable and unique person.

When the end had come, I went into the Cromwell Hospital in London that morning. She was having her bath. We went for a short walk together round the floor, and then she went back to bed. She had not been able to eat anything for many days as she had terrible nausea if she did. I had luncheon in her room; afterwards she got up, we had another little walk together round the floor of the hospital and then she sat up in a chair in her room. I had been unable to sleep at nights, and so they had very kindly rigged a camp bed up beside her chair: I used to sleep there beside her in the afternoons.

We were sleeping, both of us. I was lying on my bed beside her chair and we were holding hands. I was woken by the spasmodic twitching of her hand in mine. She gave a cry, and she was dead. I don't think that she even woke from her sleep.

She died, as we had walked through life together, hand in hand.

Once, years ago and after the Portuguese revolution when we were looking for another home, we had gone the Azores. Standing overlooking the mysterious lakes at the bottom of the huge crater of Sete Cidades, we were talking about Atlantis. We wondered if we had ever lived before, as we had identical memories of half-remembered things in Verona and perhaps Greece, or somewhere like that. I can now only hope and pray that we will meet again, some time or somewhere, as when she died I died too, in spirit if not, alas, in body. There were so many things that we still wanted to do, so many places we wanted to visit and never did, so much of the excitement and amusement of life still to be enjoyed. However, to be honest, we did have our fair share of it in this life.

Our children live on; both have had and are still having fascinating lives, Marcus as a geologist in Brazil and elsewhere, Juanita married to a Portuguese air force colonel. They too have travelled all over the world and had unique experiences. We were very lucky with our children: both turned out to be delightful, accomplished people with the same enjoyment of life as we had. We were lucky, too, in the people whom they married: both have companions with whom, after some twenty years, they are still in love. But that is their story and, perhaps, one day they too will write it.

When Honor died, our son came from Brazil and our daughter from Portugal and spent the next three months with me to try to help me to get over the shock. Nobody could have done more than they did, and we spent the time in a cottage in Gloucestershire, visiting old family houses, lunching in quiet country pubs, fishing in the dusk of the summer evenings and driving for miles through lovely, unspoilt countryside. However, I will never get over my beloved Honor's death.

With apologies to Fitzgerald for misquotations:

> And when thou thyself, with shining
> Feet shall pass
> Amongst the guests star-scattered
> On the grass
> And in thy joyous errant
> Pass the spot
> Where thou and I, made one, turn
> Down an empty glass.

TAMÀM SHUD
(It is finished)